FOURTH EDITION

CONVENTIONAL WISDOM AND AMERICAN ELECTIONS

EXPLODING MYTHS, EXPLORING MISCONCEPTIONS

JODY C BAUMGARTNER
and PETER L. FRANCIA

ROWMAN & LITTLEFIELD
Lanham • Boulder • New York • London

Executive Editor: Traci Crowell
Assistant Editor: Deni Remsberg
Executive Marketing Manager: Amy Whitaker
Interior Designer: Rosanne Schloss

Credits and acknowledgments for material borrowed from other sources, and reproduced with permission, appear on the appropriate page within the text.

Published by Rowman & Littlefield
An imprint of The Rowman & Littlefield Publishing Group, Inc.
4501 Forbes Boulevard, Suite 200, Lanham, Maryland 20706
www.rowman.com

6 Tinworth Street, London SE11 5AL, United Kingdom

British Library Cataloguing in Publication Information Available

Library of Congress Control Number: 2019949766
ISBN: 978-1-5381-2916-6 (pbk. : alk. paper)
ISBN: 978-1-5381-2917-3 (electronic)

♾™ The paper used in this publication meets the minimum requirements of American National Standard for Information Sciences—Permanence of Paper for Printed Library Materials, ANSI/NISO Z39.48-1992.

Brief Contents

Contents

Illustrations

BOXES

FIGURES

About the Authors

DR. JODY C BAUMGARTNER is the Thomas Harriot College of Arts and Sciences Distinguished Professor at East Carolina University. He has numerous books, authored and edited, to his credit. In 2017, he edited *The Internet and the 2016 Presidential Campaign* with Terri Towner, and in 2018, *Political Humor in a Changing Media Landscape: A New Generation of Research* with Amy Becker. He has also written or collaborated on numerous articles and book chapters on political humor, the vice presidency, and other subjects.

DR. PETER L. FRANCIA is the Thomas Harriot College of Arts and Sciences Director of the Center for Survey Research and is a professor in the Department of Political Science at East Carolina University. He is the author of numerous academic publications on various topics related to American elections. His books include *The Financiers of Congressional Elections: Investors, Ideologues, and Intimates*, coauthored with John C. Green, Paul S. Herrnson, Lynda W. Powell, and Clyde Wilcox; *The Future of Organized Labor in American Politics*; and the volume, *Guide to Interest Groups and Lobbying in the United States*, coedited with Burdett A. Loomis and Dara Z. Strolovitch. Francia's insights on American politics have been included in the press accounts of national media outlets including CNN, National Public Radio, and the *Wall Street Journal*.

Preface

THIS IS THE FOURTH EDITION of *Conventional Wisdom and American Elections*. From its inception, the project has been our attempt to deconstruct several of the myths and misconceptions surrounding campaigns and elections in the United States. This is necessary because elections, especially presidential elections, generate a seemingly limitless supply of theories, opinions, and predictions from journalists, scholars, and political pundits. The ideas that these observers put forth make their way into popular accounts about elections. Unfortunately, many oversimplify complex subjects or overhype the latest political fads. It is perhaps inevitable that some exaggerated assertions and misinformation become part of the conventional wisdom about American elections. Our objective is to try and set the record straight on several of these subjects.

For example, it is now commonplace for commentators to emphasize the negative tactics and practices of the campaigns of presidential candidates. In 2016, some commentators suggested that the presidential campaign was the "nastiest" ever, with the campaigns of President Donald Trump, Hillary Clinton, and their supporters, going to "new extremes" of negativity. But these claims are not new. In fact, they seem to be repeated every four years.

Claims about negative campaigns reflect a misunderstanding about the role that negative campaign tactics have always played in U.S. elections. For instance, critics of Thomas Jefferson stated that his election in 1800 would bring about legal prostitution and the burning of the Bible. Opponents of Andrew Jackson charged that he was a murderer and that his wife was a bigamist. Perhaps most scurrilous of all, Jackson's opponents even accused his dead mother of being a prostitute.[1]

These and many other falsehoods about American elections persist in the minds of citizens. Based on our experience as college educators, we have identified eleven widely held myths and misconceptions about elections in the United States. Changes between editions of the book are based on the fact that new myths or misconceptions seem to emerge during each presidential election cycle.

The conclusions that we draw throughout the book are based on the most current political science research. In some instances, the literature is clear in debunking popular myths about American elections. On other issues, research findings are more mixed. In either case, we clarify the issues such that readers can discern between those which scholars have largely resolved and those in which honest debate remains.

PLAN OF THE BOOK

The basis of any election campaign is to understand who voters are and what they want. The first chapters of the book are devoted to exploring three misunderstandings that have arisen in recent years about the voting public. In chapter 1, we look at two groups of voters who are often portrayed as being quite similar, namely, so-called independent and swing voters. These two groups receive a disproportionate amount of attention from the media throughout the campaign. This is true in spite of the fact that there is little consensus as to how to define either group, there are fewer of either than is widely believed, and relatively few of them actually vote. Further, as the chapter makes clear, most people who do vote cast their votes in a partisan fashion most of the time. In the end, independent and swing voters rarely decide election outcomes, unless the margin of victory is especially narrow.

Chapter 2 explores the myth that voter turnout in the United States is steadily declining, pointing to the fact that traditional measures of voter turnout are faulty. Although turnout has declined somewhat in recent decades, the decline is not nearly as precipitous as some would have us believe. The chapter also examines the various factors that influence voter turnout and the subject of youth voter turnout. Finally, the chapter examines the evidence surrounding voter identification laws and voter fraud.

In chapter 3, we cover the frequently trumpeted myth that a viable third party will emerge in the United States due to the declining approval voters express toward the Democratic and Republican Parties. Third-party success, however, almost never materializes, and in the rare cases when it does, proves to be short-lived. Chapter 3 reviews how the electoral system itself explains why the rise of a third party in the United States is unlikely to materialize in any significant and sustained way.

Chapter 4 examines the various misconceptions surrounding the influence of money in U.S. elections. As we discuss in this chapter, raising significant sums of money is a necessary condition for candidates to wage competitive campaigns, but contrary to popular narrative, it does not guarantee victory on Election Day. Likewise, money matters in shaping some important aspects of public policy, but it does not buy an elected official's roll-call vote on important legislation. Money *does matter* in politics, but in ways that are more nuanced and complex than the overly simplistic notion that American democracy is "for sale to the highest bidder."

Chapter 5 deals with the "veepstakes," a guessing game about who presidential candidates will choose as their running mates. This entertaining game pervades media coverage of the campaign. Unfortunately, however, much of this coverage fails to provide a complete picture of what presidential candidates look for in a running mate. The chapter goes beyond issues of "balancing" the ticket and examines other factors that have emerged in the past several decades as being important in vice presidential selection.

In chapter 6, we explore the belief that presidential campaigns have become nastier in modern times. In addition to discussing what negative campaigning really is, we survey several of the truly vicious campaigns throughout our nation's history.

Chapter 7 turns the spotlight on the media, in particular, the mismatch between what most people expect from the news media, which is objective and accurate reporting, and what we can reasonably expect. Although there is some debate about the extent and direction of media bias, our purpose in this chapter is to emphasize a fundamental reality about the American news media: the news media are a business, which means that commercial considerations ultimately drive content.

Another frequently repeated claim during almost every presidential campaign is that presidential debates can be "game changers." Yet as decades of evidence from the Gallup Poll and other sources reveal, debates have a minimal effect on voters. While a strong debate performance certainly can yield favorable media coverage for a candidate, presidential debates tend to reinforce voters' preexisting beliefs rather than change their evaluations of the candidates. We examine the claims surrounding presidential debates in chapter 8.

Many Americans hold misconceptions about public opinion polls. While some think that polling data paint a precise and error-free representation of American political opinion during presidential campaigns, others see polls as a form of modern-day voodoo. Both views miss the reality. Chapter 9 reviews the basics of public polling methodology and discusses potential problems with, and misuses of, polls.

Chapter 10 asks the provocative question of whether congressional elections, especially those to the House of Representatives, are truly democratic. The chapter begins by establishing the fact that congressional elections are becoming increasingly less competitive and then provides insight into the various advantages incumbents have in congressional elections.

In the final chapter, we examine the ubiquitous claims following presidential elections that the winning candidate and his political party have won a "mandate from the people." As we discuss, the public's general lack of policy knowledge complicates these "mandate" claims. In this chapter, we review how difficult and rare it is for a winning presidential candidate to have earned a true policy mandate, as well as the consequences that often follow for presidents who claim a mandate when none truly exists.

ACKNOWLEDGMENTS

In the course of writing and preparing this book, we benefited from a great deal of assistance. Preparation of the previous editions was helped greatly by numerous people, including reviewers, students, and colleagues at East Carolina University (ECU), as well as colleagues from other institutions. Their suggestions helped improve the overall clarity and quality of this book.

For this current edition of the book, we thank Menna Abdel Salam and Chris Rudkowski, two of our students at ECU, who helped with proofreading and research. We thank those who provided reviews for the fourth edition: Sean Foreman (Barry University), Michael Coulter (Grove City College), Michael J. Faber (Texas State University), Ngozi C. Kamalu (Fayetteville State University), N. Alexander Aguado (University of North Alabama), and John Dinan (Wake Forest University). We also owe a debt of gratitude to our editor at Rowman & Littlefield, Traci Crowell, for her helpful suggestions and assistance with this project. Finally, none of this would be possible—or worthwhile—without the love, support, and patience of our families. Many sincere and heartfelt thanks to all.

1

The "Independent" and "Swing" Voter Myth versus the Reality of Mobilizing the Base

DESPITE DECADES OF POLITICAL SCIENCE RESEARCH, many commonly held assumptions about voting are not as simple as some political observers portray them to be. For example, during each election cycle, Americans are treated to any number of news accounts that discuss the growing numbers and power of two related blocs: the independent and the swing voter.[1] As one account proclaimed in 2018, "outcomes of the midterm elections will be decided by swing voters."[2]

The much-vaunted independent voters are those who have presumably eschewed attachments to either of the two major parties. Popular accounts often portray these voters in a favorable light for shunning party labels and for making their voting decisions based on a thorough examination of the issues of the day and the candidates' stands on them.[3] The independent voter is therefore the virtuous citizen, voting in a manner consistent with the model presented in high school civics courses. Swing voters are typically portrayed in a similar way, waiting to make their voting decisions until the last minute, after all of the information from the campaign has been received and processed. They too are reluctant to allow partisanship to dictate their vote.

A common theme throughout nearly every election cycle is that these voters comprise a growing percentage of the electorate.[4] Related stories focus on how these nonpartisan segments of the electorate have the power to decide the election.[5] Yet these stories ignore the reality that most voters are actually partisans. In other words, political science research conclusively demonstrates that if we examine how people cast their votes, rather than how they see themselves, there are actually few "true" or "pure" independents among the electorate.

This matters. To claim that independent and swing voters may "decide" the election is misleading. Although Donald Trump won the so-called independent vote in 2016 by four percentage points (46% to 42%), Mitt Romney won this group in 2012 and lost to Barack Obama.[6] The fact is that although parties and candidates expend a fair amount of effort trying to persuade the relatively few independent voters, most of the campaign, particularly in the latter stages, is spent making sure both that their partisan base is registered and that it will turn out to vote. In the real world of presidential campaigns, much of the focus is on the mobilization of these partisans rather than the persuasion of a relatively small number of moderate independents. In spite of hyperbole to the contrary, partisan turnout typically decides elections.

THE INDEPENDENT VOTER

A widely held tenet of American politics is that since the 1950s the number of independent voters is growing. News accounts of the partisan preferences of American voters routinely reflect this belief. In recent years, the rise of the independent voter has been a popular subject. Headlines routinely claim that the number of "independent voters [is] burgeoning" and that "more voters are steering away from party labels."[7] Because they are growing in number, these so-called independents are presumably the most important bloc of voters in any given election.

Indeed, over the past several decades, many who observe American politics frequently have equated the increased numbers of independent voters with the decline of political parties. One textbook was explicit, referring to the "decline of both parties and resultant upsurge of independents."[8] A book from the early 1970s sounded the alarmist note that "the party's over."[9] One of the leading texts on party politics was a bit less dramatic but still suggested that "the American electorate is somewhat less partisan now than it was prior to the 1960s."[10]

In fact, it is true that the number of people registering as independent has been increasing over the past several decades.[11] Using a simple measure of partisan identification, we see that there has indeed been a rise in independents since as far back as the 1950s. This is consistent with a trend toward what some refer to as partisan dealignment,[12] or a growing movement away from attachment to parties within the electorate. A good deal of research suggests that the public sees political parties as being less central to government and the political system. Many people, in other words, view parties as less relevant to the business of government. But these people are not so much *non*partisans as they are *a*partisans.[13] They simply do not believe parties matter.

There is, however, more to the story. In 1952, the Survey Research Center and the Center for Political Studies of the Institute for Social Research at the University of Michigan conducted a wide-ranging national survey related to presidential and congressional elections. They conducted similar surveys in the presidential and midterm elections that followed. In 1977, the National Science Foundation began funding these surveys and, in the process, established the American National Election Studies (ANES).[14] The stated mission of the ANES "is to inform explanations of election outcomes by providing data that support rich hypothesis testing, maximize methodological excellence, measure many variables, and promote comparisons across people, contexts, and time."[15]

One of the many questions over the years that the ANES has asked concerns partisan identification, or the psychological attachment, if any, an individual has toward a political party. The interviewer asks respondents, "Generally speaking, do you usually think of yourself as a Republican, a Democrat, an independent, or what?" Other choices include "other" and, starting in 1966, "no preference." If the respondent answers either "Republican" or "Democrat," there is a follow-up question: "Would you call yourself a strong (Republican/Democrat) or a not very strong (Republican/ Democrat)?" If the respondent answers "independent," "other," or "no preference" to the first question, the question that follows is "Do you think of yourself as closer to the Republican or Democratic party?"[16]

The importance of the ANES surveys for the study of voting behavior would be difficult to overstate. For decades, political scientists have used the information that the ANES collects, and for most, these data represent the gold standard. After an initial study produced in 1954 using ANES data, a research team in 1960 produced what is arguably the most important work in the study of American voting behavior, *The American Voter*.[17] This book alone has spawned a veritable mountain of research since its publication, produced by several generations of scholars. Indeed, it is impossible to study American voting behavior without coming face-to-face with the theories and conclusions of *The American Voter*.

One of the primary findings of the book is that the majority of voters cast their ballots based on their partisan identification. While some have challenged the central role of partisan identification in vote choice,[18] political science research has, over time, clearly demonstrated its powerful influence. This partisan identification develops primarily during childhood under the influence of one's parents.[19] Although some have questioned the validity of the ANES partisan identification measure,[20] it has stood the test of time and is now a standard component of how political behavioralists model the study of voting. Other polling organizations (e.g., Gallup) ask similar questions measuring this concept.

The reason many claim that independent voters are growing in number and importance is that the number of people answering "independent" to the first party identification question has increased—and fairly significantly—since 1952. Measured in this way, the percentage of independents has almost doubled (from 23% to 37%) since the early 1950s (see table 1.1).

However, if we examine this group of independents further and include their responses to the *second* question, we see that the percentage of people

Table 1.1 Democratic, Republican, and Independent Identification, 1952–2016 (in percentages)

Year	Democrats	Independents	Republicans
1952	49	23	28
1954	49	23	28
1956	46	25	31
1958	51	20	29
1960	47	23	30
1962	48	22	30
1964	52	23	25
1966	46	28	25
1968	46	30	25
1970	44	31	24
1972	40	36	23
1974	39	40	22
1976	40	38	23
1978	39	40	21
1980	41	36	23
1982	44	32	24
1984	37	36	27
1986	40	35	26
1988	36	37	28
1990	39	36	25
1992	35	39	25
1994	33	36	30
1996	37	36	27
1998	37	37	26
2000	34	41	24
2002	34	36	31
2004	33	39	28
2008	34	40	26
2012	35	38	27
2016	35	37	28

Sources: Data for 1952 through 2012 from Harold W. Stanley and Richard Niemi, *Vital Statistics on American Politics 2013-2014* (Washington, DC: CQ Press, 2013), table 3.1 (rows do not total 100 percent because those who expressed no preference or a preference other than those presented are excluded). Data (weighted) for 2016 from the 2016 American National Election Survey.

who claim to be closer to *neither* party is rather small. This fits with an intuitive understanding of what an independent actually is. Table 1.2 presents the data again, but this time divides the independents into three categories: those who claim to "lean" toward either one of the two major parties and "pure" independents. Although the percentage of these pure independents has fluctuated over time, and although there was a slight rise in 2012 and 2016, it only briefly (from 1974 to 1978) constituted more than 15 percent

Table 1.2 Partisans, Independent "Leaners," and Pure Independents, 1952–2016 (in percentages)

Year	Democrats, and Independents "Leaning" Democrat	Pure Independents	Republicans, and Independents "Leaning" Republican
1952	59	5	36
1954	58	8	34
1956	53	9	38
1958	58	8	34
1960	53	10	37
1962	56	8	36
1964	61	8	31
1966	55	12	32
1968	56	11	34
1970	54	13	32
1972	51	15	33
1974	52	18	31
1976	52	16	33
1978	53	16	31
1980	52	15	33
1982	55	13	32
1984	48	13	39
1986	50	14	37
1988	48	12	41
1990	51	12	37
1992	49	13	37
1994	46	11	42
1996	51	10	39
1998	51	12	37
2000	49	13	37
2002	50	7	44
2004	50	10	40
2008	51	11	38
2012	47	14	39
2016	46	15	39

Sources: Data for 1952 through 2012 from Harold W. Stanley and Richard Niemi, *Vital Statistics on American Politics 2013–2014* (Washington, DC: CQ Press, 2013), table 3.1 (rows do not total 100 percent because those who expressed no preference or a preference other than those presented are excluded). Data (weighted) for 2016 from the 2016 American National Election Survey.

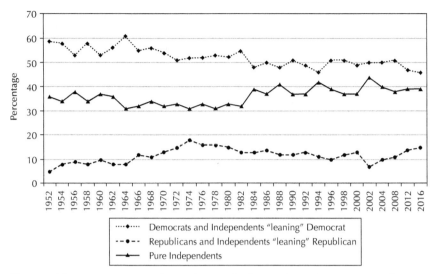

Figure 1.1 Percentage of Partisans, Independent Leaners, and Pure Independents, 1952–2016.
Data for 1952 through 2012 from Harold W. Stanley and Richard Niemi, *Vital Statistics on American Politics 2013–2014* (Washington, DC: CQ Press, 2013), Table 3.1. Data (weighted) for 2016 from the 2016 American National Election Survey.

of the electorate. Figure 1.1 shows the average percentage of partisans and "leaners" (independents who think of themselves as "closer to the Republican or Democratic party"), and pure independents, by decade. Again, while there is an increase in the percentage of independents during this time, it is hardly dramatic.

One conclusion to draw from these data is relatively straightforward: it is not necessarily the measure of partisan identification that is the culprit in propagating the myth of the rising independent voter, but rather how some have used the data from this measurement. A second problem is that an understanding of how leaners and independents actually vote receives short shrift. For example, most leaners are actually partisans in their voting behavior. And, as suggested earlier, partisans tend to be loyal to candidates from their own party. Figure 1.2 shows that partisan loyalty in national elections has increased since the 1980s. Greater than 80 percent of partisan identifiers vote for their party's candidates in elections to the House, Senate, and the presidency. In only a very few cases does the number fall below 75 percent. In other words, partisanship clearly matters when it comes to voting.

Moreover, it is worth remembering another lesson from *The American Voter* and subsequent analyses (e.g., *Myth of the Independent Voter* by Keith et al.). Research strongly suggests that many independent voters are

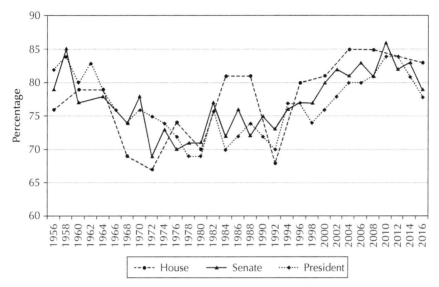

Figure 1.2 Party Line Voting in U.S. Elections, 1952–2016.
From Thomas E. Mann, Norman J. Ornstein, Michael Malbin, and M. E. Reynolds, 2018, *Vital Statistics by Brookings*, Table 2.19.

neither attentive to, nor involved in, politics. While they might be independent, many are not politically active, and they vote at much lower rates than do partisans.[21] It is a mistake, therefore, to focus disproportionate attention on how these individuals might vote in any given election, because many simply will not do so.

WHAT ABOUT SWING VOTERS?

Perhaps no other group of Americans is celebrated in news accounts throughout presidential campaigns more than the elusive[22] and all-powerful "swing voters." Accounts describe them as being nothing short of "supervoters,"[23] or individuals who "decide national elections."[24] In 2008, one popular website went so far as to include an "interactive calculator" to help readers determine for themselves if they belonged in this category.[25] More recently, one political strategist claimed, "swing voters hold the key in 2020."[26]

There are several problems with this focus on so-called swing voters. First, there is no common, agreed-upon definition or understanding of what a swing voter is. As one account surmises, "Political science has committed to neither a single term nor a common definition for this phenomenon."[27] Many, it seems, are actually the independents discussed earlier. Second, even using the most generous definition of a swing voter, they constitute only a minority of the voting public. Third, consistent with the earlier discussion of independents, many behave in a partisan manner in terms of their actual voting behavior. Finally, political science research indicates that swing voters actually "decide" very few elections. The little amount of research on the subject suggests that the demographic profile of swing voters varies from election to election.[28] It is, for example, entirely too simplistic to lump them into a single category like soccer or hockey moms, security moms, NASCAR dads, or Walmart moms as some political observers have done over the years.[29]

So who—or what—is a swing voter? One definition might be that a swing voter is someone whose "candidate preference tends to be variable, and whose ultimate decisions will determine the outcome of the election."[30] Other possible definitions include individuals who are "relatively uncertain about who they will vote for," "persuadable" or "potentially persuadable" voters, those whose votes are "up for grabs," those who have "not developed a committed preference for one candidate," or those who are "undecided."[31]

Political scientists have a few different concepts that seem to correspond, if only imperfectly, to understandings like these. For example, Philip Converse identified a class of less engaged and informed individuals he termed "floating voters," or those who might be persuaded to vote for either party's candidate.[32] V. O. Key Jr. identified a different group of (also less informed) voters he referred to as "party switchers," or those who might cast their ballot for the candidate from one party in one election and the other party's candidate in the next.[33] These two possibilities illustrate one of the problems in coming to a common definition of a swing voter: Does the concept refer to voting behavior in a single election (floating voters) or across multiple elections (party switchers)?

The way that most news organizations and polling firms define a swing voter is based on another approach, namely, the "strength of support" questions in preelection polling. Since Gallup began doing it in 1944, polling organizations attempt to gauge the level of commitment poll respondents have toward their preferred (if any) candidate. For example, in 2016, Rasmussen Reports asked respondents throughout the fall the following question: "If the 2016 presidential election were held today, would you vote for Republican Donald Trump, Democrat Hillary Clinton, Libertarian Gary Johnson or Green Party candidate Jill Stein?" Regardless of who respondents expressed a preference for, they were then asked, "are you sure that you will vote for this candidate or is it possible that something could change your mind between now and Election Day?" Those who claimed that they might change their mind "between now and Election Day" were (and are) classified as swing voters.[34]

It is also common to include those who claim to be undecided as swing voters. This "undecided" category can include those who claim to be "leaning" toward one candidate or the other after expressing no preference. However, there is some evidence that the "undecided" vote may be overreported, perhaps due to the fact that respondents may be reluctant to tell the interviewer what their preference is.[35] Survey firms employ various strategies to measure strength of support for a candidate throughout the campaign, with the idea being that the weakly committed might be considered swing voters.[36] Here too, the undecided voters and those with no preference, but who are leaning toward a particular candidate, are often categorized as swing voters.

The point is that such "strength of support" questions help pollsters determine who the committed voters are. All others fall into the swing voter category. By this measure, swing voters sometimes can make up a sizable segment of the electorate, especially depending on which election it is and at what point during the campaign that respondents are asked the question. One problem is that this measure is so broad that it makes the concept almost meaningless. Swing voters cannot be a critical *subgroup* or *faction* if they constitute a large *majority* of the electorate. Moreover, as noted, there is no consensus that this is the proper way to determine what a swing voter is. Recent research by two political scientists using different methods suggests that the actual percentage of "persuadable" voters (those not firmly committed to either candidate) might be closer to one-fifth of the electorate.[37]

Some research suggests as well that many of the so-called swing voters are self-identified independents,[38] most of whom, as this chapter discussed earlier, exhibit partisan voting patterns. Others have found that many of the so-called persuadable swing voters—those who express only soft support for their candidate—vote for their preferred candidate in the end.[39] In 2004, for example, as many as 85 percent of Bush supporters who said there was a chance they might vote for Kerry, voted for Bush. The percentages for Kerry were similar.[40] This is typical. While the percentages of soft supporters voting for their preferred candidate have been lower in previous elections, research suggests that election campaigns reinforce existing preferences, as opposed to changing minds.[41] Relatively few people, in other words, are actually persuaded to switch during a campaign.

Finally, and this is perhaps the central question: Do swing voters decide elections? As a group, these voters are generally less engaged in politics.[42] Moreover, most of these voters do not really start to focus on the campaign until the fall of the general election and their numbers decrease as the campaign wears on. In the end, many do not even vote.[43] In a fairly sophisticated analysis, a prominent political scientist who specializes in the dynamics of electoral choice and presidential elections determined that the only winning presidential candidate since 1952 who needed the swing vote bloc (as he defined and measured swing voters) to win was John Kennedy in 1960.[44] As a rule, it seems that swing voters do not decide elections.

THE PARTISAN CORE

Thus far we have illustrated that most voters are, at least in terms of how they vote, partisans. How does this reality translate into actual campaign activity during a presidential campaign? It is certainly true that campaigns spend a great deal of time and money attempting to reach what campaigns refer to as "persuadables" (the small percentage of likely voters who are undecided and who may be swayed). There is, in other words, some effort made to capture the votes of the independent or swing voters.

But as the campaign draws to a close, attention shifts to turning out the vote among the partisan core. This is, after all, where the bulk of the votes will come from in an election. Turning out the vote entails efforts to register new voters and getting both them and the party faithful to the polls on Election Day. Party leaders have historically gone to extraordinary lengths—in some cases outside the law—to ensure that they mobilize the votes needed for victory. For example, if the infamous Tammany Hall machine in New York City needed extra votes to put their candidate over the top, they might import extra voters from New Jersey or Pennsylvania.[45] Parties were also not averse to buying votes. Stephen Dorsey, one of the campaign managers of the 1880 Garfield campaign, reportedly bought 30,000 votes in Indiana for two dollars apiece.[46]

Modern get-out-the-vote (GOTV) efforts are very systematic and sophisticated, conducted at both the state and local levels. Research demonstrates that voters are more likely to vote if political parties, candidate organizations, or other interested groups contact them,[47] and voter turnout can be the critical difference in an election outcome. One dramatic example of this is the story of a local school board election in upstate New York. According to the account, one of the candidates, using information from their campaign lists, identified three people who had not yet voted. The candidate drove to the homes of these individuals and persuaded them to go vote. In the end, the candidate won by exactly three votes.[48]

While perhaps not as obvious, there are numerous examples of how GOTV efforts have affected presidential election outcomes. Some political observers attributed Jimmy Carter's close win in 1976 to organized labor's role in Democratic registration and GOTV efforts,[49] as well as the party's successful drive to register African Americans. In 1984, Republicans, who often rely on volunteers, housewives, small-business owners, religious conservatives, and retirees in their effort to turn out the vote,[50] mounted a sophisticated and successful effort, contributing to Reagan's victory.[51]

In 2000, the Democratic Party had an estimated 40,000 volunteers making personal contacts with voters. The National Association for the Advancement of Colored People (NAACP) used telephone messages from President Clinton and African American leaders urging people to vote.

In addition to reminders from church leaders about the importance of voting, this helped double voter turnout from what it had been in 1996 among African Americans in Florida. Republicans were active as well. In the last week of the campaign, they made approximately 85 million telephone calls and sent over 110 million pieces of mail. During the final two weeks, they distributed roughly 16 million pieces of campaign literature to people's doors, 1.2 million yard signs, and over one million bumper stickers. The National Rifle Association, pro-life, and other groups helped in this effort.[52]

After the 2000 election, Bush's main strategist Karl Rove estimated that the campaign had lost some four million conservative voters who had stayed home. Rove subsequently built a GOTV operation designed to increase turnout in 2004. Built around the purchase of commercial databases to pinpoint potential voters, the campaign targeted appeals to members of thirty-two different subgroups in 2004.[53] The campaign also registered approximately 3.4 million voters who had recently moved and reached out to roughly seven million identified Republicans who did not vote consistently. For its part, the Kerry campaign spent $60 million in GOTV efforts, doubling the amount spent by Democrats in 2000. In the last three weeks of the campaign they made approximately sixteen million telephone calls, sent twenty-three million pieces of mail, and delivered eleven million flyers.[54]

Although Barack Obama had an enormous amount of personal appeal, his campaign understood that the presidency is won "on the ground." Obama's 2008 campaign was unprecedented in organization, execution, and scope. The team used "its record-breaking fundraising to open more than 700 offices in more than a dozen battleground states, pay several thousand organizers, and manage tens of thousands of volunteers."[55] Obama used the Internet to recruit and organize an army of volunteers for voter registration and turnout efforts. This translated into a systematic grassroots effort. For example, Ohio was broken down into 1,231 "neighborhoods" that contained 8 to 10 precincts, and importantly, also included rural areas that Kerry had ignored in 2004.

While the Obama campaign faced an "enthusiasm gap" four years later in 2012, in which polling data showed supporters were less enthusiastic than they had been in 2008, it was able to overcome this by focusing, again, on turnout efforts.[56] In virtually every demographic group, Obama's vote totals exceeded polling expectations as the result of these efforts. By contrast, the Republican Party, and the Romney campaign in particular, were at a technological disadvantage, which directly affected mobilization efforts.

However, by 2016, this technological advantage for the Democrats seemed to have been erased. Republicans and the Trump campaign were better able to target and mobilize blocs of voters and potential voters, at least by contrast with Hillary Clinton's presidential campaign and the Democrats. While Clinton mobilized more first-time voters than did Trump (57% to 38%, according to exit polls[57]), voter turnout among the critical African American population fell a full seven percentage points from 2012—this in spite of the fact that "a record number of Americans cast ballots."[58] Perhaps more important, in terms of targeting and mobilizing critical blocs of voters, Clinton's "ground game did not come through in critical places like Philadelphia, Pittsburgh, Detroit, and Milwaukee," cities in three states that virtually all analysts agree Clinton should have won.[59]

CONCLUSION

The conventional wisdom that independent and swing voters are a growing segment of the electorate and decide elections oversimplifies the more complex reality of American election campaigns. As this chapter has illustrated, despite increases in the percentage of self-identified independents, independent "leaners" behave in a distinctly partisan manner on Election Day, casting legitimate doubts as to whether "independents" are increasing in both number and importance. Similarly, even if we could identify who swing voters are with any precision, there are probably fewer of these voters than popular accounts suggest, and, in almost all cases they do not, as a bloc, decide elections, unless perhaps when the margin of victory is exceptionally close.

In short, two of the most widely discussed aspects about American voters—the rise of the independent voter and the importance of the swing voter—require several caveats and a more nuanced discussion than the conventional wisdom typically provides. The plain fact is that party identification still heavily influences most voters in midterm and presidential elections. Indeed, as the final section of this chapter illustrates, the mobilization of core partisan voters is a matter of high priority in modern campaign strategy.

FURTHER READING

Aldrich, John H., Jamie L. Carson, Brad T. Gomez, and David W. Rohde. *Change and Continuity in the 2016 Election.* Thousand Oaks, CA: CQ Press, 2019.

Keith, Bruce E., David B. Magleby, Candice J. Nelson, Elizabeth Orr, Mark C. Westyle, and Raymond E. Wolfinger. *The Myth of the Independent Voter.* Berkeley, CA: University of California, 1992.

Mayer, William G., ed. *The Swing Voter in American Politics.* Washington, DC: Brookings Institution, 2008.

2

To Vote or Not to Vote
Three Myths about Voter Turnout

VOTER TURNOUT IS ONE OF the most thoroughly studied subjects in political science. One could literally fill an entire room with the amount of scholarship that has been devoted to understanding how and why voters and potential voters exercise their most fundamental of democratic freedoms. The reason for this is simple: voting is central to democratic citizenship. If one accepts the Founding Fathers' belief that government derives its legitimacy from the consent of the governed, then participation by citizens in free, fair, and regular elections is necessary for a functioning democracy to exist.

Historians and political scientists frequently trace the evolution of American democracy in terms of when and how certain groups like women, African Americans, and young adults received the right to vote. Indeed, political observers and scholars often view expanding democratic participation and increasing voter turnout as a measure of democratic progress. However, even though voter turnout is so often under the microscope, several commonly held assumptions about the subject are dubious.

Perhaps the most common misconception is the belief that American voter turnout has been in general decline. In previous years some observers have gone so far as to label the situation a "turnout crisis."[1] Nonetheless, research on the subject calls this idea into question, concluding that any decline in turnout might not be as serious as many have suggested.[2] Moreover, discussions about declining voter turnout in the United States typically ignore the fact that the modest voter turnout decline that does exist appears to parallel a decline in most other established democracies.

A more recent controversy regarding voter turnout revolves around discussion of alleged voter fraud and voter identification laws. In what has developed into a divisive partisan issue, rhetoric surrounding these issues has become heated and sometimes exaggerated. On the one side, we hear claims of rampant voter fraud used as justification for stricter voter identification laws. As one account claims, "Unfortunately, in some U.S. cities, voter fraud has been so common and so pervasive for so long that it's more likely to be a punch line than a felony."[3] On the other side, we hear charges that voter identification laws are unnecessary and serve only to suppress the vote, particularly among young and minority voters. Implementing these laws across the fifty states would presumably result in "catastrophic consequences."[4]

There is very little evidence to support either contention. Voter fraud, especially fraud perpetrated by impersonation or stealing another's identification, is exceptionally rare. Indeed, it is almost nonexistent. Likewise, voter identification laws have had only a very modest effect on voter turnout, with some studies suggesting that they have had no significant impact at all.[5]

Given the importance of voter turnout, electoral integrity, and voting rights to a healthy democracy, these issues warrant serious attention and objective discussion. In the pages that follow, we first review the factors that political science research has suggested can affect voter turnout. We then discuss the idea that most political observers use flawed measures of voter turnout, which result in inaccurate—in particular, lower—estimates of voter turnout. Finally, we examine and debunk the claims that suggest American democracy is in crisis, whether because of low turnout, election fraud, or voter suppression.

WHAT AFFECTS VOTER TURNOUT?

Discussions about voting behavior in the United States often begin with the premise that Americans do not vote in percentages equal to the past or that they do not vote in numbers proportionate to citizens in other democracies. Most American government textbooks frame the discussion of voting in the United States in terms of low voter turnout, noting correctly that the United States ranks near the bottom of the world in voter turnout.[6] During the campaign of 2014, a number of stories featured discussion about the "abysmally low turnout" in the United States.[7] The picture these accounts present, at least implicitly, is that our democracy is in decline.[8]

Many scholars have echoed these sentiments. Works such as *The Disappearing American Voter*, *Why Americans Don't Vote*, *Why Americans Still Don't Vote* (emphasis added), *Why America Stopped Voting*, and *Where Have All the Voters Gone?* all suggest that American turnout is in decline.[9] One author, for example, explicitly refers to a "turnout problem."[10] Another summarizes, "In ever larger numbers over the past three decades, Americans have been tuning out campaigns and staying home on Election Day. Turnout has fallen in virtually every type of American election."[11]

There are a variety of explanations offered for the decline in voter turnout in this research. We can divide these explanations into two broad categories: individual-level and institutional factors. Individual-level factors include various characteristics of individual citizens. As it happens, some people are more likely than others to vote. Institutional factors focus simply on the rules governing the administration of elections. A final set of factors includes various aspects of the campaign itself. We will discuss each of these in turn.

Individual-Level Factors

The first set of factors affecting voter turnout deals with characteristics of individuals themselves. For example, research suggests that voting is a habit. The more a person does it, the more likely he or she is to keep doing it.[12] This helps explain why younger citizens are less likely to vote than their older counterparts.[13] People who feel connected to their communities are also more likely to vote, if only because they have something to protect or advocate (e.g., lower property taxes for homeowners).[14]

Another reason why people do not vote is that many are either not interested in, or are cynical about, government, politics, and politicians.[15] It is common, for example, to hear people complain that campaigns are too long, too negative, and focus too much on personality rather than on the issues. This is significant because these negative perceptions can lead to cynicism about campaign politics, the political system, and the belief that voting has the potential to affect change. These feelings are important because an individual's sense of political efficacy (the confidence an individual has in their own political understanding and abilities), trust in government, and sense of duty associated with citizenship are often significant predictors of voting.[16] Along these lines, people who identify with, or feel attached to, a political party are more apt to vote than people who claim they are independents (see previous chapter).[17]

Related to these general attitudes about politics and the individual's place in the political system is knowledge about politics. Those who are more knowledgeable about politics are more likely to vote. In fact, formal education itself has a similar effect on an individual's likelihood of voting. The more educated one is in terms of formal schooling, the more likely that individual is to vote.[18] This may be the result of the fact that our system of government, like the institutional arrangements governing elections, is fairly complex. Individuals can easily become confused about their choices and the implications of those choices.

In addition to education, the academic literature overwhelmingly confirms that other socioeconomic, demographic, and background variables can affect turnout, including income, gender, race and ethnicity, marital status, residential mobility, religiosity, and organizational memberships.[19] Figure 2.1, for example, shows that while voter turnout has increased in the past three decades for whites and non-whites, this increase was especially pronounced among African Americans in the 2008 and 2012 elections.

Age has been the focus of a few studies.[20] In the late 1960s and early 1970s, at the height of the Vietnam War, young people who opposed the military draft mobilized around the slogan, "old enough to fight, old enough to vote." Eventually, this led to ratification of the Twenty-Sixth Amendment in 1971, which lowered the voting age from twenty-one to eighteen. In 1972, the first election after the amendment's ratification, youth voter turnout (defined as eighteen to twenty-four year olds) reached an impressive rate of 54.6 percent.[21] However, in the years that followed, youth turnout rates have been consistently lower than those for older Americans (see figure 2.2). In spite of commentators' frequent predictions

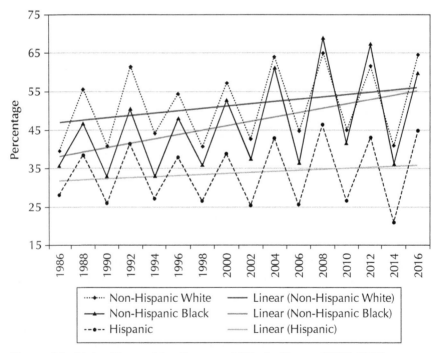

Figure 2.1 Voter Turnout by Race and Ethnic Group, 1986–2016.
Source: Michael P. McDonald, "United States Election Project," http://www.elec tproject.org/home/voter-turnout/demographics.

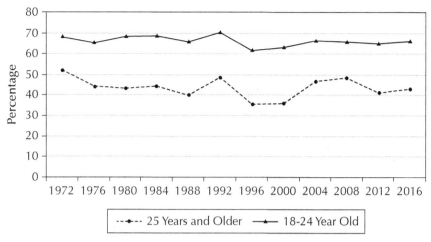

Figure 2.2 Youth Voter Turnout in Presidential Elections, 1972–2016.
Sources: For 1972–2008, see the Center for Information & Research on Civic Learning and Engagement, http://www.civicyouth.org/wp-content/uploads/2007/10/72_12_cps_voting_WithLogos.xls. Data for 2012 and 2016 from U.S. Census, https://docs.google.com/spreadsheets/d/1lSd27SlEirIlKHOFWADswBv6cyN5i8 4zd08z69xS3Wk/edit?usp=sharing.

that a given election will be the "big year" for young voters, these expecta-tions nearly always fall short.[22]

Institutional Factors: The Rules

A second set of factors that affects voter turnout deal with institutions, or the rules governing the administration of elections. The act of voting in the United States is more difficult than it is in other democracies. This, many believe, drives turnout down. Borrowing from economists, some political scientists hold that individuals are "rational actors" who weigh the costs of voting against its perceived benefits. For example, filling out a registration form, traveling long distances to reach a polling place, and then waiting in a line to cast a ballot might be too much of a cost when compared with the perceived benefit of casting one vote.

Institutional factors may be important because they can reduce the costs of voting by making the process more accessible and convenient for citizens. State laws dictate most of the rules and requirements for voting. This includes standards for voter registration, the location of polling places, the times that these polling places will be open, absentee ballot require-ments, and more.[23]

Despite the idiosyncrasies of each state's voting laws and requirements, several general aspects of election law in the United States are important to understand in a discussion of possible reasons as to why people do not vote. Many studies suggest that restrictive laws, such as registration requirements, or in particular, deadlines that force citizens to register early in the election season, result in decreased voter turnout.[24] For example, in most states, people are required to register to vote before Election Day. The length of time varies from state to state, but it is usually at least a few weeks prior to the election. This is not the case in other established democracies, where voters are automatically "registered" simply by virtue of being a citizen. In the United States, some people—even the best intentioned—simply forget to register until it is too late or to reregister after moving. The result is that they cannot vote.

In most other democracies in the world, voting takes place on weekends or special holidays dedicated to voting. In the United States, Election Day is on a Tuesday. This is significant because most people work on Tuesdays. In order to vote, people have several rather inconvenient options. They can rise early and go to the polls before work, or they can vote during a lunch break, during work (with the boss's permission), or after work. This added inconvenience (or cost, in the language of rational choice theory) may reduce the likelihood of voting.

There are also more elections in the United States than in any other country. In most European democracies there are only a few elections (e.g., representative to parliament, representative to the European Union, and a scattering of local offices) held in any given four- or five-year period. By comparison, the U.S. system offers a bewildering array of elections almost every year. There are, for example, primary and general elections for the U.S. House of Representatives and other offices every two years (all even-numbered years). In some states and cities, citizens vote in primary and general elections for governor, state legislature, mayor, city council, and so on, during odd-numbered years. Elections to decide on ballot propositions can also occur in any year and at different times of the year. In some rare instances, citizens might even have to vote in a recall election. Put simply, the decentralized system of elections in the United States asks Americans to vote with great frequency.

In addition, voting in the United States can be a somewhat complicated affair. In most democracies, citizens might be asked to cast a vote for a political party and maybe for a single member of parliament from their district, and perhaps for a few other offices. Our system of federalism and separated government means there are a multiplicity of offices that voters must decide on, from president down to county commissioner, local sheriff, circuit court judges, and more. In total, there are over one million elective offices in the United States, and ballots rarely simplify matters by giving voters the option of voting a straight-party ticket for all offices.[25] The array of choices citizens face at the voting booth can be intimidating, especially to first-time voters, who are inexperienced and more likely to be lacking in information about the process and the choices facing them. In fact, it may be so intimidating that they decide to stay home.

Finally, with respect to the rules governing elections, plurality-winner rules in single-member districts decide nearly all elections for federal office in the United States. This is unlike electoral systems in most other democracies, which employ a system of proportional representation, either completely or combined with plurality-winner/single-member districts. Some research has suggested that voter turnout is lower in plurality-winner/single-member district systems because they tend to produce two-party systems, which provide citizens with fewer choices, presumably reducing the incentive for citizens who support minor-party candidates to vote.[26]

Citizens can become especially frustrated with only two choices. Candidates in a two-party system often blur their differences in an attempt to capture the "median voter," who falls in the middle of the ideological spectrum.[27] In short, the choices facing citizens on Election Day may not seem as clear as they would like them to be, which reduces the incentive to vote.

While some of these rules may depress voter turnout, there have been several efforts in recent years to ease the burden on citizens to vote. The first, and perhaps most prominent, was the National Voter Registration Act of 1993 (the Motor Voter Bill) that requires motor vehicle offices nationwide to accept voter registration applications, and allows other government agencies and programs to do so as well. In fact, some states, including Oregon, California, West Virginia, and Vermont, have automatic registration for any citizen who interacts with the DMV (Department of Motor Vehicles).[28] Mail-in and online voter registration also has become common in many states. Additionally, as of 2019, twenty-one states plus the District of Columbia allow same day (Election Day) registration.[29]

Many states are doing more to reduce the burden of voting itself. All states have absentee ballots that allow individuals to vote from a location other than their designated polling place and at a time that is convenient to them. In twenty-eight of these states "no excuse" absentee voting is allowed, meaning that individuals do not have to have a reason for requesting an absentee ballot, and early voting is allowed in thirty-five states. Three states (Oregon, Washington, and Colorado) conduct their elections entirely by mail. Finally, more than half of the states require that private businesses give employees time off to vote, and many provide that the employee be paid for this time (at least in some cases).[30] Table 2.1 presents a summary overview of how laws governing voter registration and voting vary by state.

Interestingly, evidence is mixed about whether institutional reforms have had significant and substantive effects on voter turnout.[31] In fact, one school of thought suggests that making voting easier by reducing the institutional costs associated with it mainly benefits those who would vote in any event.

Table 2.1   Summary: Laws Governing Voter Registration* and Voting, by State (2018)

Average number of days required to register to vote before election	18.6
Number of states that require citizens to register to vote from 28 to 30 days before election	19
Number of states that allow same day registration	21
Number of states that allow online voter registration	37
Number of states that allow citizens to change their voter registration information online after already registered	4
Number of states that have automatic registration for any citizen that interacts with a government agency	18
Vote by mail for all elections	3
Early voting allowed	39
Photo ID required	17
Number of states that allow "no excuse" absentee voting**	28

Sources: Heather Perkins, "Elections," in Book of the States, 2018, chap. 6, The Council of State Governments, 2018, http://knowledgecenter.csg.org/kc/conten t/book-states-2018-chapter-6-elections; The National Conference of State Leg-islatures, http://www.ncsl.org/research/elections-and-campaigns/same-day-reg istration.aspx; http://www.ncsl.org/research/elections-and-campaigns/automat ic-voter-registration.aspx; http://www.ncsl.org/research/elections-and-campaig ns/early-voting-in-state-elections.aspx; http://www.ncsl.org/research/elections-and-campaigns/voter-id.aspx.

*North Dakota does not require voter registration.

**Not applicable in Colorado, Oregon, and Washington, which conduct their elections by mail.

No overview of these institutional-level factors would be complete without noting, at least in passing, the wide variation in voter turnout between the states. Table 2.2 details turnout among the states in the 2016 presidential election. Voter turnout ranges from lows of 42.3 percent (Hawaii) and 50.2 percent (West Virginia) to a high of 74.1 percent in Minnesota.

Campaign-Specific Factors

A final set of factors that affect voter turnout has to do with the campaign itself. Competitive elections tend to see higher voter turnout, quite likely because individuals are more likely to believe their vote will make a differ-ence. This may be one reason why voter turnout was so low in 1996, a year few thought Bob Dole had a real chance to defeat the incumbent President Bill Clinton. In addition, elections that generate more media coverage tend to stimulate greater interest, which in turn leads to greater turnout.[32] Simi-larly, candidates, parties, interest groups, and ordinary citizens can play a role in stimulating interest in the campaign as well by talking to other citizens. Individuals who meet or are contacted by a candidate are far more

Table 2.2   Voter Turnout, by State, 2016

State	Percentage (VEP)	State	Percentage (VEP)
Hawaii	42.3	Alaska	61.0
West Virginia	50.2	Illinois	61.6
Tennessee	51.1	Montana	61.8
Texas	51.4	Missouri	62.2
Oklahoma	52.3	Nebraska	62.8
Arkansas	52.8	Ohio	62.9
New Mexico	54.5	Pennsylvania	63.6
Arizona	54.9	Connecticut	63.7
Mississippi	55.2	Vermont	63.7
Indiana	56.4	Delaware	64.2
California	56.5	New Jersey	64.4
South Carolina	56.7	Florida	64.5
New York	56.8	North Carolina	64.5
Utah	56.8	Michigan	64.7
Nevada	57.4	Washington	64.7
Kansas	57.7	Virginia	66.1
Kentucky	58.6	Oregon	66.2
South Dakota	58.6	Maryland	66.4
Alabama	58.8	Massachusetts	67.2
Georgia	59.1	Iowa	68.4
Rhode Island	59.1	Wisconsin	69.5
Idaho	59.2	Colorado	70.0
Wyoming	59.5	Maine	70.7
Louisiana	60.0	New Hampshire	71.4
District of Columbia	60.4	Minnesota	74.1
North Dakota	60.8		

Source: Michael P. McDonald, "United States Election Project," http://www
.electproject.org/home/voter-turnout/voter-turnout-data.

likely to get involved than those who have not.[33] One especially interesting recent research finding is that personalized campaign messages and appeals are a particularly effective method of generating increased turnout.[34] This is especially true with regard to person-to-person contact, which can be extremely effective in getting people to vote. In other words, one person can make a difference by simply talking to friends, family, coworkers, or associates.[35]

In sum, there are a multiplicity of factors that affect whether individuals will exercise their most fundamental of democratic freedoms. They are important to understand because, as noted earlier, voter turnout confers the "consent of the governed"—a vital component to the legitimacy of democratic government. In the next section we turn our attention to the myth of the "vanishing voter," focusing on how voter turnout is measured and reported.

VOTER TURNOUT IN THE UNITED STATES

What can we make of the claim that American democracy is in peril because of ever-lower and dangerous levels of voter turnout? Is voter turnout in the United States in decline? To suggest that this is the case misrepresents the reality. The fact is that when measured correctly, voter turnout has remained relatively constant—indeed, increased somewhat—over the past few decades. Moreover, any decline in voter turnout in the United States is quite consistent with developments in other countries. But this particular myth is rooted in a faulty method of calculating voter turnout.

Determining voter turnout would seem to be a fairly straightforward calculation: the number of votes cast (the numerator) is divided by the number of potential voters (the denominator). On the one hand, it is relatively easy to tabulate the number of votes counted in any given election. On the other hand, tabulating the number of potential voters is not as simple a task as one might think. For this, most people typically utilize census data, in particular, a count of all people who are eighteen or older. This is referred to as the voting-age population (VAP).

Until fairly recently, the VAP measure was the accepted standard in calculating voter turnout rates. However, political scientists Michael McDonald and Samuel Popkin have noted that the VAP measure is problematic because it fails to accurately tabulate the number of *eligible* voters. Age, they note, is not the only criterion for a person to be considered eligible to vote. Noncitizens are ineligible to vote, as are prisoners and felons in many states. Several states even prohibit ex-felons from voting. Most accounts of voter turnout throughout American history fail to consider the actual eligible population.

McDonald and Popkin suggest that the decline in voter turnout in the past fifty to sixty years has been systematically overestimated because of an increase in the number of those eighteen years of age or older who are non-citizens or felons. McDonald and Popkin also examine residency requirements in various states, which they estimate disenfranchise approximately 1 percent of the VAP in any given election.[36] Finally, they note that the census has become more accurate over the past half century. In 1940, the Census Bureau estimated that its count missed approximately 5 percent of the population. Many of these "missed" citizens were likely to be poor and less educated, and therefore less likely to vote, resulting in potentially biased turnout statistics. This number shrank to less than 2 percent in 1990.[37]

More simply, the number of people incorrectly counted as potential voters—the voting-age population—has grown relative to those who have reported voting. These discrepancies have collectively created a situation whereby the statistics have *overestimated* the number of people eligible to vote, thus *underestimating* voter turnout. This problem is especially acute in states that have greater populations of voting-age people who are not eligible to vote (for example, legal immigrants who are not citizens). This explains much of the reason that previous estimates using the VAP statistic appear to have overstated declines in voter turnout.

A final aspect of our discussion centers on the calculation of the number of votes cast. Many experts believe that one of the reasons voter turnout was so high in the late 1800s is that there was a good deal of election fraud in various states and localities.[38] For example, some research suggests that in certain areas of the country corrupt election officials "stuffed" ballot boxes or deliberately reported false returns, often inflating the vote totals for the candidate of the party in power.[39] This would, of course, lead to inflated rates of voter turnout. Unfortunately, no complete data are available to estimate the effects of vote fraud on voter turnout.

McDonald and Popkin's research points to another fact worth considering. The numerator in the voter turnout equation relies on the number of votes cast for president (during presidential election years) or the number of votes cast for members of Congress (during midterm election years). However, this method systematically undercounts the number of votes cast because some citizens, albeit only a small percentage (approximately 2%), show up to the polls to vote for ballot propositions or local offices but abstain from casting votes for higher offices.[40] This would not have been possible until the widespread adoption of the Australian ballot in the 1890s, a period that corresponds with yet another fairly sharp decline in turnout.[41]

Table 2.3 shows estimates of the turnout rate using the VAP as well as the voting eligible population (VEP). Importantly, the VEP calculation only corrects for felons and noncitizens who are ineligible, not for the mentally incompetent, those disenfranchised by residency requirements, or census undercounting. In other words, the corrections are conservative. The final column shows a fairly significant increase in the difference using these two methods to calculate the turnout rate. The point is that VEP estimates of turnout suggest a less dramatic decline in voter turnout than do those based on VAP.

Regardless of whether one calculates voter turnout using VAP or VEP, it is still true that turnout in the United States has declined slightly over the past century and remains lower when compared with turnout in other established democracies. Yet, the way in which some political observers present this fact often makes the situation appear bleaker than it actually is. For example, figure 2.3 presents turnout rates in the United States from 1828 to 2016. Here, the decline in voter turnout appears to be dramatic.

However, figure 2.4 presents data measuring voter turnout from 1920 (when the size of the electorate effectively doubled) to 2016. Here, the trend line shows a slight increase. In fact, since 1972, turnout in presidential

Table 2.3 VAP versus VEP: Voter Turnout Rates in U.S. Elections, 1972–2016

Year	VAP Turnout Rate	VEP Turnout Rate	Difference
1972	55.2	56.2	1.0
1974	38.2	39.1	0.9
1976	53.5	54.8	1.3
1978	37.9	39.0	1.1
1980	52.8	54.7	1.9
1982	40.6	43.0	2.4
1984	53.3	57.2	3.9
1986	36.5	39.0	2.5
1988	50.3	54.2	3.9
1990	36.5	39.8	3.3
1992	55.0	60.6	5.6
1994	38.9	41.8	2.9
1996	48.9	52.6	3.7
1998	36.1	39.0	2.9
2000	51.2	55.6	4.4
2002	36.3	40.5	4.2
2004	55.4	60.7	5.3
2006	37.1	41.3	4.2
2008	56.9	62.3	5.4
2012	53.6	58.6	5.0
2014	33.2	36.7	3.5
2016	54.7	60.1	5.4

Source: Michael P. McDonald, "United States Election Project," http://www.electproject.org/home/voter-turnout/voter-turnout-data.

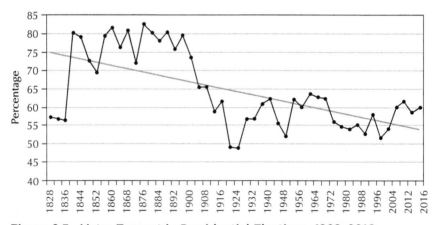

Figure 2.3 Voter Turnout in Presidential Elections, 1828–2016.
Source: United States Election Project, "National General Election VEP Turnout Rates, 1789–Present," http://www.electproject.org/national-1789-present.

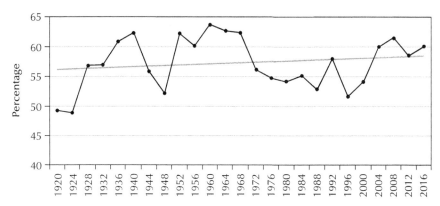

Figure 2.4 Voter Turnout in Presidential Elections, 1920–2016.
Source: United States Election Project, "National General Election VEP Turnout Rates, 1789–Present," http://www.electproject.org/national-1789-present.

elections has generally hovered consistently in the mid to high 50 percent range; in four years (1992, 2004, 2008, and 2016) it has exceeded 60 percent. This only reinforces the point that voters do not appear to be "vanishing."

In spite of this, U.S. voter turnout rates are consistently lower when measured against turnout in other established democracies. It is also true, however, that voter turnout has been declining in other nations over the past fifty years.[42] As table 2.4 indicates, average voter turnout from the 1950s to the 2010s has declined significantly in other established democracies. The table also makes clear that although U.S. voter turnout is lower than all of the others, the decline in the United States during this period is less than in any of these countries.

It is worth noting, however, that voter turnout in the 2014 election was unusually low in the United States at just 35.9 percent of the VEP.[43] This

Table 2.4 Decline in Voter Turnout, Six Established Democracies, 1950–2016

	Canada	France	Germany	Japan	United Kingdom	United States
Mean, 1950s	69.6%	71.3%	84.1%	73.7%	79.1%	59.3%
Mean, 2010s	54.2%	58.6%	66.0%	55.8%	61.1%	54.8%
Decline	15.4%	12.7%	18.1%	17.9%	17.9%	7.1%

Note: Cell entries for the United States are for presidential election; entries for all other countries are for parliamentary elections. All figures are calculated based on VAP.

Source: International Institute for Democracy and Electoral Assistance, http://www.idea.int/vt.

reinforced the alarmist view that American democracy is in trouble.[44] However, turnout in 2016 was at 60.1 percent, the fourth highest since 1972, and in the 2018 midterm election turnout was 49 percent,[45] the highest for a midterm election since 1966. In other words, the 2014 election notwithstanding, based on the data presented here, it is difficult to argue that voter turnout in the United States has reached crisis lows.

VOTER FRAUD AND VOTER ID LAWS

Significant controversy arose in the aftermath of the hotly contested presidential election of 2000 about African Americans waiting in long lines to vote or being denied the vote in certain areas of northern Florida. Others asserted that many absentee ballots from members of the military were unjustly disqualified.[46] In 2004, there were problems with voting machines and long lines at many inner city polling stations in Ohio, a state that was expected to be central to victory for both candidates. Democrats complained that these long lines likely decreased voter turnout in these areas, which may have cost its presidential nominee, John Kerry, critical votes.[47] In 2008, much ado was made about the activities of the pro-Obama group, the Association of Community Organizations for Reform Now. Republicans claimed the group was organizing registration and voting efforts for individuals who were not actually eligible to vote.[48]

Rhetoric concerning alleged disenfranchisement and voter fraud has evolved to the point where there are now two easily identifiable sets of charges and claims, each associated with one of the two major parties. Republicans, claiming to have evidence of widespread voter fraud, insist on the need to secure the "integrity" of elections by enacting laws that demand citizens produce photo identification in order to vote.[49] Democrats counter these claims by asserting that evidence of voter impersonation—the type of fraud that identification laws intend to eliminate—is exceedingly rare. They claim that voter identification laws are a ploy by Republicans to suppress turnout among lower income and minority citizens who traditionally support the Democratic Party.[50]

Is there any merit to these claims? Is voter fraud a problem? Do voter identification laws suppress turnout, particularly among minorities and lower income citizens? The evidence suggests that both charges are exaggerated. On the one hand, anecdotes of voter fraud and disenfranchisement due to identification requirements abound. However, despite the fact that claims about widespread voter fraud or suppression make for good partisan rhetoric, neither claim is widely supported by evidence.

There have been several systematic studies during the past decade examining the extent to which voter fraud may be a problem in national elections, and most come to a similar conclusion.[51] In-person voter fraud, where an individual claims to be someone he or she is not in order to vote, is extremely rare. Documented cases of voter fraud in any given national election rarely number higher than a few dozen.[52] In one of the most comprehensive studies on voter fraud, Justin Levitt of the Brennan Center for Justice at New York University's School of Law reported that "there have been a handful of substantiated cases of individual ineligible voters attempting to defraud the election system. But by any measure, voter fraud is extraordinarily rare."[53] Levitt notes the lack of incentive to commit voter fraud given the harsh federal penalties (five years in prison and a $10,000 fine) and additional state penalties for the inconsequential benefit of an additional vote.

Levitt concludes that purported cases of voter fraud can be typically traced to benign errors, such as clerical and typographical errors.

> Often, what appears to be voter fraud—a person attempting to vote under a false name, for example—can be traced back to a typo. . . . For example, despite having died in 1997, Alan J. Mandel was alleged to have voted in 1998; upon further investigation, Alan J. Mandell (two "l"s), who was very much alive and voting at the time, explained that local election workers simply checked the wrong name off of the list.[54]

One report from North Carolina in 2010 appeared to indicate a clear case of voter fraud. A conservative think tank, Civitas, presented evidence showing that some 2,214 voters in the state cast ballots at the ripe age of 110.[55] However, upon further investigation it was shown that these numbers were the artifact of an old voter registration law, which, before 1960, only required people to provide proof that they were of legal age to vote. A person did not have to provide an exact date of birth. For those who did not report a date of birth, the state entered a default year of 1900. Of course, none of those voters were actually born in 1900. All proved to be both alive and eligible to vote. What appeared to be voter fraud was not.[56]

If there is no evidence of widespread or systematic voter fraud, why the push for identification laws? Part of the reason is that they were included as one of the recommendations of the blue ribbon Commission on Federal Election Reform, formed after the 2000 presidential election and chaired by former President Jimmy Carter and former Secretary of State James Baker III.[57] Critics, of course, as noted earlier, allege more cynical reasons they believe are rooted in efforts by Republicans to gain an electoral advantage by disenfranchising young and minority voters who disproportionately vote for Democrats. In fact, some Republicans have added fuel to this suspicion by admitting to this motivation publicly, as one North Carolina Republican did on the *Daily Show with Jon Stewart* in 2013.[58] Democrats not only question Republican motives but also claim that voter identification laws could have a significant impact in reducing voter turnout.[59]

However, scholarly research on this subject is largely inconclusive. Some published research does support the claim that such laws have a negative effect on voter turnout, especially among minorities.[60] One study, while finding little evidence of an overall relationship between voter identification laws and voter turnout, did find that these laws seemed to depress turnout among lower income and less educated citizens.[61] Importantly, however, other studies find no effect.[62]

What explains these differing conclusions? The simple fact is that there are numerous methodological difficulties associated with estimating the effects of voter identification laws—indeed, any laws—on voter turnout.[63] These difficulties include the fact that because voting is done by secret ballot, it is difficult to ascertain with any certainty exactly who did and did not vote. For example, it is well understood that surveys asking people if they voted in previous election(s) overestimate voter turnout.[64] Why? Because many people are reluctant to admit to researchers that they did not vote. One review of research on the effects of voter identification laws on voter turnout concludes, "None of this is to say that voter identification laws are unproblematic. It is just difficult to prove that they are associated with lower turnout."[65]

CONCLUSION

Over the past several decades, a myriad of observers have pushed the notion that American democracy is in crisis, whether due to low voter turnout or, most recently, voter fraud and voter suppression. Yet, as this chapter makes clear, American democracy is not in crisis. Voter turnout is not in serious decline, even in the aftermath of several states passing voter identification laws, and voter fraud is nearly nonexistent.

Of course, this is not to suggest that American democracy is perfect, nor that voter fraud or voter suppression are not important issues worthy of our attention. A democracy requires fairness in the electoral process for citizens to respect election outcomes and the legitimacy of government. But proper and informed perspective on these issues is critical.

FURTHER READING

Hill, David. *American Voter Turnout: An Institutional Approach.* New York, NY: Routledge, 2018.

Leighley, Jan E., and Jonathan Nagler. *Who Votes Now? Demographics, Issues, Inequality, and Turnout in the United States.* Princeton, NJ: Princeton University Press, 2014.

Springer, Melanie Jean. *How the States Shaped the Nation: American Electoral Institutions and Voter Turnout, 1920–2000.* Chicago: University of Chicago Press, 2014.

3

End of the Two-Party System?

The Myth of the Rise of Third Parties

IN 1968, FORMER ALABAMA GOVERNOR George Wallace ran for president as a candidate of the American Independent Party, famously declaring, "there's not a dime's worth of difference" between the Democratic and Republican parties.[1] One book, published decades later, used Wallace's statement in its title.[2] Presidential candidate Ralph Nader also repeated this claim during his 2000 and 2004 campaigns.[3] Nader, among others, was known for referring to the two major parties as "Tweedledum and Tweedledee," a reference to the twins in Lewis Carroll's *Through the Looking-Glass and What Alice Found There*.[4] Many Americans agree with this assessment of the two major political parties in America. For example, a 2014 Gallup poll revealed that 35 percent of respondents believe that the two parties were "pretty much the same" when asked if there were "important differences between Republicans and Democrats on issues that matter to you."[5] In fact, many voters not only fail to see differences between the parties but also often respond favorably to poll questions about the need for a third party.[6]

Of course, Americans have always been somewhat ambivalent about political parties. This may be in part due to the fact that most learn at an early age that George Washington warned of the destructive and divisive potential of political parties in his 1796 Farewell Address.[7] However, dissatisfaction with the two major parties is near an all-time high. A 2018 Gallup poll found that 57 percent of Americans believed that "a third major political party is needed" because the Democratic and Republican parties do "a poor job" of "representing the American people."[8] Indeed, over the past decade, support for a third party has averaged over 50 percent. Of those polled, "only about four in 10" have a positive view of the Republican and Democratic parties, reflecting a rather "tepid" view of each "for much of the last decade."[9] One observer put it simply, "The American people have finally had enough of a two-party system."[10]

Citing the perceived similarities and declining popularity that voters express toward the Democratic and Republican parties in public opinion polls, political pundits frequently trumpet the notion that a viable third party is on its way and will soon advance into a position where it can seriously compete with the two major parties. These predictions of third-party success, however, almost never materialize, and, in the rare cases when they do, prove to be short-lived.

In this chapter, we review the two structural reasons why the rise of a third party in the United States is unlikely to occur in any significant and sustained way despite the declining popularity of the two major parties. First, the American electorate is predominately moderate, meaning that parties and candidates are competing for a large share of votes in the middle of the ideological spectrum. While it might be possible for a third party to emerge in such an electoral environment, it is more likely that competition would, over time, settle into one between the two parties—leaving the weaker party behind.

Yet, a moderate electorate is not enough to ensure the stability of a two-party system. The second reason we are unlikely to see a third party succeed in the long term is the electoral system. In particular, rules that specify that only one winner will be selected from each electoral district and that the winner will be the individual who receives the most (not the majority of) votes, all serve as powerful disincentives for supporters of third or minor parties.

PARTY SYSTEMS IN COMPARATIVE PERSPECTIVE

Most democracies have multiparty systems, and parties in these systems represent a broad range of the ideological spectrum. For example, in most European democracies, there is a significant socialist or social democratic party on the left. Great Britain has the Labour Party, France has its Socialist Party, and Germany has the Social Democratic Party.[11] These same countries also have conservative or Christian democratic parties that oppose them from the right side of the ideological spectrum. Examples include Great Britain's Conservative Party, France's Rally for the Republic, and Germany's Christian Democratic Union (with its smaller sister party, the Christian Socialist Union). In addition to these main parties of the left and right, most European democracies, as well as other established democracies, have minor parties that win a significant share of the vote in elections to the European Parliament, national parliaments, and local elections (for a listing of some of these parties, see table 3.1).[12] An impressive show of minor-party strength occurred in France where ultranationalist candidate

Table 3.1 Examples of Minor Parties in European Democracies

Party Type	Examples
Classic Liberal	Free Democratic Party (Germany), Liberal Democrats (Great Britain)
Green	German Green Party, The Greens (France)
Regional	Scottish National Party (Great Britain), Northern League (Italy)
Nationalist/Populist	National Front (France), Austrian Freedom Party
Radical Socialist/Communist	The Left (Germany), French Communist Party

Jean-Marie Le Pen of the National Front Party finished a surprising second in the presidential election of 2002. A decade later in 2012, Le Pen's daughter, Marine, ran a strong presidential campaign herself, finishing with 18 percent of the vote, slightly higher than the vote share received by her father in the first round of balloting in 2002.[13]

By comparison, the United States has always had a two-party system, and the same two parties have dominated national politics since 1860. Both of these parties occupy a relatively small space on the spectrum of major political ideologies of the world. To be more specific, both American political parties come from the same classic liberal tradition. Both embrace, as a matter of faith, classic liberal ideas about individual freedoms. These ideas find acceptance in the economic realm of a market economy and in the political realm of democratic governance. In this narrow sense, it is true that there is not a "dime's worth of difference" between the Republican and Democratic parties.

It is within this relatively small ideological slice of classic liberalism that American politics takes place. However, there is a wide gulf separating the two parties when it comes to their prescriptions for American society. Party activists, members, and supporters hold sharply different opinions on most issues of public policy.[14] Members of Congress have grown more polarized over time as well, suggesting that elites in the two parties find few issues on which to agree.[15] The two major American political parties are, in fact, quite different from each other in terms of the positions they take on any variety of issues. Yet, the differences between Republicans and the Democrats are not as great as the differences between major parties in some other democracies.

Several theories have been advanced to explain the stability of the two-party system in the United States. Political scientist V. O. Key suggests that there is a lasting duality of interests in American society that, while shifting (East–West, North–South, urban–rural), naturally coalesces to form a two-party system.[16] Another theory is the social consensus theory, which suggests that because the United States did not have a feudal past, there has historically been agreement on the basic values that provide the foundation for the republic (democratic government, a market economy). Therefore, two parties have always been needed to forge compromise.[17] These theories are centered primarily on the idea that parties are an outgrowth of social forces. Our discussion first takes this bottom-up approach, focusing on the idea that the American electorate is a generally moderate one.

A RELATIVELY MODERATE ELECTORATE AND THE MEDIAN VOTER THEORY

Compared to citizens in many other countries, research suggests that the American electorate is fairly moderate.[18] Although some issues, such as abortion or gay marriage, can be fairly divisive, relatively few people claim to be extremely liberal or extremely conservative.[19] If we accept that aggregate opinion is moderate on most issues, it can be depicted as a bell-shaped curve, or a "normal" distribution. In figure 3.1, the horizontal axis represents the hypothetical positions that can be taken on any given issue, ranging from extremely liberal (Democratic) on the left to extremely conservative (Republican) on the right. The vertical axis represents the number of people who take these positions. For example, at the extreme right end of the x-axis, there are relatively few individuals classified as extremely conservative Republicans. A majority clustered in the middle area of the spectrum indicates that most people are relatively moderate. The shaded area of the figure represents the number of voters who are one standard deviation off the mean, or the midpoint, and are the individuals who are closest to the

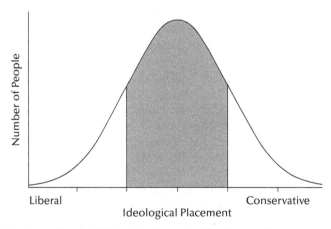

Figure 3.1 Hypothetical Distribution of a Moderate Electorate.

middle. This shaded area represents 68.3 percent of the distribution, or the total area of the figure—a clear majority.

Parties competing for votes among a moderate electorate will attempt to moderate their program and message, or "move to the center," in order to capture the greatest number of votes. This is known as the "median voter theory." Originally the work of economists, it was first articulated in an article by Duncan Black and subsequently expanded upon in Anthony Downs's influential *An Economic Theory of Democracy*.[20] Downs's theorem suggests individuals will vote for the party or candidate that is closest to them on the ideological spectrum. Because voters in the United States cluster in the middle of the spectrum (in statistical terms, are normally distributed), parties and candidates naturally moderate their message and move to the center. This tendency has the effect of reducing the effective number of parties, as only a limited number can reasonably compete for the same bloc of votes.

The notion that there are few discernible differences between the two major parties is based on the fact that candidates sometimes moderate their party's policy positions when campaigning for office. This then explains the myth of Tweedledum and Tweedledee. As candidates from both parties moderate their messages or issue positions, their resulting messages will appear to be, or might actually be, quite similar.

ELECTORAL SYSTEMS: RULES AND THEIR EFFECTS

An electoral system is a set of rules that govern how votes will translate into seats in government office. While it might be tempting to believe that one could simply count votes and award seats to those who received the most votes, this might not always be the answer. For example, imagine a scenario in which three candidates, Smith, Jones, and Brown, are running for president. The election is held and the votes are distributed as follows:

- Smith: 35 percent
- Jones: 33 percent
- Brown: 32 percent

In this case, we might simply award the presidency to Smith, as she received more votes than either of the other two candidates. This would mean, however, that she would take office even though 65 percent of the voting public (almost two-thirds) did *not* vote for her. Electoral systems must sometimes deal with complex issues like this and others.

Electoral systems address two main questions: how many winners will there be, and how will winners be determined? Regarding the number of winners, there are several alternatives. For example, at-large elections often determine city council races. Under such a system, voters select a list of candidates for *all* of the seats on the council, and the seats are then awarded to those individuals who receive the most votes. Alternatively, some city and town councils, and even a few state legislatures, have so-called multimember districts, where voters elect at least two candidates to represent the district. Philadelphia, Cincinnati, and Seattle are a few cities that use an at-large system to select their city councils, while the state of Maryland uses the multimember district system to select members to the state legislature.[21]

However, in most elections in the United States, including all elections to federal office, there is only one election winner per district. In U.S. House elections, only one candidate wins a seat in Congress in each of the 435 districts. Similarly, although each state has two senators, elections to the Senate are staggered so that no state elects both its senators in the same election year. Finally, in every state except Maine and Nebraska, the winner of the popular vote for president receives all of the Electoral College votes awarded to that state.[22] This system, where there is only one winner from each election district, is known as a single-member district (SMD) system.

A second aspect of an electoral system deals with the rules that determine a winner. Does the winner require a plurality (the most), a majority, or some other minimal threshold of the vote to win office? In parliamentary systems, it is common to select multiple representatives from the entire country or a region according to the principle of proportionality. Under this system, known as proportional representation, citizens vote for a party. Each party then receives seats in parliament based on the proportion of votes it earns in the election. For example, in a national legislature with one hundred seats, a party that receives 30 percent of the vote would win thirty seats. The formulas governing proportional representation rules are typically much more complex,[23] but the proportional principle still applies.

In the United States, plurality-winner rules determine the winners in federal elections. Referred to by some as "winner takes all" or "first past the post," the winner is the candidate who receives the most votes, even if no candidate receives a majority of the votes. In the example election used earlier between Smith, Jones, and Brown, Smith won a plurality of the votes with 35 percent. With the exception of Louisiana and Georgia, plurality-winner rules apply to all elections to the U.S. House and Senate.

It is important to understand how different electoral systems work because they have a direct effect on the political system in general and the party system in particular. The French political scientist Maurice Duverger suggested long ago that countries with SMD, plurality-winner electoral systems tend to have two-party systems.[24] There are some exceptions. For example, although the British use a SMD, plurality-winner electoral system, there is a significant third party (the Liberal Democrats) and two significant regional parties (the Scottish National Party and the Welsh Plaid Cymru).

To illustrate the difficulties that third parties confront, consider the following hypothetical example. Figure 3.2 shows the geographic distribution of party support in a "country" for three political parties. The figure shows that Republicans enjoy the support of all of the inhabitants who live in the outer region of the country, delineated as "A." Democrats are supported by those who live in the inner ring of the circle, labeled as "B." Finally, those who live in the center ("C") support the New Party. Support for Republicans amounts to 44 percent of the electorate, Democrats 41 percent, and for the New Party, 15 percent.

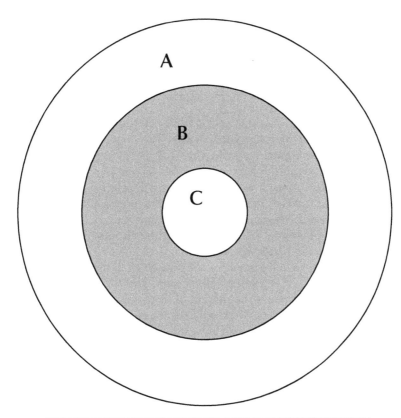

Area	All Inhabitants Support	Percentage of Vote
A	Republican Party	44%
B	Democratic Party	41%
C	New Party	15%

Figure 3.2 Hypothetical Example #1: Geographic Distribution of Party Support.

Imagine now that this country elects a 100-person legislature under a straight proportional representation (multimember district) system. In other words, each party will be awarded seats in the legislature directly proportional to the percentage of votes it receives. Republicans, with 44 percent of the vote, receive forty-four seats; Democrats, forty-one seats. Although the New Party is clearly the smallest of the three parties, it receives fifteen seats in the legislature, allowing it some voice in governance. In fact, depending on the ideological orientation of the New Party, either the Republicans or the Democrats will attempt to align with the New Party in order to gain majority (greater than 50%) status in the legislature.[25] They might offer to select a few of the New Party's leaders for prominent positions in the administration or adopt an issue position important to the New Party. In such a case, we might even be justified in claiming that the New Party is easily as powerful as the two larger parties, because without New Party's cooperation neither has a majority. The point is that the New Party has every incentive to continue on its course, as do its supporters (voters, donors, volunteers, candidates).

Imagine now that this same country has determined to elect its legislature by way of SMD–plurality-winner rules. The same regions of the country support the same parties and by the same percentages. For simplicity, let us reduce the size of the legislature in this second hypothetical example to ten seats. Voters in each electoral district will select one representative in the legislature, and that individual will be the one who receives the most votes in that district (see figure 3.3). In district one (-1-), the Republican candidate, with 44 percent of the vote, wins the election and a seat in the legislature. District two sees similar results.

In fact, with their 44 percent of the vote in each district, Republicans win all districts. As this example illustrates, the SMD–plurality-winner electoral system exaggerates the margin of victory for the winner (and the margin of loss for the loser). With only 44 percent of the vote nationwide, Republicans win 100 percent of the seats (10) in the legislature. Indeed, such distorted outcomes occur in real life. In the 2018 midterm elections, Republicans in North Carolina who ran for a seat in the U.S. House won nine of twelve contests (75%) despite winning only 51 percent of the two-party vote statewide.[26] Most elections to the House follow a similar pattern, as do elections in other countries that use SMD–plurality winner rules (e.g., Great Britain).

Returning to our hypothetical example, it is not hard to imagine a swing in the percentage of votes between the Democrats and the Republicans in at least a few districts from one election to the next. Democrats, in other words, are unlikely to be locked out of the legislature in the long term. In contrast, the New Party, with only 15 percent of the vote, is unlikely ever get enough votes in any of these districts to win a seat in the legislature.

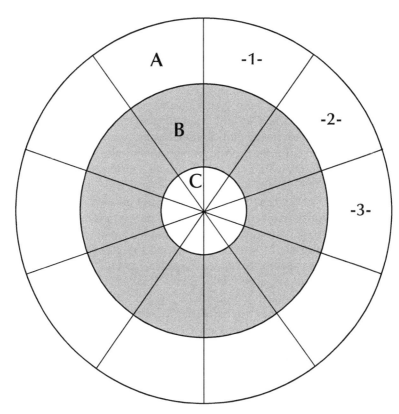

Area	All Inhabitants Support	Percentage of Vote
A	Republican Party	44%
B	Democratic Party	41%
C	New Party	15%

Figure 3.3 Hypothetical Example #2: Geographic Distribution of Party Support with Ten Single-Member Districts.

Over time—after repeated elections—voters, candidates, and supporters of the New Party will begin to see that it is politically expedient and strategically wise to align with one of the larger two parties. Politically, there might be a variety of incentives for the New Party to do so. First, it faces an obvious choice: align with one of the two major parties and share power or be consigned to an eternity in the political wilderness. It has no prospect of gaining *any* power otherwise. Second, the larger parties could offer incentives to the New Party to join forces. These might include, for example, adopting a focus on a policy important to the New Party, modifying a position on an existing issue to account for the New Party's position, and offering legislative leadership positions to prominent members of the New Party.

Beyond what the party itself does, over time voters and supporters will move toward one of the two major parties as well. Duverger identifies what he calls a "psychological factor" that pushes out third parties. According to this explanation, voters do not want to waste or "throw away" their votes on a likely loser. In the end, SMD–plurality-winner electoral systems erode the ability of third parties to compete and survive. This is Duverger's law: in SMD–plurality-winner electoral systems, third parties are practically squeezed out of the system.

If the effects of the electoral system were not enough to discourage the formation and long-term viability of third or minor parties, other election-related laws have that effect as well. For example, debates between political candidates at all levels of government during the general election season regularly feature a Democrat and a Republican. Only rarely do debate sponsors or the major-party candidates themselves consent to allow a minor-party or independent candidate to join. In 1992, independent presidential candidate Ross Perot debated the Republican president George H. W. Bush in his reelection bid and his Democratic challenger, Bill Clinton. This was an exception. In 1996, as the Reform Party candidate, Perot was not included in the presidential debates. During the 2016 presidential election, Libertarian Party candidate and former New Mexico governor Gary Johnson was excluded, as was Green Party candidate Jill Stein.

Historically, campaign finance laws, at least for presidential elections, were also designed to privilege major parties and their candidates. Candidates for their party's nomination may receive what are known as federal "matching" funds from the government. This means that the government will "match" the first $250 of an individual's contributions to a candidate.[27] The total amount a candidate receives in matching funds is capped at half of the national spending limit for the primary campaign (in 2016 the national spending limit was approximately $48.07 million).[28] In order to be eligible to receive this money a candidate must raise at least $5,000 in twenty different states.

This is a somewhat difficult hurdle to clear, although in 2016 the Libertarian candidate Gary Johnson and the Green Party candidate Jill Stein did so.[29] But major-party candidates can draw on the resources of state and local party activists, making it much easier to meet this requirement than for a candidate not affiliated with the two established parties (having said this, the past few elections have seen the major-party presidential candidates eschew federal matching funds).

Major-party candidates are also entitled to receive money for the general election campaign (in 2016, approximately $96 million).[30] A third-party

BOX 3.1 | **Various State Measures Governing Ballot Access for Minor Parties and Independent Candidates**

Filing fees: Most states require that candidates pay a fee to get their name on the ballot. In some cases, the amount is a minimal flat fee. As of 2018, Pennsylvania charges $200 for individuals running for president.[1] In other states this flat fee can be a few thousand dollars. Other states charge a percentage of the salary associated with the office being sought. As of 2018, South Carolina charges one percent of the $174,000 annual salary for a member of Congress (either representative or senator) multiplied by the length of the term, or $100, whichever is greater. Candidates for the U.S. Senate, for example, paid $1,740 times six, for a total of $10,440.[2] Because minor parties and independent candidates typically have fewer resources than do the major and their candidates, these fees can be troublesome.

Filing dates: All states have deadlines that all candidates and parties must adhere to in order to have their names on the ballot. For the major parties accustomed to these deadlines and with organizations in each state, this is typically not a problem. However, minor parties and independent candidates must not only find out when these dates are but also in many cases gather petition signatures to allow them on the ballot prior to the deadline.[3]

Petition signature requirements: Many states require that minor-party and independent candidates submit a petition in order to gain access to the ballot. Like filing fees (if any) these rules vary greatly. Some states demand a minimal absolute number of signatures be submitted. Hawaii, for example, only requires twenty-five signatures for candidates to either house of Congress.[4] To run for the Senate in Virginia, an individual must collect 10,000 signatures[5]; in Iowa, 1,500 from ten different counties.[6] Here too the major parties have an organizational advantage.

Political parties: Here the questions are more basic. Do the rules for independent candidates vary from those governing access for political party candidates? And how do minor parties automatically gain access to the ballot? In Arkansas, a party that wins three percent of the vote in the most recent presidential or gubernatorial election has officially recognized-party status, and thus ballot access for its candidates in the next election.

Fusion: A few states (e.g., Connecticut, Delaware, New York, and South Carolina) allow for a greater competitive advantage for minor-party and independent candidates by providing for fusion voting, where two parties nominate the same candidate.

Sore loser laws: These laws prohibit candidates who lost in their party's primary to run again in the general election as an independent or under a different party label. These statutes were intended to privilege the two major parties by not allowing intraparty dissent to morph into the formation and success of a new party.

Further Reading

"Getting on the Ballot: What It Takes," *The Canvas: States and Election Reform*. National Conference of State Legislatures. Issue 27, February 2012.

http://www.ncsl.org/documents/legismgt/elect/Canvass_Feb_2012_No_ 27.pdf.

Hall, Oliver. "Death by a Thousand Signatures: The Rise of Restrictive Ballot Access Laws and the Decline of Electoral Competition in the United States," 29 *Seattle U. L. Rev.* 407 (2005).

Winger, Richard, ed. *Ballot Access News.* http://ballot-access.org/.

[1]Office of the Philadelphia City Commissioners, "Nomination Petitions and Filing Fees," n.d., http://www.philadelphiavotes.com/en/candidates-a-campai gns/nominating-petitions.

[2]South Carolina State Election Commission, "Filing Fees," n.d., https://www .scvotes.org/filing-fees.

[3]See, for example, The Federal Election Commission, "2010 Congressional Primary Dates and Candidate Filing Deadlines for Ballot Access," n.d., http:// www.fec.gov/pubrec/fe2010/2010pdates.pdf.

[4]State of Hawaii Office of Elections, "Candidate Filing," n.d., https://electio ns.hawaii.gov/candidates/candidate-filing/.

[5]Virginia Law, "Code of Virginia § 24.2–506," n.d., https://law.lis.virginia.gov/ vacode/title24.2/chapter5/section24.2-506/.

[6]Candidates Guide to the General Election, "General Election Candidate Qualifications – Partisan Offices," November 6, 2018, https://sos.iowa.gov/elec tions/pdf/candidates/2018gencandguide.pdf.

or independent candidate is eligible to receive public funding in this phase of the election if the third party's nominee from the previous presidential election managed to garner 5 percent of the national vote in the general election. While this may seem a small percentage, the reality is that very few third-party candidates ever reach this threshold. In 2000, Ralph Nader, as the Green Party candidate, narrowly missed it (earning roughly 3% of the popular vote), meaning that the Green Party was not eligible for public funds in that or the next election.[31] Without public funds, third-party candidates must self-finance their campaigns or raise funds privately—a difficult task given that few donors are interested in giving to a candidate who will almost certainly lose.[32] Consequently, third-party candidates, unless independently wealthy, are unable to generate the hundreds of millions of dollars necessary to wage a viable presidential campaign. In turn, this makes it difficult to win even 5 percent of the vote in the general election and thereby qualify for public funds.

Finally, laws in several states make it difficult for minor-party candidates to appear on the ballot. To be fair, the rationale for this is not necessarily to ensure the continued duopoly of the Democratic and Republican parties. Instead, these laws are designed to discourage frivolous candidacies that could result in a lengthy and unmanageable ballot for voters. Elections, including the printing of ballots, cost money. In addition, presenting voters with too many choices may be confusing and lead to lengthy waiting times at the polls. A cluttered ballot might even be so confusing that it turns away potential voters, reducing turnout. Each of the states has its own individual ballot access rules, with some states providing stricter requirements for third-party candidates than others (see box 3.1).

A number of states have third parties that are officially recognized. In a few cases, third parties can be marginally competitive in some areas. Nonetheless, electoral rules, particularly the electoral system, make it all but impossible for a third party to enjoy long-term national success.

IS A THIRD PARTY REALLY NEEDED?

Dissatisfaction with the two major parties is often—although not always—grounded in the idea that there are few discernible differences between them. As noted at the outset of this chapter, many believe that the major parties simply do not offer enough actual choice, and that a third party could and would add fresh ideas or new perspectives to policy debates. This assumption, however, bears closer examination. Are there actual meaningful differences between the Republican and Democratic parties? The short answer is a resounding yes.

As evidence, we can look first to the platforms of the parties themselves. A party platform is a document that outlines, often very specifically, the positions the party takes on a variety of issues. The platform is the party's official policy document, and it is here that we can see numerous differences between the parties themselves.

Much of the difference between the two parties in the past two decades is in the positions each takes on social and cultural issues, such as abortion and civil rights.[33] The Republican Party has consistently held the more conservative or traditional positions on these so-called cultural issues. For example, Republicans generally oppose abortion rights, gay marriage, and embryonic stem-cell research, and favor school prayer. Most Democrats, conversely, favor a women's right to choose an abortion, legal marriage for same-sex couples, embryonic stem-cell research, and oppose school prayer.

Many Republicans oppose affirmative action, while a large percentage of Democrats favor such programs that are designed to redress past discrimination. Democrats usually support hate crime legislation, while Republicans typically (with some exceptions, such as when President George H. W. Bush signed the Hate Crimes Statistic Act in 1990) oppose it. Additionally, many Democrats favor legislation regulating certain aspects of gun ownership (e.g., waiting periods for the purchase of handguns). Most Republicans perceive these laws as an infringement on their Second Amendment rights and oppose them.

On issues related to education, Democrats generally advocate putting more money into public schools, whereas a large number of Republicans believe that the problem of failing schools should be addressed by some measure of privatization (namely, school vouchers or charter schools). Democrats are more likely to be in favor of legislation and regulation to protect the environment; Republicans less so. The George W. Bush administration's withdrawal from the Kyoto Protocol on greenhouse gas emissions or Donald Trump's withdrawal from the Paris Accords, and Democrats' scathing criticism of these decisions by the last two Republican presidents are examples of this difference. Democrats are generally in favor of greater government involvement in the realm of health care in order to reduce the number of uninsured and underinsured. Republicans typically oppose government involvement in managing the nation's health-care system. The fierce partisan battles waged in Congress and the deep public divisions that continue to exist over the Affordable Care Act (Obamacare) exemplify these sharp divisions.

On economic matters, Republicans tend to favor policies that emphasize individual initiative and limited government intervention, whereas Democrats are more inclined to see a role for government regulation in economic matters. For example, Republicans are generally in favor of tax cuts (broadly defined), while many Democrats prefer using tax revenues to reduce the federal deficit or to increase federal spending on programs addressing poverty and social needs. Democrats often call for increases in the minimum wage to assist the working poor. Many Republicans believe that this is harmful to business and ultimately to workers because wage increases may force business to cut costs with layoffs. Finally, Republicans have historically been the party that takes a more hawkish stand on foreign policy disputes and favor greater military spending when compared to those in the Democratic Party.

In short, there are significant differences between the issue positions of the two parties. Of course, presidential candidates sometimes stray from the official party line. However, presidential candidates have always been central to the process of drafting these documents.[34] The first party platform was written in 1832 when the first Democratic National Convention met to renominate Andrew Jackson.[35] The document was actually written as an address for Jackson to deliver to the convention, making it a very candidate-specific document. This has been the case throughout history. But because direct primaries and caucuses—rather than the party itself—effectively decide the party nomination, presidential candidates are free to ignore the platform if they so choose. A rather obvious example occurred in 1996, when Republican presidential hopeful Bob Dole freely admitted that he had not even read the Republican platform.[36]

Another reason for the blurred differences between the two parties on the presidential campaign trail is that both candidates are attempting to appeal to the middle of the electorate. This blurring of the lines by presidential candidates, however, should not lead one to conclude that the parties themselves are similar. Most research overwhelmingly demonstrates that the moderate rhetoric of presidential candidates is a poor indicator of how members of the two parties actually govern, especially in the U.S. Congress. Increasingly, the evidence shows that Democrats and Republicans find very little upon which to agree when casting their roll-call votes on legislation in Congress.[37] Evidence makes clear that the Democratic and Republican parties do not look alike, as some have suggested.[38] Political activists, individual donors, and interest groups all exert pressure on elected officials to stand firm on certain core party principles, making moderation more difficult.[39] In addition, elected officials often represent districts with heavy concentrations of voters from their own political parties, creating little incentive to reach across party lines and develop a more pragmatic approach to governing.[40] According to political scientist Keith Poole, "Moderates have virtually disappeared" from the U.S. Congress in the past few decades, especially in the House of Representatives.[41]

The result is growing polarization in Congress, underscoring the fact that there are clearer and more pronounced differences between the parties than at any time in recent memory. The statements of presidential candidates should not be confused with the positions of the parties they claim to represent. Candidates are not parties. There is a party line (or to be more precise, two party lines), even if candidates do not always follow that party line. Each party's platform reflects fundamental differences in the positions of both parties. It is also important to remember that these differences are not simply words in some irrelevant party platform that are ignored by elected officials. Members of the two major parties do govern differently— even if the rhetoric of their presidential candidates can sometimes make the parties seem very similar.

CONCLUSION

There are a number of minor or third parties in the United States today, a few of which sometimes attract a moderately respectable following. These include the Green Party, which stands for grassroots democracy, social justice, "ecological wisdom," diversity and equity, and economic decentralization.[42] The Libertarian Party, the nation's third largest, holds a "vision for a world in which all individuals can freely exercise the natural right of sole dominion over their own lives, liberty, and property."[43] Other parties (e.g., the Constitution Party) are popular in selected areas, while many states have state-specific minor parties (e.g., Hawaii Independence Party). But, with few exceptions (e.g., Sen. Angus King of Maine, Sen. Bernie Sanders of Vermont, former Alaska Governor Bill Walker), these parties typically do not win higher elective office.

The reason for this is very straightforward: the rules of the game work against them. The reality is that the SMD–plurality-winner electoral system creates a powerful incentive for candidates, supporters, and parties to move eventually to one of the two existing major parties. In addition, other electoral rules work to marginalize or disadvantage minor parties. While the desire for a third party—more choice—is legitimate, it is extraordinarily unlikely that the United States will ever have anything but a two-party system.

FURTHER READING

Hershey, Marjorie Random. *Party Politics in America*. 17th ed. New York, NY: Routledge, 2017.

McCarty, Nolan, Keith T. Poole, and Howard Rosenthal. *Polarized America: The Dance of Ideology and Unequal Riches*. Cambridge, MA: MIT Press, 2006.

Reichley, A. James. *The Life of the Parties: A History of American Political Parties*. Lanham, MD: Rowman & Littlefield, 1992.

White, John Kenneth, and Daniel M. Shea. *New Party Politics: From Jefferson and Hamilton to the Information Age*. Boston, MA: Bedford/St. Martin's, 2000.

Zeigler, L. Harmon. *Political Parties in Industrial Democracies*. Itasca, IL: F. E. Peacock, 1993.

4

Buying Elections?

Campaign Finance Law and Money's Influence in Elections and Politics

CONCERN ABOUT THE INFLUENCE OF MONEY in American elections is nearly timeless, with the cause of campaign finance reform dating back as far as the enactment of the Naval Appropriations Bill in 1867 (which prohibited government officials from raising money from naval yard workers). Despite numerous laws passed at the federal and state levels to mitigate the political influence of campaign contributions, a recent *New York Times/* CBS News poll showed that 84 percent of Americans hold the opinion that "money has too much influence" in U.S. campaigns.[1] In another survey, 57 percent of Americans completely or mostly agree with the statement, "Politics and elections are controlled by people with money and by big corporations so that it doesn't matter if I vote."[2]

Although past efforts to reform the campaign finance system have been unable to quell continued public concern about the influence of money in American democracy, support for campaign finance reform remains high. According to a 2018 poll from the Pew Research Center for the People & the Press, 65 percent of Americans view new campaign finance laws as an effective way to reduce the role of money in politics.[3] In the 116th U.S. Congress (2019–2020), several lawmakers introduced new campaign finance reform legislation, such as the For the People Act sponsored by Rep. John Sarbanes of Maryland. Although the Sarbanes bill is unlikely to become law, its introduction suggests that the issue of how to best legislate money in politics is far from a settled matter.

In this chapter we present the essentials of campaign finance law and the influence of money in American elections and policymaking. We begin with a review of past scandals involving corruption and bribery, as well as the reforms and court rulings that followed, to provide the necessary background and context about why the public is so suspicious of money's influence in politics. But while understanding this history makes it easier to appreciate why so many Americans are cynical about the influence of money in politics, it is easy to go too far with that cynicism, oversimplifying a more complex reality. For instance, the notion that American democracy is "for sale to the highest bidder" (as some have alleged[4]) may make for good headlines, but is ultimately too reductionist and fails to capture the nuances of how money does and does not affect American elections and policy.

As we will discuss later in this chapter, money may be necessary for a candidate to wage a competitive campaign, but it does not guarantee victory on Election Day. Likewise, money matters in shaping public policy, but not in ways that are easily observable. We close the chapter with a discussion on the latest efforts to reform the campaign finance system and conclude with some final thoughts on the implications of what continued increases in campaign fundraising and spending may mean for the future of American elections and politics.

MONEY, CORRUPTION, AND REFORM: A BRIEF HISTORY

Ohio millionaire and former U.S. Senator Mark Hanna once remarked, "There are two things that are important in politics. The first is money, and I can't remember what the second is."[5] Hanna uttered his half-serious quip in the year 1895, a time when stories about "robber barons" and wealthy industrialists contributing vast sums of money to political candidates dominated what is known as the Gilded Age of the late nineteenth century. Charges of vote buying and allegations of graft in the legislative process were common. Political cartoons frequently cast politicians and party leaders as corrupt (see photo 4.1). In one notable example, the publication *Puck*, known for its political satire, famously depicted U.S. Senator James Blaine, a presidential contender, as the "tattooed man" with each tattoo representing examples of his corruption (see photo 4.2).

Investigative journalists, known as "muckrakers," drew further attention to political corruption with their reporting. By the early twentieth century, reformers, known as "progressives," called for new federal laws limiting the power and influence of large corporations and wealthy donors. In particular, they pushed for restrictions on corporate lobbying and campaign contributions from big business.

Congress eventually took major steps to reform the nation's campaign finance system following charges from Democratic presidential candidate Alton Parker that President Theodore Roosevelt exchanged favors with corporate and banking interests for their financial support in his 1904 presidential campaign.[6] Unable to dampen the suspicion of improper dealings, Roosevelt, in his address to Congress in 1905, proposed a federal law eliminating all corporate contributions and requiring disclosure of

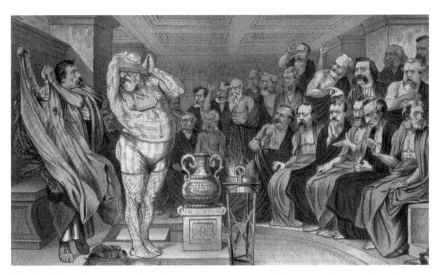

Photo 4.1 Big money's grip on government: Bernhard Gillam's "Phryne Before the Chicago Tribunal" (a depiction of James Blaine covered in his scandals, originally published in *Puck*, June 4, 1884).

campaign expenditures. Congress passed the Tillman Act of 1907, which banned corporations and interstate banks from contributing directly to federal candidates. Several years later, Congress passed additional regulations on campaign contributions. The first federal disclosure requirements (i.e., public reporting of campaign contributions and expenditures) took effect in 1910 for U.S. House elections and in 1911 for U.S. Senate elections. Congress also set limits on campaign expenditures for all congressional candidates.

By the early 1920s, however, national attention was again drawn to a major scandal involving bribery when allegations surfaced that Secretary of the Interior Albert Bacon Fall secretly leased U.S. naval petroleum reserves in Teapot Dome, Wyoming, to Harry Sinclair of the Mammoth Oil Company in exchange for cash and interest-free loans. Fall would become the first presidential cabinet member to go to prison for crimes committed while in office. In response, Congress amended the Federal Corrupt Practices Act in 1925 to require quarterly disclosure reports for all contributions made to an elected official. This would serve as the primary law regulating federal campaign finance for much of the twentieth century.[7]

However, the reforms of the early 1900s never created a regulatory agency to monitor and enforce campaign finance rules and restrictions. Federal campaign finance law relied on congressional oversight, which due to partisan pressures, proved to be highly ineffective. Early legislation also failed to establish a clear and comprehensive set of penalties for those who

Photo 4.2 Big money's grip on government: Thomas Nast's "The Brains" (a depiction of Boss Tweed of the Tammany Ring, originally published in *Harper's Weekly*, October 21, 1871).

violated the law. Candidates could avoid liability for violating the spending limit and disclosure requirements by simply claiming they had no knowledge of spending on their behalf. Consequently, campaign finance remained effectively unregulated and lacked proper disclosure.

Even with the passage and strengthening of the Federal Corrupt Practices Act, stories of powerful interests wielding too much influence over the political process continued. In 1935, Congress passed another law, the Public Utilities Holding Act, which banned political contributions from public utility companies. Attention turned to organized labor in the 1940s as Congress passed the Smith–Connally Act in 1943 and the Taft–Hartley Act in 1947, which together prohibited labor unions from contributing money and making expenditures to federal campaigns in primary and general elections.

The nation's campaign finance system finally reached its breaking point in the early 1970s when news surfaced that Richard Nixon's Committee to Re-Elect the President laundered unreported campaign funds to pay for the silence and perjury of those responsible for breaking into the Watergate hotel in 1972.[8] The committee also raised money illegally for a slush fund by applying pressure on major American companies to make secret contributions. Those that did not contribute risked losing access to the Nixon administration and faced the threat of audits from the Internal Revenue Service. The Watergate scandal ultimately led to the resignation of President Nixon and pressured Congress to reform the nation's campaign finance system.

Congress passed the Federal Election Campaign Act (FECA) in 1971, which attempted to strengthen contribution and spending limits in federal elections. An amendment to that law in 1974 created the Federal Election Commission (FEC) to oversee and enforce federal campaign finance rules and regulations, as well as administer the reporting and public disclosure of campaign finance information. The law also gave the FEC authority to oversee a newly created system of public funding for presidential elections (created under the Revenue Act of 1971). The FECA of 1971 and its amendments in 1974 became the foundation of the modern campaign finance system. Although several court rulings later weakened the law— notably the case of *Buckley v. Valeo* (1976), which struck down limits on campaign expenditures as a violation of the U.S. Constitution's right to free speech—the campaign finance regime set in place in the 1970s held together for much of the next two decades.

By the late 1990s, however, campaign professionals discovered ways to channel huge sums of unregulated donations, known as "soft money," to party committees. Soft money was the result of a 1979 amendment to FECA that allowed individuals and interest groups to give unlimited amounts to political parties for "party-building activities" (e.g., buying office equipment, building mailing lists) and to help state and local candidates. This provision soon became a way for companies, labor unions, and wealthy individuals to make contributions to parties that in some cases exceeded hundreds of thousands of dollars. Parties often earmarked this money to use in particular races for generic party advertising and issue advocacy (i.e., political ads promoting a particular cause—not a candidate).[9]

By the end of the twentieth century, soft-money fundraising had become so prevalent that concerned groups and citizens were again arguing that Congress needed to pass stronger campaign finance reform legislation.[10] When the energy company Enron went bankrupt due to accounting fraud, reports surfaced that its executives had used soft-money donations to help the company avoid federal regulations.[11] So, once again, scandal served as a catalyst for additional reforms to the campaign finance system. (For a complete timeline of campaign finance scandals and reform, see box 4.1.)

BOX 4.1	History of Major Campaign Finance Scandals and Reforms

1867: Congress passes the first federal campaign finance law by enacting the Naval Appropriations Bill.

1896: William McKinley's fundraising for his presidential campaign, under Ohio millionaire Mark Hanna, draws scrutiny.

1907: The Tillman Act becomes federal law.

1910: Congress takes additional action by passing the Publicity Act (also known as the Federal Corrupt Practices Act).

1925: Following the Teapot Dome Scandal, Congress strengthens the Federal Corrupt Practices Act.

1971: Congress passes the Federal Election Campaign Act and the Revenue Act.

1974: Congress amends the Federal Election Campaign Act in the aftermath of the Watergate scandal.

1976: The Supreme Court strikes down portions of FECA in *Buckley v. Valeo*.

1979: "Soft money" is born under a new amendment to FECA.

1996: In *Colorado Republican Federal Campaign Committee v. Federal Election Commission* the Supreme Court rules that political parties could make unlimited campaign expenditures provided that they were independent of the candidate.

2002: The Enron scandal paves the way for the Bipartisan Campaign Reform Act.

2003: BCRA survives a challenge in the Supreme Court.

2007: The Supreme Court, in *Wisconsin Right to Life, Inc. v. FEC*, rules that ads that did not contain express advocacy, even within 60 days prior to a general election, were not corruptive to outweigh free-speech rights.

2010: The Supreme Court expands the rights of corporations to spend money in elections in *Citizens United v. FEC*.

2014: The Supreme Court strikes down overall contribution limits in *McCutcheon v. FEC*.

Source: Information adapted from the Center for Responsive Politics; see https://www.opensecrets.org/resources/learn/timeline.

CURRENT LAW AND THE DEBATE SURROUNDING IT

In 2002, Congress passed the Bipartisan Campaign Reform Act (BCRA), which provided significant changes to FECA. Of note, BCRA banned soft-money contributions to political parties to eliminate the large six-figure donations that had become common throughout the 1990s. BCRA also placed new regulations on so-called issue advocacy ads. These issue advocacy ads differ from campaign ads in that they do not include "express advocacy," defined by the Supreme Court as "explicit words of advocacy of election or defeat" such as "vote for," "re-elect," or "help defeat." Under BCRA, any ad[12] that referred to a clearly identified candidate for federal office within sixty days of the general election or thirty days of a primary election qualified as "electioneering communications," or a campaign ad. BCRA required that interest groups pay for these electioneering communications with political action committee (PAC; see box 4.2a and box 4.2b) funds as opposed to general treasury funds.

Senator Mitch McConnell, a staunch opponent of BCRA, led the first major legal challenge to the new law, and in 2003, the Supreme Court heard *McConnell v. FEC*. In a major victory for BCRA supporters, the Court upheld the ban on the use of soft money by national party committees, ruling that there was sufficient governmental interest in "preventing the actual or apparent corruption of federal candidates and officeholders"[13]

BOX 4.2a │ What Is a PAC?

What is a PAC? A political action committee is a legal entity formed by an organized group (a corporation, union, citizen action group, etc.) whose primary purpose is to raise money for, and to spend money to elect and defeat, candidates running for federal office.

How much money can a PAC raise? PACs may receive up to $5,000 from any one individual, PAC, or party committee per calendar year.

How much money can a PAC contribute and spend? A PAC may make direct campaign contributions of up to $5,000 to a candidate running for federal office per election (primary, general, or special). It can spend unlimited amounts on independent expenditures.

BOX 4.2b │ What Is a Super PAC?

What is a Super PAC? A Super PAC is an independent expenditure-only committee. It differs from a traditional PAC in that it does not make any direct campaign contributions to candidates running for federal office.

How much money can a Super PAC raise? Super PACs may receive unlimited donations from corporations, unions, associations, and individuals.

How much money can a Super PAC spend? A Super PAC may spend unlimited amounts of money supporting or opposing a candidate running for federal office provided that this spending is not coordinated with a candidate's campaign.

to justify the restriction. The Court also upheld regulations on electioneering communications, reasoning that because corporations and unions could still finance electioneering communications through their PAC funds, BCRA did not result in an outright ban on expression. According to the Court, issue ads aired in the final days of the election were the "functional equivalent of express advocacy."[14] The ruling thereby left the law relatively intact.

Yet, BCRA faced additional constitutional challenges. In 2007, the Supreme Court, now under Chief Justice John Roberts, signaled a major shift in campaign finance regulations in the case of *Wisconsin Right to Life, Inc. v. FEC*, which reversed some of BCRA's core provisions. The Court ruled that ads that did not contain express advocacy (or its functional equivalent), even if aired within sixty days of the general election or thirty days prior to a primary, were not sufficiently corruptive to outweigh the free-speech rights of Wisconsin Right to Life, Inc.[15] This ruling signaled the emerging antiregulatory direction of the Roberts court.

The decision in *Wisconsin Right to Life, Inc. v. FEC*, however, created only a minor stir compared to the Court's later ruling in *Citizens United v. FEC* in 2010. This latter case traces its history back to the 2008 Democratic presidential nomination season. Citizens United, a conservative nonprofit organization, planned to release *Hillary: The Movie*—a documentary that attacked then-Senator Hillary Clinton, who at the time was running for the Democratic presidential nomination. The documentary highlighted Clinton's involvement in various scandals during her years of public service in Arkansas and Washington.[16]

To make the film widely available, Citizens United sought to sell it as a DVD directly to consumers and to show the film in a small number of selected theaters. It also offered to pay $1.2 million to a consortium of cable operators for the documentary to be offered through an "on demand" service at no charge to cable subscribers.[17] However, as noted earlier, federal law under BCRA barred corporations from funding electioneering communications from their general treasuries, a provision upheld in *McConnell v. FEC*.[18] Citizens United financed *Hillary* from various corporate sources and sought to pay for its distribution and advertising with funds from its general treasury, not from its political action committee (Citizens United Political Victory Fund). This raised a host of legal questions, notably whether *Hillary* was equivalent to a lengthy negative campaign advertisement, and if so, whether Citizens United was thereby subject to the electioneering communication financing requirements as specified in BCRA.

Fearing criminal and civil penalties, Citizens United went to district court to seek a preliminary injunction to prevent the FEC from applying and enforcing its interpretation of BCRA's electioneering communication requirements on the film based on the legal argument that the law violated its members' First Amendment rights. Given the Supreme Court's earlier willingness to weaken BCRA's electioneering restrictions in *Wisconsin Right to Life*, the group sought to challenge the law further. The U.S. District Court, however, ruled against Citizens United and denied the injunction, arguing that *Hillary: The Movie* amounted to express advocacy and therefore *Wisconsin Right to Life* did not apply (that case had only involved *nonexpress* issue advocacy). It also noted that previous court rulings, notably *McConnell v. FEC*, had upheld BCRA's communication provisions.[19]

Citizens United appealed the ruling to the U.S. Supreme Court. In a controversial 5 to 4 ruling, the Court overturned the lower court's ruling on First Amendment grounds, and FECA's prohibition on corporations from using general treasury funds to finance electioneering and express advocacy communications. Similar to the rationale in *Buckley v. Valeo*, the majority wrote that "independent expenditures, including those made by corporations, do not give rise to corruption or the appearance of corruption."[20] In the absence of corruption, the Court reasoned that the government had no compelling interest or justification to curb the free-speech rights of Citizens United or any corporation or political organization that remained independent of a candidate and a candidate's campaign organization.

The Court's ruling in *Citizens United v. FEC* received near-instant condemnation from those in the campaign finance reform community. Fred Wertheimer of the pro-campaign finance reform group Democracy 21 labeled the decision "the most radical and destructive campaign finance decision in Supreme Court history."[21] Keith Olbermann, then a host on MSNBC, went as far as to claim that the case "might actually have more dire implications than *Dred Scott v. Sandford*."[22] Years later, the Citizens United ruling is still routinely cited by its opponents as allowing corporations and wealthy donors to "buy" elections, or that American democracy is "drowning" in money.[23] While it is undeniably true that money spent in U.S. elections has increased considerably since the Citizens United ruling,[24] the effects that additional money in American elections and politics may have requires deeper examination. In the pages that follow, we review the findings in the academic literature that paint a clearer picture of what money does and does not buy in American elections and politics.

WHAT MONEY DOES AND DOES NOT BUY IN ELECTIONS

The most obvious answer to what money buys in context of a political campaign is simple. Money buys professional staff to perform vital campaign services, such as polling, fundraising, and event planning. It also pays for travel, opposition research, and the biggest expense of all, advertising.[25] A typical U.S. Senate campaign, for example, often spends more than 40 percent of its overall budget on advertising.[26] Major presidential candidates spend an even higher percentage, often more than 70 percent.[27] Of course, advertising is important because it allows candidates to spread and amplify their campaign message to thousands, and sometimes even millions, of voters. Advertising can serve to mobilize voters by generating interest in the election and persuade voters when candidates address issues and problems that people care about deeply.[28]

Aside from advertising and other basic campaign functions, the ability to raise money can affect whether a candidate decides to run for office at all.[29] For those who decide to run for office, successful fundraising, particularly early in the election cycle, makes it easier to raise money later, as early fundraising totals serve as an important sign of a candidate's strength.[30] This is especially important for donors who seek access to those with political power.[31] These so-called investors give money primarily to candidates likely to win office.[32]

During the early phase of the election, fundraising also helps determine which candidates ultimately emerge as official candidates for office. Referred to as the "invisible primary," presidential candidates often drop out of contention before votes are even cast. In the 2000 presidential election, for example, Elizabeth Dole ended her campaign before the Iowa caucuses (the first state to vote in the presidential nomination process), citing her campaign's inability to raise money as the primary reason. As Dole explained in an announcement ending her campaign, "The bottom line remains money."[33] She described being caught in "a kind of Catch-22," in which a lack of money prevented her campaign from reaching voters. By not reaching voters, her poll numbers could not increase, which made it exceedingly difficult to convince donors to contribute to her campaign.[34] As the short-lived Dole campaign illustrates, money establishes a candidate's viability, often dictating which candidates remain in an election before voters even cast their ballots.

For candidates who are successful at fundraising, increased media attention often follows. This "free" media coverage brings positive press to a campaign, which, in turn, can help boost a candidate's standing in the polls. Rising poll numbers then bring further positive press, making it easier to raise additional money, creating a virtuous cycle.

Money plays a critical role not only in the invisible primary but also during the nomination season. With no party cues for voters to rely upon, campaign advertisements and other forms of communication are more likely to be able to persuade.[35] Moreover, primary elections often experience low voter turnout. This creates a greater opportunity for campaign spending to have a significant impact when it goes toward GOTV efforts.[36]

Money can make a difference in the general election season, especially when there is no incumbent running for reelection.[37] In these open-seat races, candidates often lack name recognition, a major predictor of electoral success.[38] With a large war chest of money, candidates can buy the advertising needed to improve their name recognition. This is true for those challenging incumbents as well. Indeed, research shows that spending by challengers has a significant effect on electoral outcomes. The more money that challengers spend, the better they perform on Election Day.[39] Challengers who fail to raise and spend money have almost no chance of victory over an incumbent officeholder. In short, serious candidates for public office spend a considerable amount of time and effort on fundraising.

Importantly, however, money is not everything. Although there is correlation between increased campaign spending and a candidate's likelihood of victory, there is no guarantee that more spending will bring victory. Moreover, some scholars suggest that money may flow to candidates who were already in a strong position to win.[40]

For example, Democratic Congresswoman Nancy Pelosi spent more than $5.3 million for her reelection in 2018. Her Republican opponent, Lisa Remmer, spent a mere $12,443. Did Pelosi win because she outspent Remmer, or did money simply flow in greater amounts to Pelosi because she was all but certain to win the election? Given that donors often invest strategically by giving to candidates who are likely to win, Pelosi's overwhelming advantages as an incumbent—being better known, handling case work for her constituents, holding the top leadership position in her party and running in a heavily Democratic district—more than likely explain why she was able to raise more money than her opponent. It also explains why she won by an 87 to 13 percent margin on Election Day. Money was not the reason Pelosi won. Money flowed to her because she was already the strongest candidate in the race.

Even in elections that are likely to be competitive, money only matters if candidates have a message that connects with voters. As political scientist Michael Malbin explains, "If voters do not like what they are hearing, telling them more of the same will not change their opinion."[41] Research also shows that voters are less likely to be persuaded, no matter what the message, if they already know a great deal about the candidates running for office.[42] Indeed, the least informed and knowledgeable voters are the most persuadable, but they are also the least likely to be paying attention to politics and the election. This tends to minimize any effects that campaign advertisements and outreach efforts have on election outcomes. For incumbents, this is especially true. Incumbents are already well known to the public, making it even more difficult for them to persuade voters with advertisements and other campaign expenditures.

This said, incumbents see plenty of return for the money they raise and spend. A large war chest can deter quality challengers from running against them.[43] There is also evidence to suggest that although incumbents may not increase their vote share with increased campaign expenditures, money can increase their probability of winning.[44] After all, incumbents typically do not need to increase their vote share and win additional votes. In most cases they simply need to target and maintain the support of the constituency that previously helped elect them. Incumbent spending thereby serves a defensive purpose of ensuring reelection rather than an offensive purpose of expanding vote share.

We should also note that money does not matter nearly as much as the external political environment and the partisan makeup of the candidate's district or state, strong predictors of electoral performance and outcomes.[45] For example, a weak economy is almost always damaging to candidates of the political party in power, just as a strong economy is almost always beneficial.[46] Additionally, a popular U.S. president or presidential candidate can have "coattail" effects, helping to boost vote totals for candidates of the same political party running in down-ballot races for the U.S. Congress, or for state and local offices.[47] And, it goes without saying that districts or states dominated by voters of one political party over another effectively dictate election outcomes far more powerfully than money can.

Taken together, the view that money "buys" or "controls" elections is clearly too simplistic. As discussed, it is exceptionally difficult, almost impossible, to win elective office without money, especially for challengers and open-seat candidates. Yet money alone offers no guarantee of victory if the candidate's campaign message fails to resonate with voters or if there is an unfavorable environment.

AFTER THE ELECTION: MONEY AND THE LEGISLATIVE PROCESS

Beyond what money can and cannot do to influence elections, critics who view money as a problem in American democracy also point to the post-election period when elected officials engage in governing. Advocates of campaign finance reform often point out that legislators favor their wealthy campaign contributors at the expense of what is best for the public. This perspective is highlighted by *New York Times* reporter Jane Mayer in her book *Dark Money*. The book goes into considerable detail about how billionaire donors have sought over the years to advance and improve their own personal financial interests by using their vast sums of wealth to influence public policies.[48] In a similar vein, there is a body of research showing that elected officials respond disproportionately to the preferences of the rich, and that campaign donors can influence the legislative process by helping to shape a party's policy agenda, providing access to elected officials, adding earmarks, and adding or editing key language in a bill.[49]

Yet, research is decidedly more mixed about the influence of money on final legislative outcomes, such as bills passed and roll-call votes.[50] Indeed, several studies have concluded that campaign contributions seldom change the roll-call votes of legislators.[51] The authors of these studies often point out that campaign donors often give to elected officials who are already predisposed to favoring their position on an important policy or set of policies. Ideology and partisanship, rather than campaign contributions, serve as the primary predictor of a legislator's support or opposition to a bill. As one scholar concluded, campaign contributions "have far less influence [on policy] than commonly thought."[52]

In short, the literature finds little support for an overt quid pro quo in which a conservative legislator would support a liberal policy, or a liberal legislator would support a conservative policy, on the basis of campaign donations. However, there is evidence of more subtle influence in which money can influence other aspects of the policymaking process in ways that are favorable to wealthy interests and donors. Once again, money matters, but in more nuanced ways than is commonly understood.

WHAT'S NEXT? REPUBLICANS AND DEMOCRATS ON CAMPAIGN FINANCE REFORM

In light of what money does and does not buy, and given the past history to reform campaign finance laws, what *should* the nation's campaign finance regime look like? As with many issues, Republicans and Democrats differ quite significantly in their answers to that question. The 2016 Republican Party platform effectively called for eliminating nearly all campaign finance laws and restrictions. The rationale for that position is that campaign finance restrictions on donations and communications stifle freedom of speech and serve to protect incumbent officeholders. As the platform reads, "Limits on political speech serve only to protect the powerful and insulate incumbent officeholders. We support repeal of federal restrictions on political parties in McCain-Feingold, raising or repealing contribution limits, protecting the political speech of advocacy groups, corporations, and labor unions, and protecting political speech on the internet."[53]

Democrats offer a much different response. Upon becoming the majority party in the U.S. House at the start of the 116th Congress (2019–2020), House Democrats introduced the For the People Act, a bill designed to create stricter campaign finance regulations. One of the bill's major provisions would require politically active nonprofit organizations to disclose donor identities for those who contribute more than $10,000.

The legislation also attempts to regulate digital ad spending with the creation of a public database that would disclose all such ads of $500 or more and create a system of government "matching" funds for all federal candidates. While such a system already exists for presidential candidates, the For the People Act would expand the system to congressional candidates as well. In addition, the proposed legislation would provide a

six-to-one match on small contributions of less than $200. A $100 donation would thus generate an additional $600 in government matching
funds, magnifying the impact of small donations. While Democrats in the
U.S. House have made this bill a high priority, Republicans, who control
the majority in the U.S. Senate, have pledged to block its passage.

CONCLUSION

Somewhat remarkably, the policy debate about money in politics, which
traces its roots back to the nineteenth century, remains squarely on the
legislative agenda in the twenty-first century. Differences separating
Republicans and Democrats run deep on this issue, suggesting that hope
for bipartisan agreement on any future reform to the current laws remains
unlikely. The debate over campaign finance will continue because money
will continue to play a central role in elections and politics. The Center for
Responsive Politics reported that more than $5.7 billion was spent in the
2018 midterm elections, making it the costliest congressional election in
U.S. history.[54] The 2020 election promises to shatter even more fundraising
and campaign spending records.

What this all means for American democracy is certainly debatable.
In elections, money is clearly a necessary, but not a sufficient condition
for waging a winning campaign. In the public policy arena, money does
not buy a legislator's vote on important legislation, but it can affect other
important aspects of the legislative process. Ultimately, money matters, but
in much more complex ways than most people realize.

FURTHER READING

Mayer, Jane. *Dark Money: The Hidden History of the Billionaires Behind the Rise
of the Radical Right*. New York, NY: Doubleday, 2016.
Mutch, Robert E. *Campaign Finance: What Everyone Needs to Know*. New York,
NY: Oxford University Press, 2016.
Powell, Lynda W. *The Influence of Campaign Contributions in State Legislatures:
The Effects of Institutions and Politics*. Ann Arbor, MI: University of Michigan
Press, 2012.
Smith, Bradley A. *Unfree Speech: The Folly of Campaign Finance Reform*. Princ-
eton, NJ: Princeton University Press, 2001.

5

The Veepstakes

Balancing the Ticket and Other Myths about Vice Presidential Selection

EVERY FOUR YEARS, political observers, commentators, and experts spill a great deal of ink predicting who the eventual winner of the presidential nomination will select as his or her vice presidential candidate. This exercise, known as the "veepstakes," has become one of the most entertaining sideshows of the presidential election season. In fact, it is so popular that speculation often starts a full year before the presidential nomination has been decided.[1] In June 2008, one writer counted more than eighty names that had been mentioned as vice presidential possibilities for John McCain, Hillary Clinton, or Barack Obama in news articles, opinion pieces, and expert commentary—and this compilation ignored most blogs and other essays written by ordinary citizens.[2] Speculation about possible Democratic vice presidential candidates in 2020 began as early as the fall of 2018, well before the 2018 midterm and before any Democrat had declared they were running for *president.*

However, one observer, noting the sheer volume of articles on the subject and their largely speculative nature, has labeled the veepstakes a "largely fact free parlour game."[3] To be fair, some speculation about the veepstakes is based on a fairly good understanding of the process of vice presidential selection. But much of this understanding, which constitutes the majority of the conventional wisdom on the subject, is rooted in a historical view of selecting a running mate. In fact, most of the conventional wisdom on this subject centers on the idea of balancing the presidential ticket. Historically this has meant selecting an individual from a larger state in a different region of the country and a different faction or ideological wing of the party (or both) from that of the presidential candidate.

In the past several decades, however, the conventional wisdom about what matters in the selection of a presidential running mate has been discarded by presidential candidates and their advisers in favor of a much more complex model. And, while many observers understand this, it is difficult to factor in all of the favorable characteristics of a running mate into a short news story or op-ed piece. This is likely why most accounts continue to focus mainly on balancing the ticket with the vice presidential pick.[4]

In the next section of this chapter, we discuss this historical model of vice presidential selection. Following that, we introduce the modern model. In each section, the focus is the same: the method of selecting presidential running mates and what types of individuals are selected. We will see that in the modern era, the process of making the choice is much more systematic, and there are many more factors that presidential candidates consider in making the choice than in the historical era.

THE HISTORICAL ERA OF VICE PRESIDENTIAL SELECTION

Until fairly recently, the vice presidency was considered to be a consolation prize of sorts. The office had few formal or informal responsibilities, and as the result of this, few men aspired to the office. In fact, history is filled with examples of notable political leaders who refused the vice presidential nomination. In 1848, Daniel Webster declined to run on the Whig ticket with Zachary Taylor, saying, "I do not propose to be buried until I am really dead and in my coffin."[5] The individuals who did run and serve as vice president in the nineteenth century were decidedly mediocre in terms of their qualifications.[6]

Because at the time the office was considered to be a political dead end, little energy or effort was expended in the process of selecting the individual who would round out the presidential ticket. One observer noted that "very little pains are bestowed on the election of a vice-president."[7] After delegates made the selection of the presidential candidate at the party's national convention, attention turned to the selection of a running mate. Balloting for the vice presidential candidate hardly ever went more than one or two rounds of voting.

The overriding concern in the selection of a running mate during this period was how to best "balance" the ticket. Other factors, such as the idea that a vice president should be somewhat compatible with the president, received little, if any, consideration. In truth, there have been a number of vice presidents who openly defied their presidents. John Calhoun, for example, actively worked in the Senate to oppose the policies of both presidents he served under (John Quincy Adams and Andrew Jackson). In fact, many vice presidents in the nineteenth century did not even live in

Washington, and of those who did, many did not meet with their president more than a few times.[8]

Vice presidential selection during this time also largely ignored considerations of the individual's competence and ability to handle the responsibilities of president. Although vice presidents and vice presidential candidates in the historical era were not completely unqualified, they were generally not men of great stature or leadership caliber, at least when compared with other leaders of the time or with vice presidential candidates in the modern era.[9] One authoritative account from the time noted:

> The convention . . . usually [gave] the nomination to this post to a man in the second rank, sometimes as a consolation to a disappointed candidate for the presidential nomination, sometimes to a friend of such a disappointed candidate in order to "placate" his faction, sometimes to a person from whom large contributions to the campaign fund may be expected, sometimes as a compliment to an elderly leader who is personally popular.[10]

The overriding concern in the selection process during this period was political: How could the vice presidential selection help the ticket win? This is where the issue of balance came into play. Although there was no precise formula, several guidelines were almost always followed when balancing the ticket, all of which were designed to broaden the appeal of the ticket as well as to unify the party. First, the vice presidential candidate typically represented a state that was from a different region of the country than the home state of the presidential candidate. From 1804 through 2016, only eleven of the major party presidential tickets have *not* been regionally balanced. The most recent of these was in 1992 when Bill Clinton of Arkansas selected Al Gore of Tennessee, another Southerner. This was done in part to broaden the appeal of the ticket in the South, a region that Democratic presidential candidates have had difficulty winning since 1968.[11]

American political parties have always been broad-based coalitions of a variety of interests. This is inevitable with a two-party system in a country as large and diverse as the United States. For example, the modern Republican Party is a loose coalition of Southern Evangelical Christians, fiscal conservatives, antigovernment individuals hailing from the mountain West, and foreign policy hawks. As such, balancing the ticket regionally was frequently an attempt to add factional balance as well. Beyond broadening the appeal of the ticket, this was done to unify the party. Because the presidential nomination could only go to a representative of one faction of the party, the vice presidential nomination was used to mollify other wings or sects within the party. This practice can be seen in the modern era as well and is often reduced to ensuring that the ticket has a certain ideological balance. The more liberal Democrat John Kennedy, for example, selected the more conservative Lyndon Johnson in 1960. The Republican Gerald Ford, a moderate, selected the more conservative Bob Dole in 1976.[12]

A final factor affecting the selection of a running mate revolved around other political considerations. Party leaders usually selected vice presidential candidates from states that had a large share of Electoral College votes. This was done because it was assumed, or hoped, that the vice presidential candidate could help win the state for the ticket. For example, New York state, which commanded anywhere from 8 to 15 percent of available Electoral College votes, fielded fourteen of the forty-eight vice presidential candidates from 1804 through 1896. Conversely, only two came from Maine: Hannibal Hamlin, Republican, in 1860 (2.6% of available Electoral College votes) and Arthur Sewall, Democrat, in 1896 (1.3%). Recent exceptions to this rule for vice presidential selection were Republican Dick Cheney in 2000, and Republican Sarah Palin and Democrat Joe Biden in 2008, each of whose home states (Wyoming, Alaska, and Delaware, respectively) have approximately one-half of 1 percent of available Electoral College votes.[13] As a historical footnote, presidential tickets have won in the vice presidential candidate's home state only about 50 percent of the time.[14]

In short, the main objective of the vice presidential pick in the historical era was to unify the party and ensure that the ticket had a broad appeal in order to prevail in November. This translated into a desire to balance the ticket regionally and ideologically, and to select a candidate from a state rich in Electoral College votes. When pundits attempt to forecast the vice presidential pick, these factors play heavily into their predictions. However, in the modern era, the process of selecting a running mate has become far more complex. We turn to a discussion of the modern system next.

THE MODERN ERA OF VICE PRESIDENTIAL SELECTION

Vice presidential selection has changed dramatically in the past fifty years. First, although delegates at the party national convention still formally nominate and select the vice presidential candidate, this process only ratifies the choice that the presidential candidate has made. Second, the process by which presidential candidates make the selection is longer and more complicated. Finally, the qualities and characteristics of modern vice presidential candidates have changed as well. While the historical factors of balance and state size still matter, a number of other considerations, including experience in public office, enter into the decision-making process as well.

One of the reasons for this new focus on experience is the increased prominence of the office of the vice presidency. Starting in the middle part of the twentieth century, the vice president has become a more important player in the American system of government. This change occurred slowly, mainly as the result of concerns over presidential succession. These concerns began when Harry Truman assumed the presidency after the death of Franklin Roosevelt in 1945 without knowing an atomic bomb was close to completion. President Dwight Eisenhower had a heart attack in 1955 and other health problems, and John Kennedy was assassinated in 1963. In 1972, Democrat George McGovern asked his vice presidential nominee, Thomas Eagleton, to withdraw from the ticket after reports surfaced that he had undergone electric shock treatment. And, in 1973, Vice President Spiro Agnew resigned in the face of corruption charges, followed by Richard Nixon's resignation in 1974.[15] All of these events served as high-profile reminders that the vice president is only "one heartbeat away" from the presidency.[16]

In large part because of these increased concerns over presidential succession, vice presidents began playing a more important role in their presidents' administrations. Although the formal role of the vice president has not changed (he or she is the president of and breaks tie votes in the Senate, and assumes the presidency in the event of presidential vacancy), vice presidents, starting with Richard Nixon (1953–1961) began taking on a number of informal roles. These included traveling abroad to meet with foreign leaders, campaigning for the party's congressional candidates in the midterm elections, acting as presidential spokesperson and presidential adviser, and other, more specialized tasks. Al Gore, for example, was charged with the task of streamlining the federal bureaucracy with his "Reinventing Government" initiative; Dick Cheney was put in charge of crafting a new and comprehensive energy policy; Joe Biden was responsible for ensuring that money from the 2009 economic stimulus package was spent as intended.[17]

Changes in the vice presidential selection process began in 1960 when, for the first time, the presidential candidates (John Kennedy and Richard Nixon) chose their own running mates. Previously, as noted, the convention made this choice, although there had been some movement toward giving presidential candidates a say in the matter beginning with Franklin Roosevelt. Of course, candidates consult with any number of advisers and party and interest group leaders, but the choice is now theirs.[18] The fact that candidates, as opposed to parties, select the running mate should by itself suggest that the factors considered in the selection have changed.

The selection process underwent another dramatic change in the 1970s. As the result of the shift to the primary system of selecting presidential candidates, the presidential nomination is now decided long before the party convention begins. This gives the presumptive presidential nominee a great deal of time to examine the experience, personal background, and political ramifications of his or her possible choices. Jimmy Carter was the first presidential candidate to engage in this lengthy vetting process in 1976, using the five weeks between the end of the primary season and the start of the convention to narrow a list of four hundred possible candidates down to approximately twelve names. His chief pollster Pat Caddell "tested the relative strengths of these names" and further narrowed the list of possibilities to seven. The campaign team then examined each of these extensively and Carter met with each to discover how compatible each would be with him, both in terms of policy and personality.[19]

If Walter Mondale, Carter's eventual choice, had been a poor vice president, this method of selecting a running mate may have become a historical footnote. But Mondale is widely acknowledged to have been an excellent vice president, the first example of the new model of active vice presidents.[20] The Carter model of extensively vetting possible vice presidential candidates has become the new standard. What was formerly a hasty and haphazard process—at best—is now lengthy and fairly systematic. The vetting process is typically headed by someone who enjoys the complete trust of the presidential candidate. In 2000, for example, Warren Christopher, who had headed Bill Clinton's search in 1992, headed Al Gore's search, while Dick Cheney was in charge of the process for George W. Bush.[21] Barack Obama relied on Jim Johnson until he resigned over controversy surrounding his Washington insider status, while Senator Lamar Alexander of Tennessee headed John McCain's search in 2008.[22] In 2012, Mitt Romney asked long-time aide Beth Myers to head his search for a running mate.

Finally, the list of characteristics that modern vice presidential candidates embody has expanded beyond those discussed earlier in the modern era. In part, this is because of the increased visibility of the office. In addition, because presidential candidates are now the ones selecting their running mates, they can pay attention to more personal factors such as compatibility. A lengthy vetting process allows more factors to be examined and considered. The selection itself occurs in context of a different social and political environment that forces presidential candidates to consider characteristics once not considered to be important. So what qualities are modern presidential candidates looking for in their selection of a running mate? We turn to that question in the following section.

VICE PRESIDENTIAL CANDIDATES IN THE MODERN ERA

It has only been in the past decade or so that research has been published that systematically examines the characteristics of vice presidential candidates.[23] Research looks not only at the characteristics of the candidates themselves but also the individuals who were being considered for the ticket but were not chosen. This short list typically includes about a half dozen people. Table 5.1 lists the eventual nominees, the year they ran, and their presidential running mates.

Table 5.1   Vice Presidential Candidates and Their Presidential Running Mates, 1960–2016

Year	Winning VP Candidate (Presidential Candidate, Party)	Losing VP Candidate (Presidential Candidate, Party)
1960	Lyndon B. Johnson (John F. Kennedy, Democrat)	Henry Cabot Lodge Jr. (Richard M. Nixon, Republican)
1964	Hubert H. Humphrey Jr. (Lyndon B. Johnson, Democrat)	William E. Miller (Barry M. Goldwater, Republican)
1968	Spiro T. Agnew (Richard M. Nixon, Republican)	Edmund S. Muskie (Hubert H. Humphrey Jr., Democrat)
1972	Spiro T. Agnew (Richard M. Nixon, Republican)	R. Sargent Shriver (George S. McGovern, Democrat)
1976	Walter F. Mondale (James E. Carter Jr., Democrat)	Robert J. Dole (Gerald R. Ford Jr., Republican)
1980	George H. W. Bush (Ronald W. Reagan, Republican)	Walter F. Mondale (James E. Carter Jr., Democrat)
1984	George H. W. Bush (Ronald W. Reagan, Republican)	Geraldine A. Ferraro (Walter F. Mondale, Democrat)
1988	J. Danforth Quayle (George H. W. Bush, Republican)	Lloyd M. Bentsen Jr. (Michael S. Dukakis, Democrat)
1992	Albert A. Gore Jr. (William J. Clinton, Democrat)	J. Danforth Quayle (George H. W. Bush, Republican)
1996	Albert A. Gore Jr. (William J. Clinton, Democrat)	Jack F. Kemp (Robert J. Dole, Republican)
2000	Richard B. Cheney (George W. Bush, Republican)	Joseph I. Lieberman (Albert A. Gore Jr., Democrat)
2004	Richard B. Cheney (George W. Bush, Republican)	John R. Edwards (John F. Kerry, Democrat)
2008	Joseph R. Biden Jr. (Barack H. Obama Jr., Democrat)	Sarah L. Palin (John S. McCain III, Republican)
2012	Joseph R. Biden Jr. (Barack H. Obama Jr., Democrat)	Paul D. Ryan (Willard Mitt Romney, Republican)
2016	Michael R. Pence (Donald J. Trump, Republican)	Timothy M. Kaine (Hillary R. Clinton, Democrat)

An examination of the characteristics of vice presidential nominees shows how complex the selection of a running mate has become. Statistical analysis has identified several factors, or characteristics of vice presidential hopefuls, that are important, although it is important to note that not every candidate possesses all of these qualities. Ultimately, statistics deal in probabilities, not certainties. In other words, the best that a statistical analysis can tell us with regard to this question is what qualities are likely to be important to presidential candidates in their decision-making.

With respect to the historical factors, research shows that presidential candidates still seek regional balance for their ticket.[24] Ideological balance, however, is no longer as important to the equation as it once was.[25] There have been many instances in the past few decades where the presidential and vice presidential candidates were from the same ideological wing of the party. For example, the elections of 2000, 2004, and 2008 all featured ideologically *un*balanced tickets. In 2008, both Obama and Biden could fairly be classified as relatively liberal. Likewise, Democrats John Kerry and John Edwards in 2004 were liberals; Al Gore and Joe Lieberman in 2000, moderates; George W. Bush and Dick Cheney in 2000, conservatives.[26] In fact, a full 50 percent of the tickets since 1960 have not been ideologically balanced. Ideological balancing of the ticket still occurs (e.g., both tickets in 2016), but it is no longer as important as in years past and is not significant from a statistical standpoint.

Similarly, state size seems to matter less in the modern era as well. In 2008, for example, neither Joe Biden nor Sarah Palin brought more than three potential Electoral College votes to the ticket. A comparable situation prevailed in 2000 with Dick Cheney, who hailed from Wyoming (three votes). As it happens, the number of Electoral College votes in the candidate's home state is less important than how competitive the state is. While presidential tickets have carried the home state of the vice presidential candidate fifteen of twenty times (75%) from 1980 to 2016,[27] coming from either a safe state or a state the ticket has no chance of winning would seem to offer no electoral advantage. Selecting a running mate from a competitive state, however, might boost the ticket's chances of winning that state.[28] While there are different ways of determining which states are competitive, we can safely conclude that they are *not* states that the presidential candidate is certain of winning or losing.

Having said this, not all vice presidential candidates come from competitive states. For example, in 2016 Donald Trump was all but sure to win in Mike Pence's Indiana, and the Obama campaign was probably not concerned about losing Biden's Delaware in 2008, a state that had gone Democratic since 1992. Similarly, the last time Palin's Alaska voted for a Democratic candidate was in 1964. Recent examples notwithstanding, statistical analysis confirms that since 1960, the competitiveness of the vice presidential candidate's home state matters.[29] John Kerry's choice of John Edwards was in part made in an attempt to win North Carolina, even though at the time of the selection, the state had not voted for a Democratic candidate since 1976 (for Jimmy Carter). And in 1992, Clinton's selection of Al Gore may have been a reflection of the fact that Gore's home state of Tennessee was perceived to be competitive. In fact, the Democratic ticket carried Tennessee in both 1992 and 1996, reversing Republican wins in 1980, 1984, and 1988.

One of the more common misconceptions in the modern era is that the presidential candidate might select their main rival from the primary season for the nomination. This is rarely the case. In fact, the modern vice presidency is built around the premise that the vice president is the president's loyal lieutenant. Because of this, a bitter primary struggle that leaves hard feelings all but precludes the nominee from selecting his or her main opponent. This, perhaps more than anything, was why Hillary Clinton was reportedly not even considered among the finalists for Obama's eventual selection or why George W. Bush's main rival, John McCain, was never considered in 2000.[30] In 2016, there was little chance Donald Trump would select one his major rivals for the Republican nomination or that Bernie Sanders would end up on the ticket with Hillary Clinton.

If the nominee's main opponent either withdraws from the race soon after it becomes obvious they will not win the nomination or stays in the race but does not campaign too aggressively, there is some chance of being selected. In 2004, for example, after it became clear that John Kerry would win the Democratic primary, John Edwards withdrew and began campaigning for him. Similarly, although Ronald Reagan's main rival George H. W. Bush had criticized Reagan in the opening caucuses and primaries, he withdrew from the race at an early stage and backed away from earlier criticisms of him. Although Joe Biden was not Obama's main opponent in 2008, he withdrew after the first contest without making any harsh public comments about Obama. The point is that doing well in the presidential primaries is no guarantee that one can eventually secure the vice presidential nomination.[31]

Having served in some capacity in the military seems to be a significant factor in vice presidential selection since 1960, although this may be changing. Since 1960, ten vice presidential candidates have not served in the military, but only two of these ran prior to 2000 (Hubert Humphrey in 1964 and Geraldine Ferraro in 1984). Since 2000, all eight vice presidential candidates (Dick Cheney and Joe Lieberman, 2000; John Edwards, 2004; Sarah Palin and Joe Biden, 2008; Paul Ryan, 2012; Tim Kaine, 2016; Mike Pence, 2016) had no military experience.[32]

In addition to military experience, youth seems to be a desirable factor in selecting a running mate in the modern age. Older presidential candidates quite often select more youthful running mates to balance the perception that they are too old for the presidency. The average age of a vice presidential candidate since 1960 was fifty-three years. Almost half the candidates from this period were younger than the average age of the group of potential running mates being considered. Several of these "youngsters" were much younger than the presidential candidate. For example, Dan Quayle was twenty-three years younger than George H. W. Bush in 1988; Sarah Palin was twenty-eight years younger than John McCain in 2008; and Paul Ryan was twenty-three years younger than Mitt Romney in 2012.

There are two other important factors in the vice presidential selection process that have emerged in the modern era. The first is political experience. Despite the example of McCain selecting the relatively inexperienced Palin, who had served less than two years as the governor of Alaska, the trend in this regard is to draw from a more experienced pool of individuals. For example, of the twenty-three nonincumbent vice presidential candidates since 1960, eleven have come from the U.S. Senate. Only three have come from the House of Representatives: William Miller, who ran with Republican Barry Goldwater in 1964; Geraldine Ferraro, who was Democrat Walter Mondale's running mate in 1984; and Paul Ryan, who was Republican Mitt Romney's vice presidential candidate in 2012. Others have brought other high-level experience to the ticket (e.g., Dick Cheney was Secretary of Defense under George H. W. Bush).[33] Just two candidates had only subnational government experience (Spiro Agnew and Sarah Palin) before running for vice president.

The point here is that unlike vice presidential selection in the historical era, political experience has become an important factor in the selection process. The good news is that political experience may translate into competence or fitness to assume the presidency in the event of a presidential vacancy. If nothing else, modern vice presidential candidates are probably more qualified than their premodern counterparts.[34] The average candidate for vice presidential office in the modern era brought nineteen years of governmental experience to the ticket, of which only five were spent in subnational (state or local government) office.

Of course, there are exceptions to this trend toward selecting more politically experienced running mates. In 1968, Richard Nixon selected the moderately well-known governor of Maryland, Spiro Agnew, as his running mate. Agnew had a total of only nine years of government experience, and Democrats aggressively exploited his inexperience throughout the campaign. After Thomas Eagleton withdrew from the Democratic ticket in 1972, George McGovern selected Sargent Shriver, who had only seven years appointive experience in various national government agencies. In 1984, Walter Mondale selected little-known, three-term House member Geraldine Ferraro, who had a total of ten years of government experience. John Kerry's choice in 2004 was John Edwards, a first-term U.S. senator with no other political experience. And in 2008, John McCain selected Sarah Palin, who, before becoming Alaska's governor, had served on the city council and as the mayor of the small town of Wasilla, Alaska (pop. 8,600). To many observers, Palin's experience was insufficient for national office, and she was widely perceived as underqualified.[35]

As this recent history illustrates, presidential candidates who fail to select a running mate capable of assuming the presidency can pay a heavy political price. While in some cases inexperienced vice presidential candidates can become vice president (e.g., Agnew, Quayle), the campaign works overtime to counter the claim that they are not qualified.

A final factor that has emerged as significant in the selection process is attention from, or exposure in, the national media. This has become especially important for the Carter model of vice presidential selection, since presidential candidates must do extensive vetting of their possible choices. Allowing the media to do this, wittingly or otherwise, makes good sense. As one account summarizes:

> No presidential candidate has the resources to fully research every aspect of a potential vice president's background . . . [presidential] nominees have increasingly in recent years turned to . . . people who not only have been fully investigated but also have extensive experience dealing with the national media.[36]

Few candidates want a surprise similar to the one McGovern received in 1972 about Thomas Eagleton's psychiatric history. Some have also argued that one of the reasons Dan Quayle had the reputation for being less intelligent than others is the fact that the Bush campaign surprised the media by selecting a relative unknown. Quayle also mishandled some early appearances.[37] The same seems true for Sarah Palin, who was both a surprise choice and unknown to most of the media elite. Conversely, Joe Biden (2008), John Edwards (2004), Dick Cheney and Joe Lieberman (2000), Jack Kemp (1996), and Al Gore (1992) had extensive experience with and exposure in the national media. This has become the norm.[38] (See table 5.2 for a summary of the characteristics of vice presidential candidates since 1960.)

In the next section, we summarize our discussion, rating several of the most recent choices according to the discussion presented here.

RATING RECENT VICE PRESIDENTIAL CANDIDATES

Analyses of modern vice presidential selections demonstrate that the old model of understanding the process no longer suffices. While regional balance is still important, ideological balance is not. Moreover, state size is less important than the vice presidential candidate's home state being competitive. Youth, military service, political experience and exposure in the national media, however, stand out as important in the modern age. As a side note, various demographic factors such as gender, race and ethnicity, and religion, often discussed now in terms of balancing the ticket, have also become significant factors in the selection process in recent years.

So what of recent selections? Bill Clinton's selection of Al Gore in 1992 flew in the face of both geographic considerations in that each were Southerners, and Gore's Tennessee was not an extremely competitive state for the Democrats (in spite of this, the Democrats did carry the state). Gore was younger, had military experience, only slightly less than average political

Table 5.2 Characteristics of (nonincumbent) Vice Presidential Candidates, 1960–2016

Year	Candidate	State (Electoral College Votes)	Regional Balance?	Ideological Balance?	Competitive State?*	Age	Military Service	Years Government Experience (Subnational, National)	Media Exposure**
1960	Lyndon Johnson (D)	TX (24)‡	Yes	Yes	Yes	52	Yes	25 (0, 25)	High
	Henry Cabot Lodge (R)	MA (16)	Yes	Yes	No	58	Yes	23 (3, 20)	High
1964	Hubert Humphrey (D)	MN (10)‡	Yes	Yes	Yes	53	No	21 (3, 18)	High
	William Miller (R)	NY (43)	Yes	No	Yes	50	Yes	18 (4, 14)	Low
1968	Spiro Agnew (R)	MD (10)	Yes	No	Yes	50	Yes	9 (9, 0)	Low
	Edmund Muskie (D)	ME (4)‡	Yes	Yes	Yes	54	Yes	25 (15, 10)	Low
1972	Sargent Shriver (D)	MD (10)	Yes	Yes	No	57	Yes	7 (0, 7)	High
1976	Walter Mondale (D)	MN (10)‡	Yes	Yes	No	48	Yes	20 (4, 16)	Low
	Bob Dole (R)	KS (7)‡	No	Yes	No	53	Yes	25 (10, 15)	High
1980	George H. W. Bush (R)	TX (26)‡	Yes	Yes	Yes	56	Yes	9 (0, 9)	High
1984	Geraldine Ferraro (D)	NY (36)	Yes	No	Yes	49	No	10 (4, 6)	Low

Year	Candidate	State (EV)							
1988	Dan Quayle (R)	IN (12)‡	Yes	Yes	No	41	Yes	12 (0, 12)	Average
	Lloyd Bentsen (D)	TX (29)	Yes	No	No	67	Yes	26 (2, 24)	High
1992	Al Gore (D)	TN (11)‡	No	No	No	43	Yes	16 (0, 16)	Average
1996	Jack Kemp (R)	NY (33)	Yes	Yes	Yes	61	Yes	23 (1, 22)	High
2000	Dick Cheney (R)	WY (3)‡	Yes	No	No	59	No	21 (0, 21)	High
	Joe Lieberman (D)	CT (8)‡	Yes	No	Yes	58	No	25 (13, 12)	Average
2004	John Edwards (D)	NC (15)	Yes	No	Yes	51	No	5 (0, 5)	High
2008	Joe Biden (D)	DE (3)‡	Yes	No	No	66	No	38 (2, 36)	High
	Sarah Palin (R)	AK (3)‡	Yes	No	No	44	No	12 (12, 0)	Low
2012	Paul Ryan (R)	WI (10)	Yes	Yes	Yes	42	No	14 (0, 14)	Average
2016	Mike Pence (R)	IN (11)	Yes	Yes	No	57	No	15 (3, 12)	Average
	Tim Kaine (D)	VA (13)	Yes	Yes	Yes	58	No	17 (13, 4)	Average

Notes: Incumbent candidates are not listed. In 1972 Sargent Shriver is listed as the choice, having run on the Democratic ticket after McGovern's first selection, Thomas Eagleton, withdrew.

*"Competitive" is when the average margin of victory from the previous three presidential elections was less than 10 percent.

**Based primarily on author calculations of number of stories that named candidates in *Time* magazine and the *New York Times* in the eighteen months prior to the selection of the vice presidential candidate.

‡Ticket won the vice presidential candidate's home state.

experience, and enjoyed an average amount of exposure in the national media. Bob Dole's selection of Jack Kemp in 1996 brought regional balance to the ticket (Kemp came from New York and Dole from Kansas). While slightly older, he also had military experience, a higher than average number of years in government, and exposure in the national media.

In 2000, both Dick Cheney and Joe Lieberman brought regional balance to their respective tickets. Both men were slightly older than the average vice presidential nominee in the modern era. Both also lacked military experience, but had above average years of political experience. Of the two, Cheney had a great deal of exposure in the national media, while Lieberman had an average amount. John Edwards in 2004 provided the Democratic ticket with regional balance. North Carolina was also somewhat competitive, although the ticket did not carry the state. Edwards was young, but boasted no military service and little political experience. He did, however, have a higher than average level of exposure in the national media.

In 2008, Barack Obama selected Joe Biden, which balanced the ticket regionally, but Biden came from a noncompetitive state that the ticket would surely have won otherwise. Biden was older and lacked military experience. However, he brought a wealth of government experience to the ticket, as well as a relatively high media profile. The selection of Sarah Palin by John McCain added regional balance to his ticket, but like Biden's Delaware, her home state of Alaska was noncompetitive. Unlike Biden she was young at the time of her selection, had a relative lack of political experience, and virtually no exposure in the national media. So why did McCain select Palin, especially given the controversy that the choice generated? First, it was an unconventional choice, highlighting McCain's reputation as a "maverick." Beyond this, it helped mobilize support from the previously lukewarm Republican base of evangelical Christians. Whether it was a strategically sound move by McCain is open to interpretation.

In 2012, Paul Ryan brought several qualities to the Republican ticket. One hope for Republicans was that his youth might help counter the perception that Mitt Romney was out of touch, especially with a younger generation that Obama had connected with so well. Second, his home state of Wisconsin, with ten Electoral College votes, was thought to be competitive in 2012. Ryan was also known as a fiscal conservative, which brought some conservative credentials to a ticket that was somewhat lacking in that department. Finally, Ryan's reputation in the House was built primarily on his focus on economic issues, which complemented Romney's focus on the still-recovering economy in 2012.

In a strategy that seemed slightly reminiscent of McCain's in 2008, Donald Trump turned to the conservative Mike Pence in 2016. Pence, middle-aged, came from a midsized, noncompetitive state (Indiana), had an average number of years experience in government, and was moderately well-known nationally. His main advantage was his social conservative credentials, particularly on the issue of abortion. The choice of Pence probably persuaded some conservatives, wary of Trump, to vote Republican.

Hillary Clinton's strategy was similar to the one her husband Bill seemed to employ in 1992, namely, to select a running mate that largely accentuated her own politics. Tim Kaine's home state of Virginia, with thirteen Electoral College votes, was considered to be competitive in 2016 and brought regional balance to the ticket. At age fifty-eight, Kaine was no youngster, but was younger than Clinton. He also brought a reasonable amount of experience to the ticket and was fairly well-known nationally. The main selling point for the selection of Kaine was the fact that he and Clinton were reportedly simpatico with respect to policy positions. In other words, like Clinton, Kaine was seen to occupy political space somewhere between the center and the progressive left.

CONCLUSION: DOES IT MATTER?

The notion of regional and ideological ticket balancing with a selection from a large state is a good way to understand vice presidential selection in a previous era, but no longer suffices. Vice presidential selection is now a complex process, dependent on a number of factors. But does the choice really matter? Does it have any real impact? On the one hand, the vice president is the constitutional successor to the president in the event of a presidential vacancy (death, disability, resignation, or impeachment). As one account summarizes:

> From 1841 to 1975 more than one-third of all U.S. presidents either died in office or quit, paving the way for the vice president to occupy the White House. Eight vice presidents became president as a result of the death of a sitting president (John Tyler, Millard Fillmore, Andrew Johnson, Chester Arthur, Theodore Roosevelt, Calvin Coolidge, Harry Truman, and Lyndon Johnson) and one, Gerald Ford, became president as the result of presidential resignation.[39]

Therefore the question of how qualified the vice president is to assume the presidency is extremely important.

But for all of the attention paid to the veepstakes by political pundits and observers, does the selection of a running mate have any effect on the outcome of the election? Some suggested that in 1992 George H. W. Bush might have been able to secure as much as eight percentage points extra without Quayle as his running mate.[40] Others were quick to suggest that McCain's loss in 2008 was in part attributable to his selection of Palin.[41] To be fair, there is no question that both of these individuals were a public relations drag on their respective tickets. But did they cost their tickets actual votes? Research on this question is notoriously difficult because it is "virtually impossible to disentangle presidential and vice presidential preferences in our system of presidential elections."[42] While a handful of studies suggest that Palin may have cost McCain some support,[43] the predominance of the evidence points in a clear direction: "the vice presidential candidate has—at most—a marginal effect on voters' choices."[44]

It is true that vice presidents and vice presidential candidates are in the spotlight more than in earlier eras. It is also true that vice presidents are a now-integral part of their president's team. However, people cast their vote for the presidential ticket based on party preference and the presidential candidate—not the vice presidential candidate. Richard Nixon once remarked that a vice president "can't help you . . . he can only hurt you."[45] Virtually all presidential scholars agree with this Nixon doctrine that vice presidential candidates can hurt but not help the ticket. So while the question of whether an individual is qualified to assume the presidency is an important one, the selection of a vice presidential candidate has almost no impact on the outcome of the election.

FURTHER READING

Baumgartner, Jody C. "The Post-Palin Calculus: The 2012 Republican Veepstakes." *PS: Politics and Political Science* 45 (2012): 605–9.

Baumgartner, Jody C. *The Vice Presidency: From the Shadow to the Spotlight.* Lanham, MD: Rowman & Littlefield, 2015.

Goldstein, Joel K. *The Modern American Vice Presidency.* Princeton, NJ: Princeton University Press, 1982.

Light, Paul C. *Vice-Presidential Power: Advice and Influence in the White House.* Baltimore, MD: Johns Hopkins University, 1984.

Mayer, William G. "A Brief History of Vice Presidential Selection." In *In Pursuit of the White House 2000: How We Choose Our Presidential Nominees*, edited by William G. Mayer, 329–331. Chatham, NJ: Chatham House, 2000.

6

Mudslinging 101

Have Presidential Campaigns Really Become Nastier?

IN ALMOST EVERY ELECTION SEASON, political observers comment on the declining quality of political campaigns. One of the most frequently made charges is that negative campaigning has grown worse over the years. For example, one analyst predicted that 2016 would be the "most negative, nasty presidential campaign in modern American history."[1] Others echoed this sentiment. An expert on negative campaigns claimed that 2016 was the "dirtiest" since 1972.[2] Critics pointed to Donald Trump's references to Hillary Clinton as a "nasty woman," his call to have Russia hack her emails and his claim that she should be imprisoned. For her part, Clinton questioned Trump's mental fitness and continually reminded voters that he was a serial womanizer. Others who opposed Trump went further, labeling him a misogynist and a bigot.

In the aftermath of the 2016 election, the British BBC asked if "this [was] the nastiest U.S. election campaign."[3] This apocalyptic view of the state of political campaigns is not new. Indeed, over the past several election cycles, observers and analysts have made claims that "negative presidential campaign ads [are] going to new extremes."[4] In 2012, for example, one analyst lamented that while "past campaigns have featured their fair share of punches . . . 2012 is setting an unprecedented tone."[5] We were treated to similar observations in 2008, which one writer characterized as history's "longest, meanest, and most expensive."[6] Another story featured a headline that read, "McCain Campaign is the Ugliest Ever."[7] Cindy McCain, the wife of Republican candidate John McCain, claimed that the Obama campaign had "waged the dirtiest campaign in American history."[8] Obama's running mate, Joe Biden, countered that the McCain campaign was "running the most scurrilous campaign in modern history."[9]

While few would dispute the fact that recent presidential elections are replete with egregious examples of political attacks, it is highly debatable that any of the recent contests were the "dirtiest" ever. In fact, negative campaign tactics have always played a pervasive role in American presidential elections. Opponents of Thomas Jefferson suggested that his victory would lead to the rise of atheism and the burning of the Bible.[10] Andrew Jackson had to endure attacks by his political opponents that his deceased mother was a prostitute.[11] These and other examples illustrate that mean-spirited, personal attacks in American campaigns are hardly new to the political landscape.

The goal in this chapter is to demonstrate that negative personal attacks during political campaigns have long been a part of American politics. Our focus is on presidential elections. Although state and local elections can be very negative, presidential races are the "Super Bowl" of campaigns. As such, perceptions of American elections are most heavily shaped by these contests. In the next section, we briefly review what it means to "go negative." We then turn to an examination of three presidential campaigns from the nineteenth century that stand out as particularly negative. These historical examples cast considerable doubt on the repeated claims that "today's campaigns are the most negative ever." Following this, we examine two more recent campaigns from the twentieth century, illustrating that even the worst of these have been no more negative than campaigns in earlier times.

"GOING NEGATIVE" AND NEGATIVE CAMPAIGNS IN THE NINETEENTH CENTURY

Evaluating how negative a campaign is, at least to some degree, a subjective endeavor. In reviewing the academic literature, there are slightly different definitions about what exactly constitutes negativity in a campaign. There is some agreement that it typically involves discrediting, criticizing, or publicizing the deficiencies of the opponent.[12] A truly balanced examination, however, would allow for the fact that some "negative" ads, such as those that compare and contrast some aspect of a candidate's record or background, should be more properly thought of as comparative or contrast ads. Although critical of the opponent, these ads present information that the voting public should know before they make their decision about who will best serve their interests if elected.[13] Indeed, there is justification for the notion that these types of ads serve the public. Some mention of the opponent's background, experience, and public record have a reasonable place in democratic campaign discourse.

Nonetheless, some political scientists suggest that negative campaigning has had a deleterious effect on American democracy. Their research finds that negative advertisements heighten political cynicism, depress voter turnout, and reduce political efficacy.[14] Others argue that negative advertisements provide important information to voters, help draw clearer distinctions between candidates, and improve voters' recall of information.[15]

Our central purpose in this chapter, however, is not to weigh into the debate about the effects of negative advertising. Rather, it is to counter the ever-present claim that today's presidential campaigns are the "dirtiest ever." With an understanding of what "negative" campaigns really are, we now turn to three historical cases to illustrate that vicious negative campaigning is nearly as old as the republic.

In his book *Mudslingers*, scholar Kerwin Swint examines the twenty-five dirtiest political campaigns in history. According to Swint, four of the five dirtiest campaigns occurred in the nineteenth century. Here we will review three of these four: the presidential elections of 1800, 1828, and 1864.

The Election of 1800
The election of 1800 pitted the Federalist President John Adams against his Democratic–Republican Vice President Thomas Jefferson. Besides the election precipitating the passage of the Twelfth Amendment, the election was significant in that it set a rather high (or low?) standard for negativity and viciousness.[16] While there were legitimate differences separating the two on many issues, supporters often focused their efforts on negative personal attacks.

Adams's supporters spread stories that Jefferson had "cheated his British creditors, obtained property by fraud, robbed a widow of an estate worth ten thousand pounds, and behaved in a cowardly fashion as Governor of Virginia during the Revolution."[17] Another attack claimed Jefferson was "mean-spirited" and the "son of a half-breed Indian squaw, sired by a Virginia mulatto father."[18] One newspaper opined that a victory for Jefferson in 1800 would result in the teaching and practice of "murder, robbery, rape, adultery, and incest" and added that the "air will be rent with cries of the distressed, the soil will be soaked with blood, and the nation black with crimes."[19] The president of Yale University believed that Jefferson's election would result in "the Bible [being] cast into a bonfire . . . our wives and daughters [becoming] the victims of legal prostitution."[20] Others attacked him as a dangerous rebel "who writes against the truths of God's word . . . without so much as a decent external respect for the faith and worship of Christians."[21]

Jefferson's supporters labeled Adams a "fool, hypocrite, criminal, and tyrant."[22] Jeffersonians also planted a rumor that Adams had intended to arrange a marriage between one of his sons and one of the daughters of King George III in a plot to reunite the United States and Great Britain. Another rumor suggested that Adams had sent his running mate, General Charles Pinckney, to England on a trip to secure four mistresses, two for each of them. To these charges, Adams famously retorted, "If this be true, [then] General Pinckney has kept them all for himself and cheated me out of two."[23]

While negativity swirled in both directions, the political environment favored Jefferson in 1800. Adams would garner just 39 percent of the popular vote compared to 61 percent for Jefferson. In the Electoral College vote, Jefferson received seventy-three Electoral College votes while Adams received sixty-five. However, because the Electoral College at the time did not distinguish between votes for president and vice president, Jefferson's running mate, Aaron Burr, also received seventy-three Electoral College votes, creating a tie and moving the election to the House of Representatives. There, Jefferson was finally elected president over Burr on the thirty-sixth ballot.[24]

The Twelfth Amendment eventually altered the chaotic process that ensued following the tie between Jefferson and Burr, giving the election of 1800 special historical significance. Many also credit it as the first seriously contested presidential election campaign. This "first" campaign certainly set a standard for negativity that one could argue makes today's campaigns seem somewhat tame.[25]

The Election of 1828

The election of 1828 matched incumbent president John Quincy Adams (the son of former president John Adams) of the Whig Party against challenger Andrew Jackson, a Democrat and former army general who led American troops to a decisive victory over the British in the Battle of New Orleans during the War of 1812. The election was a rematch of sorts of the previous election, which had ended in bitter controversy.

In 1824, Jackson faced Adams, as well as William Crawford and Henry Clay. Jackson garnered 41 percent of the popular vote, ten percentage points more than that of Adams. Yet, all four candidates received votes in the Electoral College: Jackson (99), Adams (84), Crawford (41), and Clay (37). Because no candidate received a majority of Electoral College votes, the election was decided in the House of Representatives.[26] In the House, Clay was disqualified for finishing fourth. (The Twelfth Amendment stipulates that the House may consider only the top three finishers.) However, as the speaker of the House, Clay wielded considerable influence, and because he deeply disliked Jackson[27] he threw his support to Adams. The Adams win infuriated Jackson supporters because their candidate received the most popular and the most Electoral College votes. To add to the outrage, Adams named Clay his secretary of state, prompting critics to suggest that the two had struck a "corrupt bargain."[28] This set the stage for the bitter 1828 rematch.

Jackson supporters attacked Adams for his excesses, suggesting "King John the Second" lived in "kingly pomp and splendor."[29] The charge centered on Adams's purchase of a billiards table, which Jacksonians falsely claimed was purchased at taxpayer expense. Jacksonians also questioned Adams's religious sincerity, claiming he sometimes traveled on Sundays and had "premarital relations" with his wife. These attacks came despite the fact that Adams was a direct descendant of Puritan colonists and, by all reasonable accounts, a devout Christian. Most outrageous was the Jacksonian claim that, while serving as the minister to Russia, Adams handed over a young American girl to Czar Alexander I.[30]

The Adams campaign played equally dirty in attacking Jackson. A pro-Adams political handbook claimed Jackson was "wholly unqualified by education, habit and temper for the station of President."[31] Adams's supporters further attacked Jackson with an endless barrage of charges that included adultery, bigamy, gambling, drunkenness, theft, and even murder. The latter charge involved Jackson's approval to execute six militiamen for desertion during the Creek War in 1813. A pro-Adams editor described the event as "the Bloody Deeds of General Jackson," in which Jackson himself sanctioned the cold-blooded murder of innocent soldiers.[32]

Attacks against Jackson even extended to his family. One newspaper story was particularly vicious, referring to Jackson's mother as a prostitute. According to the account, "General Jackson's mother was a COMMON PROSTITUTE, brought to this country by the British soldiers. She afterward married a MULATO MAN, with whom she had several children, of which GENERAL JACKSON IS ONE!!!"[33] Jackson also had to endure insults against his wife. Adams's supporters spread misleading stories that Jackson's wife, Rachel, was an adulterer and a bigamist. The story underlying the charge, however, was more complicated. Jackson's wife had been married previously and believed she had lawfully divorced her first husband when she began her relationship with Jackson. This, however, was not the case. By the time Jackson and Rachel became aware of this, the two had already married.[34]

In the end, Jackson defeated Adams in the 1828 election, winning 56 percent of the popular vote and 178 of the 261 Electoral College votes. However, the victory came at a deep personal cost to Jackson. His wife died a month after the election, and Jackson blamed Adams's supporters for their relentless attacks against her, referring to them as "murderers" and vowing never to forgive them. At her funeral, Jackson declared, "May God Almighty forgive her murderers, as I know she forgave them. I never can."[35]

The 1828 election certainly rises to the highest levels of negativity in American campaigns. Indeed, many scholars consider the election of 1828 to be one of dirtiest presidential contests in American history.[36] As negative as modern campaigns can sometimes become, it seems difficult to argue that the 2016 election contained anything that surpassed the attacks of the 1828 election.

The Election of 1864

The two main candidates in the 1864 presidential election were President Abraham Lincoln (Republican) and challenger General George McClellan (Democrat) of New Jersey. While Lincoln is revered today as one of the greatest presidents in American history, he was not nearly as popular in 1864. The Civil War was responsible for rising death tolls and mounting financial costs, which critics suggested were Lincoln's fault. His opponents in the Democratic Party believed that this presented them with an opportunity to win the White House.

During the campaign, Lincoln's opponents labeled him ignorant, incompetent, and corrupt. Others went further, referring to him as "Ignoramus Abe." Additional pejorative descriptions of Lincoln included ape, gorilla, Old Scoundrel, despot, liar, perjurer, thief, swindler, robber, buffoon, monster, and butcher.[37] One critic claimed the "idea that such a man as he should be president of such a country is a very ridiculous joke."[38] Another attack involved a false story that Lincoln demanded one of his officers sing him a song while passing the bodies of dead Union solders after the Battle of Antietam.[39]

Other anti-Lincoln groups relied on overtly racist appeals in their attempts to discredit Lincoln. One pamphlet labeled Lincoln as "Abraham Africanus the First" for his opposition to slavery (see photo 6.1). Another was titled "Miscegenation: The Theory of the Bending of the Races, Applied

Photo 6.1 "Abraham Africanus" ad, 1864. *Source*: Answers.com, http://www.answers.com/topic/united-states-presidential-election-1864.

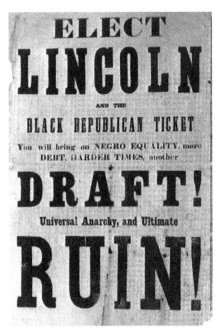

Photo 6.2 "Elect Lincoln" ad, 1864. *Source*: Illinois Periodicals Online, http://www.lib.niu.edu/2001/iht820144.html.

to the American White Man and Negro," and claimed that Lincoln favored "race mixing" and actively encouraged and supported the "intermarriage" between whites and blacks. Many anti-Lincoln newspapers aggressively publicized the pamphlet.[40] Another claimed his election with the "Black Republican Ticket" would "bring on NEGRO EQUALITY, more DEBT, HARDER TIMES . . . Universal Anarchy, and Ultimate RUIN!" (see photo 6.2). Yet a third, labeled "The Lincoln Catechism," outlined the "despotism" and horrors another Lincoln term would bring (photo 6.3).

Lincoln supporters attacked McClellan personally as well, labeling him a "coward" and criticizing his "defeatism" and "lack of patriotism."[41] Some even suggested that Democratic opposition to the war constituted treason. Republicans ridiculed McClellan as "Little Mac," and attacked his military credentials as a general, noting that he had "nothing to offer but a tradition of defeat."[42] In Pennsylvania, Republicans warned in one poster that a McClellan victory would lead to anarchy, despotism, and the end of civilization.

The election concluded with a clear victory for Lincoln that ultimately had significant implications for American history. Lincoln's presidency would also be remembered for its high ideals. However, even "Honest Abe" could not avoid negative campaigning in the election of 1864.

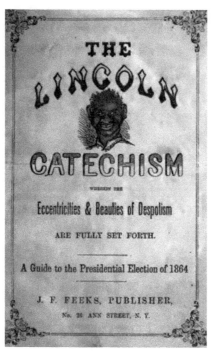

Photo 6.3 Lincoln "Catechism" ad, 1864. *Source*: Communities Digital News, http://www.commdiginews.com/politics-2/the-lincoln-catechism -and-president-barack-obama-31745/.

MODERN "NEGATIVE" CAMPAIGNS

Extreme examples of negative campaigning exist in the modern era as well. Similar to the nineteenth century, modern campaigns have continued the practice of ruthlessly attacking the opposition. Yet, unlike the nineteenth century, modern campaigns could package negative messages into thirty-second (or less) television advertisements capable of reaching millions of citizens. Television also provides a "perfect medium" for tapping into voters' "surface feelings."[43] The emotional appeals of television can have the effect of mobilizing citizens to vote and to participate in the political process.[44] In the television era, two campaigns stand out as particularly negative: the presidential elections of 1964 and 1988.[45]

The Election of 1964
The presidential election of 1964 was a contest between two candidates with sharply different views about the proper role of government. The political ideologies of the incumbent president, Democrat Lyndon Johnson of Texas,

and his Republican challenger, Senator Barry Goldwater of Arizona, could not have been more different. Johnson believed in an active role for government to combat poverty, racism, and other social ills, whereas Goldwater campaigned on a conservative platform, claiming that smaller government was essential to expanding individual freedom and liberty. Indeed, Goldwater himself promised voters a "choice rather than an echo."[46]

As the incumbent president, Johnson faced little serious opposition for the Democratic nomination. Goldwater's nomination, however, divided the Republican Party. Moderates, led by Governors Nelson Rockefeller of New York and George Romney of Michigan, refused to support or campaign on Goldwater's behalf. Goldwater alienated former president Dwight Eisenhower as well, referring to his presidential administration as a "dime store New Deal."[47] When asked about the presidential prospects of Eisenhower's brother, Milton Eisenhower, Goldwater told *Time* magazine, "One Eisenhower in a generation is enough."[48] Goldwater also exacerbated tensions with moderate Republicans in his acceptance speech at the Republican convention in San Francisco, famously remarking that "extremism in the defense of liberty is no vice . . . [and] that moderation in the pursuit of justice is no virtue."[49] Reacting to the speech, Senator Kenneth Keating of New York and others from the New York delegation walked out of the convention in protest.

Goldwater not only faced divisions within his own party but also was up against his own tendency to make highly controversial public statements, which the Johnson campaign eagerly exploited. In particular, the Johnson campaign made use of several Goldwater statements in its advertisements to paint him as a dangerous, prowar candidate. In one short, twenty-second television ad, viewers see a nuclear explosion as an announcer recites: "On October 24, 1963, Barry Goldwater said of the nuclear bomb, 'Merely another weapon.' Merely another weapon? Vote for President Johnson. The stakes are too high for you to stay home."[50]

The aforementioned advertisement, however, is less well known than the so-called "Daisy Girl" commercial, which one scholar dubbed, "the Mother of all televised attack ads."[51] In this ad, a young girl plucks the petals of a daisy while the ad transitions into a nuclear countdown that ends in an atomic explosion. Although the ad never mentions Goldwater by name, it clearly makes a less than subtle suggestion that a Goldwater victory would lead the nation into nuclear war (see photo 6.4). Interestingly, while the "Daisy Girl" ad would go on to become one of the most controversial commercials in presidential election history, it was only aired once (on CBS' *Monday Night at the Movies*, September 7, 1964). Yet, because the ad generated near-instant controversy, all three networks replayed it the following day. The Goldwater campaign reacted in outrage

WiscAds
"DAISY GIRL"
Lyndon Johnson, 1964

[Girl]: One...two...

three...four...five

seven...six...six

eight...nine...nine
[General (fade over)]: Ten...

nine...eight...seven...six...five

four...three...two...one

zero! [sounds of
explosion]

[Lyndon Johnson]: These are
the stakes, to make a world in
which all of God's children

can live, or to go into the dark.

We must either love each other,
or we must die.

[Narrator]: Vote for President
Johnson on November Third

The stakes are too high for
you to stay home.

Photo 6.4 "Daisy Girl" ad, 1964. *Source*: University of Wisconsin Advertising Project.

at the ad and filed a complaint with the Fair Campaign Practices Committee. The attention that the ad generated helped more people see the ad and likely increased its effects.

Perhaps equally vicious was a Johnson spot that attacked Goldwater's opposition to a treaty banning atmospheric testing of nuclear weapons. The so-called "Ice Cream" ad suggests that Goldwater's opposition to a nuclear test ban treaty could lead to the poisoning—and even death—of innocent children. The sixty-second advertisement features a young girl licking an ice cream cone, while a female announcer warns of Strontium 90 and Cesium 137 (present in nuclear fallout) and the potential dangers of electing Goldwater.

The Johnson campaign also went after Goldwater for his opposition to the 1964 Civil Rights Act. One ad goes so far as to tie Goldwater to the Ku Klux Klan. As a cross burns in the background surrounded by Klan members, a narrator quotes Robert Creel, the leader of the Alabama Ku Klux Klan, who offers his support for Goldwater, stating: "I like Barry Goldwater. He needs our help"[52] (see box 6.1). Other Johnson spots suggested that Goldwater would destroy Social Security and that he harbored animosity toward Americans living on the East Coast with one ad quoting Goldwater as saying, "sometimes I think this country would be better off if we could just saw off the Eastern Seaboard and let it float out to sea."[53] The Johnson campaign added to the assault by altering Goldwater's slogan of "In your heart, you know he's right," to "In your guts, you know he's nuts."[54]

The Goldwater campaign hit back at the Johnson campaign. Goldwater ran advertisements suggesting that Johnson was corrupt and morally deficient, noting his connections to disgraced figures such as Billy Sol Estes, who had been involved in a scam to swindle the Department of Agriculture out of millions of dollars. In one ad, Goldwater accused Johnson of "running a country" by "buying and bludgeoning votes."[55] Goldwater also used his advertisements to make dire predictions. In an ad titled "Moral

---

BOX 6.1 | **Transcript of "KKK" Ad, 1964**

MALE NARRATOR (set against backdrop of KKK members burning a cross): "We represent the majority of the people in Alabama who hate niggerism, Catholicism, Judaism, and all the -isms of the whole world."

So said Robert Creel of the Alabama Ku Klux Klan.

He also said, "I like Barry Goldwater. He needs our help."

Source: The Living Room Candidate, http://www.livingroomcandidate.org/commercials/1964.

Responsibility," Goldwater warned that the Johnson administration was "not far from the kind of moral decay that has brought on the fall of other nations and people. The philosophy of something for nothing . . . is an insidious cancer that will destroy us as a people unless we recognize it and root it out now."[56]

Like Johnson, Goldwater was willing to use children in his ads. In one spot, a boy rides a bicycle as an announcer tells the audience, "Don't look now young man, but somebody has his hand in your pocket. It's the hand of big government. It's taking away about four months pay from what your daddy earns every year—one dollar out of every three in his paycheck. And it's taking security out of your grandmother's Social Security."[57]

Despite Goldwater's counterattacks, Johnson won the election in a landslide, with victory in 44 states totaling 486 Electoral College votes (compared to 52 for Goldwater). Johnson also won 61 percent of the popular vote. However, the size of Johnson's triumph was only part of the story. The presidential election of 1964 was what one scholar claimed the "moment when the negative TV ad was born."[58] This pioneering election set a negative tone that few campaigns have since matched.

The Election of 1988

Vice President George H. W. Bush faced Massachusetts Governor Michael Dukakis in the presidential election of 1988. The election followed the two-term presidency of Republican Ronald Reagan. Bush assumed the role as Reagan's heir apparent and pledged to continue the "Reagan Revolution" of lower taxes, famously proclaiming at the Republican convention, "Read my lips, no new taxes." In contrast, Dukakis campaigned on a platform to balance the federal budget, after the deficit increased under Reagan, and to cut military spending for increased spending on education, health care, and other social programs.

In the early stages of the election, Dukakis led in most polls.[59] However, with the assistance of political consultant Lee Atwater, the Bush campaign went on the attack, calling into question Dukakis's patriotism, ability to lead the military, environmental record, and his commitment to fighting crime. The Bush attacks effectively cut into the Dukakis lead and ultimately propelled Bush to frontrunner status in the late stages of the election.

Perhaps the most memorable negative advertisements against Dukakis was the infamous "Willie Horton" spot, which suggested that Dukakis was ineffective in fighting violent crime during his time as governor of Massachusetts. The ad featured the picture of a convicted murderer, Willie Horton, who raped a Maryland woman during a weekend furlough from a Massachusetts prison. An announcer tells viewers, "Dukakis not only opposes the death penalty, he allowed first-degree murderers to have weekend passes from prison."[60] The final screen read simply, "Weekend

Prison Passes: Dukakis on Crime." Significant controversy followed. Critics charged that the ad was racist because it featured an African American, which some claimed was an attempt to exploit "racist fears" about crime.[61] A similarly themed ad, "Revolving Door," also attacked Dukakis's record on crime, although without the image of Willie Horton. The ad, nevertheless, suggested that a Dukakis victory was a "risk" for the nation (see photos 6.5 and 6.6).

The Bush campaign attempted to paint Dukakis as not only weak on crime but also weak on military and defense issues. Dukakis had attempted to address this perceived problem by visiting the General Dynamics plant in Michigan and riding in an M1 Abrams tank for a campaign photo op. While in the tank, Dukakis wore a large helmet and grinned awkwardly (see photo 6.7). Instead of failing to dispel the attack that he was unfit to be commander-in-chief, the "Dukakis in the tank" footage became synonymous with public relations disasters. Dukakis was pretending to

NARRATOR: Bush and Dukakis on crime

Bush supports the death penalty for first-degree murderers.

Dukakis not only opposes the death penalty,

He allowed first-degree murderers to have weekend passes from prison.

One was Willie Horton who murdered a boy in a robbery, stabbing him 19 times.

Despite a life sentence, Horton received 10 weekend passes from prison.

Horton fled, kidnapped a young couple, stabbing the man and repeatedly raping his girlfriend.

Weekend prison passes. Dukakis on crime.

Photo 6.5 "Willie Horton" ad, 1988.

NARRATOR: As governor, Michael Dukakis vetoed mandatory sentences for drug dealers.

He vetoed the death penalty.

His revolving door prison policy gave weekend furloughs to first-degree murderers not eligible for parole.

While out, many committed other crimes like kidnapping and rape.

And many are still at large.

Now Michael Dukakis says he wants to do for America what he's done for Massachusetts. America can't afford that risk.

Photo 6.6 "Revolving Door" ad, 1988.

be something he was not. The implied message was that he could not be trusted with the job of commander-in-chief. The Bush campaign used this footage to reinforce its message that Dukakis was not a credible military leader (see box 6.2).

The attacks against Dukakis extended to other areas as well. The Bush campaign skewered Dukakis for his record on environmental pollution, citing problems with Boston Harbor. There were also false rumors spread during the campaign that Dukakis received treatment for mental illness and that his wife, Kitty, burned an American flag in protest of the Vietnam War.

The Dukakis campaign was slow in responding to the attacks, which some believe contributed to his sharp decline in the polls as the campaign progressed. Dukakis ultimately fought back by questioning Bush's honesty and claiming in one ad that the Bush campaign had taken a "furlough from the truth."[62] Other ads attacked Bush for his record in the war on drugs, blamed the Republicans for increasing the federal deficit, and poked fun at the selection of Bush's running mate, Senator Dan Quayle of Indiana, who was perceived by some as too young and inexperienced to be president. There were also rumors spread by a member of the Dukakis staff that Bush had an affair with his secretary, Jennifer Fitzgerald. Dukakis, nonetheless, failed to regain his early lead and won just 111 Electoral College votes compared to Bush's 426.

BOX 6.2	"Tank Ride" Ad, 1988

NARRATOR: Michael Dukakis has opposed virtually every defense system we developed.

NARRATOR AND TEXT: He opposed new aircraft carriers. He opposed anti-satellite weapons. He opposed four missile systems, including the Pershing II missile deployment. Dukakis opposed the stealth bomber, a ground emergency warning system against nuclear testing. He even criticized our rescue mission to Grenada and our strike on Libya. And now he wants to be our commander-in-chief. America can't afford that risk.

Photo 6.7 "Dukakis Tank Ride" ad, 1988. *Source*: The Living Room Candidate, http://www.livingroomcandidate.org/commercials/1988/.

CONCLUSION

As noted at the outset of this chapter, the 2016 presidential election campaign had its fair share of negative attacks. Yet, while there were numerous examples of nasty personal attacks, it was probably not "the dirtiest" presidential election in American history. Nor, for that matter, were the campaigns of 2016, 2012, 2008 and so on any nastier than previous campaigns. As the examples presented in this chapter make clear, vicious personal attacks and negative campaigning have been the norm for centuries. Negative campaigning has been and continues to be a part of presidential elections, and each future election will undoubtedly bring about the familiar claim that it is the "most negative ever." Such lines certainly make for flashy headlines and provocative quotations. However, as the historical record rather plainly suggests, these claims come much closer to hyperbole than they do to reality.

FURTHER READING

Boller, Paul F., Jr. *Presidential Campaigns: From George Washington to George W. Bush*. New York, NY: Oxford University Press, 2004.

Buell, Emmett H., Jr., and Lee Sigelman. *Attack Politics: Negativity in Presidential Campaigns since 1960*. Lawrence, KS: University Press of Kansas, 2008.

Geer, John G. *In Defense of Negativity: Attack Ads in Presidential Campaigns*. Chicago, IL: University of Chicago Press, 2006.

Mark, David. *Going Dirty: The Art of Negative Campaigning*. Updated ed. Lanham, MD: Rowman & Littlefield, 2009.

Museum of the Moving Image. "The Living Room Candidate: Presidential Campaign Commercials, 1952–2008." Available at: http://www.livingroom-candidate.org/.

7

Where Have You Gone, Walter Cronkite?

The "News" Just Ain't What It Used to Be

MOST AMERICANS HAVE AN IDEA, subconscious or otherwise, about what they can and should expect from the news. A commonly held presumption is that the news reported in a given day should be a fair representation of the important events or stories from that day. This sentiment is mirrored on the masthead of *The New York Times*, which claims the paper presents "all the news that's fit to print." Most also believe, unsurprisingly, that the news they get should be a true representation of those events or stories. In other words, news should be both factual and accurate. Indeed, a full 84 percent of Americans believe that fact-checking, in various forms, should be a responsibility of news organizations. Beyond this, almost two-thirds believe that news presentations should be restricted only to the facts.[1] A third idea that most share about news is that it should be objective and unbiased. One recent poll found that 78 percent of those surveyed believe that "the news media should never favor one political party over another."[2]

Still, there seems to be a fairly large and increasing gap between what people expect from the news and what they perceive they are getting. Data supporting this assertion are plentiful. For example, only 47 percent believe the news media are "doing well at reporting political issues fairly" and 56 percent at "reporting news accurately."[3] Another poll reveals that 67 percent believe that "stories and reports" in the news "are often inaccurate." A full 71 percent believe that news organizations "try to cover up their mistakes," 65 percent that they "spend too much time on unimportant stories," and 58 percent that they are "politically biased in their reporting."[4] Other polls show similar levels of dissatisfaction with news organizations and their product. Majorities, for example, believe that most members of the news media are dishonest and have a generally unfavorable impression of the national news media.[5]

What accounts for the difference in what we expect from news and what we think we are getting? The answer to this question is somewhat complicated. The modern media environment is fundamentally different than what prevailed even twenty years ago. In particular, there have been a number of changes over the past few decades in how news is produced and distributed as well as how we get our news. This chapter reviews these developments, all of which result from the simple fact that news production and distribution is a business.

In the first section, we review the news environment that prevailed until the 1990s, a time with more limited news choices, at least compared to the numbers that exist today. The second section briefly discusses the changes, mainly technological, that have transformed the modern news landscape. This includes the proliferation of partisan news sources, both on cable television and on the Internet. We also discuss the subject of bias in news coverage from traditional media sources, as well as the recent tendency of traditional news outlets to rush to print without fully checking their facts. Finally, this chapter covers the interrelated emergence of social media as a platform for news and the posting of misinformation, or "fake news," on these platforms.

The idea that "the 'news' just ain't what it used to be" is very much true. It is not, in other words, a myth. There is misunderstanding, however, about why the news often fails to live up to the lofty expectations of being completely objective at all times and in all situations. American news media are severely restricted in how they present their product by commercial considerations. The drive to make money by attracting more viewers ultimately shapes the news that we receive.

A BRIEF HISTORY OF NEWS PRODUCTION, DISTRIBUTION, AND CONSUMPTION

Most people likely assume that it is easy and obvious to identify the events and occurrences that make up the news of the day. In actuality, "news" is the product of a series of decisions by owners, editors, producers, reporters, and journalists. There are any number of newsworthy events that occur in a given day that go unreported or underreported. Individuals working in news organizations decide what stories are worthy of attention and how to present them. Commercial factors also balance these considerations. Editors, for example, are more likely to choose stories that will capture the average news consumer's attention. This explains why there is so much celebrity news, and why scandal, controversy, and sex are often prominently featured in news coverage.

Indeed, commercial considerations play a major role in driving the production and dissemination of news in the United States. To understand why, we need look no further than the powerful implications that our cherished First Amendment to the U.S. Constitution has on the organization of the media. The provision that Congress cannot make laws "abridging the freedom . . . of the press" means that that government cannot control the media. Most people correctly understand this to mean that government cannot censor the press, but do not stop to consider that it also refers to ownership of media outlets. After all, as the old saying goes, "He who pays the piper calls the tune." If government owned and operated the media, it could control the news we receive.

This is why the media environment in the United States is mainly characterized by private ownership. So-called public broadcasting, that is, National Public Radio and the Public Broadcasting System, are actually joint ventures funded by federal, state, and local governments; universities; private sponsors and foundations; and individual citizens.[6]

Unlike publicly (or government) owned media outlets, private media outlets are continually under pressure to make money. Newspapers and magazines must sell advertising space and copies; television and radio must sell airtime (i.e., commercials); and websites must attract views and generate "clicks." In all cases, more consumers (readers, viewers, listeners) means news providers can charge more money for advertising. Therefore, news media outlets are under pressure to make money by orienting their product toward what consumers want. Commercial considerations, inevitable products of the First Amendment, are never far from the minds of those responsible for news production in the United States.

Commercial factors, along with the evolution of communication technology, go a long way toward helping to explain the type of news that is provided in any given era. Printing shops produced the earliest newspapers in the United States in order to supplement income from other printing jobs. Most printers tried to maximize sales by maintaining editorial neutrality to avoid controversy. This was easier because the available technology did not allow for much immediacy in news content. The "news" was mainly older news from Europe, less controversial because of its distance from local affairs.

But news neutrality began to disappear during revolutionary times in the United States as conflict with England intensified. Pro-independence sympathizers controlled most of the printing shops and began reporting news with a pro-independence slant. After independence, this morphed into a pro-government bias, again, because most printing houses were owned by pro-government Federalists. Biased news continued to be a norm well into the nineteenth century. There was little demand for its nonpartisan alternative. Virtually all local newspapers had a particular partisan orientation or identity.[7]

The eventual shift to objective, nonpartisan news corresponded with improvements in printing technology, which made it possible to mass produce and sell newspapers at a low price. These "penny papers" found markets in urban centers and attracted major advertising dollars. By the mid-1800s, most owners and editors understood that partisan presentation of news effectively cut them off from half of their potential market. In other words, the notion of presenting objective, impartial news was not a high-minded ideal, but rather a response to commercial considerations.

A second factor responsible for the emergence of nonpartisan news was the fact that journalism began to be seen as a profession, guided by professional norms, which included objectivity.[8] Finally, newspapers became increasingly reliant on newly formed national wire services in the move toward impartiality in news production. Following the same commercial logic that drove local papers away from partisan presentation of the news, the Associated Press and United Press International understood that neutrality in reporting was necessary for them to sell stories.[9] In short, the development of news as an industry and as big business helped drive the emergence and acceptance of objectivity as a journalistic norm.

By the end of the Second World War, "news" was a mass-produced, highly commercialized product. News organizations "sought to provide an information supermarket whose aisles . . . would hopefully attract mass audiences across all classes of society."[10] During these "glory days" of news, most people got their news from one or two sources, and news was fairly homogenous. By the 1960s, the nation's "trusted" news sources were the likes of Walter Cronkite of CBS News, John Chancellor of NBC News, *The New York Times*, *The Washington Post*, *Time*, and *Newsweek*. This also meant that for the most part, news was unbiased. As one account summarizes, "For nearly four decades after WWII, mainstream journalism was notably non-ideological."[11] Importantly, the market supported this model of journalism.

From the post–Second World War era through the early 1990s, the model of journalism that prevailed is likely the one that most people have in their minds when they think about what to expect from the news. However, changes in news production, distribution, and the consumption environment, primarily driven by changes in communication technology, have worked to render these expectations out of date and largely unrealistic. In the next section we discuss these changes and how they have affected what we call the news.

CHANGES IN THE NEWS ENVIRONMENT AND THE "NEW" NEWS

Perhaps the most important change in the news environment has been the extraordinary proliferation in media sources over the past few decades. The change began with the introduction and adoption of cable television in the 1970s. By the time George W. Bush was elected president in 2000, the vast majority of households subscribed to either cable or satellite television, which included a multiplicity of channels, many offering news and opinion, from which viewers could choose.[12] The days of having only three broadcast television networks (ABC, CBS, and NBC) to choose from were long past.

By the 2000s, the World Wide Web had increased the number of potential sources of news, information, and opinion exponentially. As the first decade of the millennium wore on, more people could and did access this content. Online information became even more accessible with the widespread adoption of Internet-ready smartphones. One estimate (likely conservative) suggested that by 2016 at least three-quarters of Americans owned a smartphone with which they could access online content.[13]

Together, these changes ushered in an era of an extremely fragmented media universe. Fifty years ago, most Americans got their news from one of the three broadcast television networks, a local newspaper, and perhaps a local radio station. These news organizations, in turn, understood that if the content they provided was ideologically biased, or favored one political party or the other, they risked losing up to half of their potential audience—and thus, revenue. In the new news and information environment, numerous specialized television channels and websites emerged.

This had two main effects, both of them related to the commercial nature of news production and delivery. First, specialized media outlets target their content and messages to relatively small and narrow segments of the market. Second, these organizations are in fierce competition for viewers. These two developments have fundamentally changed news as we know it.

For example, the cable news market has now segmented into distinct partisan camps and is now reminiscent of the nineteenth-century era of the partisan press. Fox News began in 1996 as a conservative counterbalance to the perceived liberal bias of the dominant media establishment. Programming on Fox is generally acknowledged to be more conservative in nature, in spite of its claim to be "fair and balanced." MSNBC, also launched in 1996, began as a fairly nonpartisan cable news channel, but took a sharp turn to the left in 2007 in order to attract progressive viewers. Both can be fairly thought of as partisan political media outlets. In addition, by the early 2000s, there were any number of websites catering to the tastes of both liberals and conservatives.

Many believe that the success and prominence of these media outlets is evidence of bias in the news. Bias, as it relates to news, refers to the idea that the selection and presentation of a particular story explicitly or implicitly reflects the political views of some person or persons involved in the news production process. However, strictly speaking, most of what we see on Fox, MSNBC, or various websites is not biased *news*, but rather *opinion*. The biggest personalities on cable news are not reporters, but rather commentators. The views they express are the cable news equivalent of editorial and opinion pages of newspapers. The fact that they are voicing their opinion is not evidence of bias in the news.[14]

We should also remember that media bias is, in many respects, in the eye of the beholder. Partisans, in other words, see bias, even when it may not exist. In 2018, Gallup found that "perceptions of media bias are strongly related to one's political leanings."[15] A few years earlier, Gallup found that "partisans . . . perceive the media very differently. Seventy-five percent of Republicans and conservatives say the media are too liberal. Democrats and liberals lean more toward saying the media are 'just about right,' at 57% and 42%, respectively. Moderates and independents diverge, however, with 50% of independents saying the media are too liberal and 50% of moderates saying they are just about right."[16]

This said, there has been a proliferation of television and Internet news and opinion sources that display a clear partisan bias in the news stories they produce, what aspects of the stories they cover are highlighted and which are slighted, and how stories are generally framed.

On television, Fox News and MSNBC lead the way in this regard, although the conservative-leaning BlazeTV is deserving of mention as well. Liberal-progressive websites include *HuffPost*, *Salon*, *Slate*, *Buzzfeed*, and the *New Yorker*; conservative sites include *Breitbart*, the *Daily Beast*, *Townhall*, *WorldNetDaily*, and *Newsmax*. For example, one analysis showed that during the 2016 election, Fox News and the *Weekly Standard* were more favorable to Trump. The same analysis showed a pro-Clinton bias in news coverage by *Slate*.[17]

As previously noted, these media outlets are satisfying a commercial demand. Research shows that most people select the outlets they acquire news from based on their own ideological or partisan leanings. Conservatives, in other words, watch Fox News, while liberals tune in to MSNBC.[18] This is known as the "uses and gratification" theory of media consumption.[19] People use the media that best fits with their views.

Until fairly recently, studies consistently showed no systematic ideological or partisan bias—either left or right—in news produced on traditional ("legacy") media like the broadcast networks, *The New York Times*, etc. In his summary of the academic literature, Adam Schiffer writes, "the preponderance of evidence finds no overall, systematic bias in the mainstream press toward one side of the political spectrum."[20] That conclusion, however, is not universally accepted. Tim Groseclose, in his book *Left Turn*, argues otherwise, finding that news reporting is slanted in a liberal direction.[21] Indeed, there is some evidence that Democrat Barack Obama received more favorable press coverage than Republican John McCain during the 2008 presidential election. According to the analysis in one academic report, Obama received 68 percent more coverage than McCain, and the ratio of positive to negative coverage was 2:1, while McCain's was the reverse, 2:1 negative to positive.[22]

Another consequence of the explosion of media sources is that television and websites are in fierce competition for viewers. This competition is at least partially responsible for two, somewhat-related developments. The first is the recent tendency of news outlets to rush to print without fully checking facts. The rush to print has as much to do with the twenty-four-hour provision of news as with anything else. In the old days, reporters could spend an entire day covering an event, talking to sources, gathering background information, and more. Now, stories have to be up on a website—or in a tweet—quickly, constantly updated throughout the day. Although we are not excusing any individual news organization, or the press as a whole, this has likely contributed to what seems to be an increase in stories that are either partly or wholly inaccurate over the past few years. Such incorrect reporting has led to a growing chorus of media critics who claim Americans are receiving "fake news."

For example, in 2017, ABC News' Brian Ross wrongly reported that Lt. General Michael Flynn had violated federal law, acting under President Trump's instruction. CNN wrongly connected financier Anthony Scaramucci, who very briefly worked as Trump's communications director, with a Russian investment fund, and later went on air with a "bombshell" report suggesting Trump and his campaign had been given access to hacked Democratic National Committee (DNC) emails before WikiLeaks went public with them. Fox News ran a story wrongly suggesting that DNC staffer Seth Rich was connected to these leaked or hacked emails. A *New York Times* editorial incorrectly suggested that the 2017 congressional baseball shooting and the 2011 shooting of U.S. Rep. Gabrielle Giffords (D-AZ) were both the results of political incitement.[23]

The problem of inaccurate reporting has been exacerbated in recent years by the fact that "breaking news" is often "reported" first on Twitter or other social networking sites. This problem is especially acute inasmuch as most Americans get at least some of their news from various social networking sites. One study found, for example, that "a majority of U.S. adults—62%—get news on social media, and 18% do so often."[24] News, accurate or otherwise, gets spread and consumed rapidly in the modern age. Little wonder so many are concerned about the rise of fake news.

In addition to the growing problem of less-than-accurate or unreliable reporting, there has also been a rise in plagiarism and, in some cases, outright fabrication of stories in the news. These outright fabrications often come from websites that attempt to look like credible news sources, but in reality publish stories that are often outright falsehoods. This is done primarily to make money and, in some cases, to try to influence election outcomes. In one well-known example, the fake news website *The Denver Guardian* falsely claimed that an FBI agent investigating Hillary Clinton had been found dead in a Maryland house fire.[25]

In other instances, erroneous information comes from real and respected journalists, who, in the rush to print to stay ahead of their competitors, make major mistakes or plagiarize. Former *New York Times* reporter Jayson Blair, for example, authored multiple articles from 2002 to 2003 containing numerous fabrications. Other offenses include those by well-known journalists like CNN's Fareed Zakaria, who faced plagiarism accusations in 2012 for lifting a passage from an article authored by Jill Lepore published in the *New Yorker* magazine. In 2011, the *Washington Post* suspended Sari Horwitz for plagiarizing two stories written about the shooting of Congresswoman Gabrielle Giffords. While it is difficult to agree precisely on what constitutes plagiarism, there is consensus that it has been on the rise in both print and television journalism as the 2000s have worn on.[26]

OTHER ASPECTS OF CAMPAIGN COVERAGE THAT LEAVE US WANTING

Over the years media scholars and observers have identified several other aspects of campaign news coverage that is lacking. All are, like those previously discussed, rooted in the commercial nature of the news industry. Here we review the most glaring of these deficiencies.

Horse Race Coverage

Most campaign coverage falls into the category of what political scientist and media scholar Thomas Patterson labels "horse race" coverage.[27] These types of stories focus on, or are framed around, the competitive or strategic aspect of the campaign: who is leading, who fell behind, and why. Horse race coverage dominates news about the campaign from the preprimary season through Election Day.[28] As much as three-quarters of all coverage of the 2016 presidential campaign was comprised of stories focused on the horse race,[29] and it has dominated campaign coverage in both print and television news since at least the 1970s.[30]

The reason horse race coverage dominates campaign news is that it makes for a more exciting story. All other things being equal, more exciting stories sell better. Because news organizations can only present a certain number of stories in any given day, horse race coverage pushes out other types of stories, including an examination of issues, policy positions of the candidates and parties, qualifications, and so on.

Horse race coverage affects campaign coverage in other ways as well. For example, as one expert suggests:

> the tendency of journalists to construct their candidate narratives around the status of the horse race also affects the candidates' images. . . . A candidate who is doing well can normally be expected to be wrapped in a favorable image—his

or her positive attributes will be thrust into public view. A candidate who is doing less well has his or her weakest features put before the public.[31]

The Press as King Maker or Winnower

The decisions that news organizations make about the deployment of their resources and the stories that they run often have a profound impact on who will eventually win the party nomination. In part, this is because most people do not know much, if anything, about many of the aspirants for their party's nomination. This is especially true in years when there are many candidates vying for the nomination. In the year preceding the election, media organizations make decisions about which candidates they will and will not cover. These decisions translate directly into the amount of coverage a given candidate receives in print or on television. The rule of thumb is that better-known candidates are more likely to be receive coverage than their lesser-known opponents.

This is due to simple economics. News organizations cannot assign a reporter to cover every candidate and every campaign event. Generally, news organizations focus on candidates who are leading in early, preprimary polls (those taken the year prior to the Iowa caucuses). Of course, this means that candidates who are not doing well in public opinion polls receive less attention, thus making it more difficult for them to raise their public profile, attract campaign contributions, and, ultimately, do well. To overstate the case somewhat, many of the hidden decisions that news organizations make about whom to cover become self-fulfilling prophecies.[32]

The most recent example of this was in 2016. During the nomination season, coverage of Donald Trump significantly outstripped that of any other candidate for the Republican Party's presidential nomination. One report found that among the top Republican presidential candidates, Senator Marco Rubio received only half as much press attention as Trump.[33] Ted Cruz and John Kasich did little better, also failing to secure coverage anywhere close to that given to Trump.[34]

In 2012, four of the twelve Republican aspirants received the lion's share of the coverage. Mitt Romney, Rick Santorum, Newt Gingrich, and Ron Paul were the subjects of the overwhelming amount of press coverage throughout the spring.[35] Of course, these four were the frontrunners, but there is evidence that to some extent "news coverage drove [their] surges."[36] In 2008, the candidates leading in the polls as 2007 drew to a close included Democrats Barack Obama, Hillary Clinton, and John Edwards, and Republicans John McCain, Mitt Romney, Rudy Giuliani, and Mike Huckabee. Not surprisingly, these individuals captured most of the press attention and coverage throughout the nomination season.[37]

Winnowing also occurs in the substance of the coverage. Most reporters and pundits all but dismiss marginal or long-shot candidates.[38] Few are as blunt about it as Ted Koppel, host of ABC's now-canceled *Nightline*, who hosted a Democratic debate in December of 2003. Before the debate Koppel asked staffers:

> How did Dennis Kucinich and Al Sharpton and Carol Moseley Braun get into this thing—the debate? Nobody seems to know. Some candidates who are perceived as serious are gasping for air, and what little oxygen there is on the stage will be taken up by one-third of the people who do not have a snowball's chance in hell of winning the nomination.

Koppel's (and others') dismissal of minor candidates is rooted in the fact that news organizations have limited resources with which to cover the campaign. Moreover, likely losers usually do not make for good stories.[39]

The amount and substance of news coverage about presumed frontrunners has the effect of forcing lesser-known candidates to withdraw from the race earlier than they might otherwise. It is highly unlikely that Carly Fiorina, Jim Gilmore, or George Pataki (among others) could have captured the Republican presidential nomination in 2016 under any circumstances. The same applies to Democrats Martin O'Malley, Lincoln Chafee, and Jim Webb. However, each was a recognized candidate whose inclusion in the race added something to the democratic process. Whether intentional or not, bias in the form of noncoverage or less-than-favorable coverage contributed to their early withdrawal and thus detracted from the democratic process.

The Expectations Game

In addition to helping winnow the field of primary candidates by way of devoting less coverage to those who are doing poorly in the polls, the press handicaps the primaries. This expectations game starts long before the primaries begin, escalating during the fall of the year prior to the Iowa caucuses. Pundits regularly report on who is leading in the polls, who is raising how much money, who is endorsing which candidate, and more. Based on this, they typically anoint a front-runner who is therefore expected to win either the Iowa caucus, the New Hampshire primary, or both. If the presumed front-runner loses either, they then frame the resulting story line in terms of the uphill battle faced by the candidate in upcoming contests. Interestingly, however, if the front-runner wins, but does worse than expected, the media frame the story in terms of a loss or setback.

In 1992, for example, media accounts declared George H. W. Bush, who most experts expected to win in New Hampshire by a large margin, the loser after placing first, "only" sixteen percentage points ahead of Pat Buchanan. This was the result of Bush falling short of expectations and Buchanan exceeding them. A similar situation occurred in that year's

Democratic primary in New Hampshire when Bill Clinton finished a surprising second in the aftermath of a sex scandal. In 2008, many expected John Edwards, who had spent much of the previous four years campaigning in Iowa, to win the state. After losing by a large margin to Barack Obama and essentially tying for second place with Hillary Clinton, his candidacy never recovered.

In addition, because the nomination season begins early, the media often pay a disproportionate amount of positive attention to the underdog, or candidate trailing in the race. For example, John McCain was the media favorite throughout the 2000 Republican nomination season, in part because he trailed George W. Bush in numerous national polls. However, although McCain won several important primaries and caucuses, Bush's grip on the nomination was never in serious doubt.

During the latter part of 2003, when Howard Dean was the front-runner for the Democratic nomination, he was the recipient of much negative press. Shortly after his loss in Iowa, however, coverage became more favorable.[40] The media also paid what seemed to be an inordinate amount of attention to Republican John Kasich during the middle to the latter part of the 2016 nomination season, especially considering that he won only 5 percent of the party's delegates.[41] The reason for this focus on the underdog is simply that it makes for a more exciting and compelling story.

A focus on the negative. Similar to its ability to anoint a winner, the press can also help drive candidates from the field with a focus on mistakes, scandals, and gaffes. This is especially true during the nomination season. In 1988, Democratic candidate Senator Joe Biden was charged with plagiarizing parts of his speeches. He withdrew from the primary race after a flurry of negative media attention. That same year, Democrat Gary Hart dropped out of the race after a widely publicized sex scandal. George H. W. Bush delivered a campaign speech in 1988 in which he mistakenly referred to September 7 as the anniversary of the attack on Pearl Harbor (the actual date is December 7). Although the audience seemed to pay little attention to the incident, all three television networks featured a story about it that evening.[42]

In addition to simple gaffes, the media often focus on more salacious stories. An inordinate amount of coverage in 1992 centered on charges that Bill Clinton had been unfaithful to his wife, had experimented with marijuana, was a draft dodger, and had burned an American flag while a student in England.[43] Of course, Clinton was able to overcome this focus on the negative and secure the Democratic nomination. This negative focus on simple mistakes, scandals, and so forth is part of a pattern in American journalism referred to by Larry Sabato as "attack journalism." Sabato uses the metaphor of "feeding frenzy" to describe how the press is drawn to, highlights, and repeats negative news from the campaign trail.[44]

The focus on the negative centers on either scandal or simple mistakes made by the candidate (or their family). In 2004, media organizations ran numerous stories about whether President Bush had lied about his National Guard service, the fact that John Kerry mentioned Vice President Dick Cheney's gay daughter Lynn during the final presidential debate, and more. Similarly, in 2008, an inordinate amount of attention was paid to the fact that Barack Obama stopped wearing his American flag lapel pin or to a comment Michelle Obama made about her husband's candidacy being the first time as an adult she was proud of her country.[45]

During the general election season of 2016, the press was overwhelmingly negative. According to one report, a full 77 percent of stories about Trump and 64 percent of those about Clinton were negative. The author of the report noted that Trump's coverage was "negative from the start, and never came close to entering positive territory. . . . During his best weeks, the coverage ran 2-to-1 negative over positive. In his worst weeks, the ratio was more than 10-to-1."[46]

Negative press about Trump included coverage of a whole series of controversies, including his fitness for office (or his presumed lack thereof), his attack on Gold Star parents Khizr and Ghazala Khan, the Trump Foundation, issues related to his tax returns, and his refusal to answer whether he would accept the results of the 2016 election outcome.[47] Perhaps the biggest controversy was the release of a video in which he boasted of "groping women without their consent."[48] Negative coverage of him immediately jumped by twenty percentage points.

The reason for news organizations' focus on the negative is best summarized by Roger Ailes's (former Republican consultant and president of Fox News) "orchestra pit" theory of politics. As Ailes explained, "If you have two guys on stage and one says, 'I have a solution to the Middle East problem,' and the other guy falls into the orchestra pit, who do you think is going to be on the evening news?"[49]

Pack journalism. Exacerbating the commercial bias of campaign coverage noted earlier is a phenomenon known by many as "pack journalism." A term originally coined by Timothy Crouse in his 1973 account of the Nixon campaign,[50] it refers to the fact that much of what appears in the news media is remarkably homogenous. Crouse argued this was because reporters who spend a great deal of time together (on the campaign trail) end up with similar ideas, but the homogeneity of news coverage has other sources as well. For example, the competitive pressure of knowing another network or newspaper is running a particular story exerts pressure on producers and editors to do the same.[51]

Other Commercial Biases

There are several other patterns evident in the news coverage of presidential primaries that reflect a commercial bias in the media. One is a focus on attractive personalities. In particular, there is a tendency for the media to give attractive personalities more positive press, especially during the nomination season. This particular bias was apparent in 2004. The highly telegenic and upbeat John Edwards received the best press of any major candidate since 1988. A full 96 percent of the coverage of Edwards by the three major television networks (ABC, CBS, and NBC) from January 1 through March 1, 2004, was positive.[52] Barack Obama probably benefited from this focus on attractive personalities in 2008 as well (see later).

News organizations also pay seemingly disproportionate attention to unusual personalities. Examples here are not hard to find. In 2004, there were numerous stories about the controversial Democratic candidate Al Sharpton, who had no chance of capturing his party's nomination. In 2008, according to one study, Republican vice presidential nominee Sarah Palin was featured in a full 28 percent of all election stories in the six weeks under examination. This fact is more surprising given that Palin was the *vice* presidential candidate. By contrast, Joe Biden, the Democratic vice presidential nominee, was featured in only 9 percent of the stories. The authors of the study suggest that Palin may have been featured in even more stories were it not for the emergent economic crisis that fall.[53]

The focus on unusual candidates was perhaps most obvious in 2015–16, with the media's near obsession with Donald Trump. During the latter part of 2015, Trump received the most press attention. This coverage was, according to one analysis, "worth millions in free [media] exposure."[54] His candidacy, perhaps like no other, highlighted the commercial nature of news production. As a report from The Shorenstein Center on Media, Politics, and Public Policy summarized:

> Journalists are attracted to the new, the unusual, the sensational—the type of story material that will catch and hold an audience's attention. Trump fit that need as no other candidate in recent memory. Trump is arguably the first bona fide media-created presidential nominee. Although he subsequently tapped a political nerve, journalists fueled his launch.[55]

Another pattern, evident during both the nomination and general election season, is an anti-incumbency bias. This is because sitting presidents (or vice presidents in the case of George H. W. Bush in 1988 or Al Gore in 2000) are not fresh "news." Challengers add something new to the race, thus making it more attractive to news consumers. While Bill Clinton received more favorable coverage than challenger Bob Dole in 1996, virtually all incumbents since Jimmy Carter in 1980 have been the recipients of negative press during their reelection campaign. This also holds true for the incumbent vice presidents George H. W. Bush in 1988 and Al Gore in 2000. In 2004, coverage of the incumbent George W. Bush on the three broadcast networks from September through November was only 37 percent positive, as compared with John Kerry's 59 percent.[56]

CONCLUSION

Most Americans want and believe they are entitled to reliable, intelligent, comprehensive journalism from news organizations. However, the reality is that if this type of news does not make news organizations a profit, it likely will not be produced. News and, in particular, news coverage of political campaigns display a distinct commercial bias.[57] This bias favors stories that news producers believe people will want to read, listen to, or watch. This often can be very different from an objective overview of what is actually happening on the campaign trail. Horse race coverage, a focus on the negative and outsized personalities, and coverage that perhaps unfairly disadvantages candidates who stand less chance of winning, are only a few of the hallmarks of the commercial bias of the press in campaign coverage.

However, the quality of news has arguably declined even further in recent years. This has been the—perhaps natural—result of a proliferation of news sources. More news outlets mean that many can, and do, focus on attracting a more partisan audience. This can leave the average viewer with the impression that *all* news is partisan, that there is no such thing as objective, unbiased news. The drive to attract readers and viewers in a nonstop, social media news cycle has also led to a situation where news organizations have become somewhat less careful about checking the facts of a story. Indeed, in a few notable instances, reporters from respected news outlets have resorted to plagiarism and even outright fabrication in order to get published. This development in combination with the rise of fake news websites has made it all the more difficult for the public to find objective and accurate reporting of the news. In all, it is certainly fair to say that the "news just ain't what it used to be." However to be completely fair, it is not at all clear how, in a commercial media environment, it could be easily improved.

FURTHER READING

Bennett, Stephen Earl, Staci L. Rhine, Richard S. Flickinger, and Linda L. M. Bennett. "Video Malaise Revisited: Public Trust in the Media and Government." *Harvard International Journal of Press/Politics* 4, no. 4 (1999): 8–23.

Bennett, W. Lance. *News: The Politics of Illusion.* 7th ed. New York, NY: Longman, 2007.

Fallows, James. *Breaking the News.* New York, NY: Vintage, 1996.

Graber, Doris. *Mass Media and American Politics.* 7th ed. Washington, DC: CQ Press, 2006.

Jamieson, Kathleen Hall, and Paul T. Waldman. *The Press Effect: Politicians, Journalists, and the Stories That Shape the Political World.* New York, NY: Oxford University Press, 2002.

Patterson, Thomas E. *Out of Order.* New York, NY: Vintage Books, 1994.

8

Game Changer?

Misconceptions about the Significance of Presidential Debates

EVERY FOUR YEARS, presidential elections dominate American politics. As Election Day approaches, the most talked-about event of the campaign season—what some political observers call the "Super Bowl of American democracy"[1]—are the presidential debates that pit the two major-party nominees against one another. Media outlets hype each debate like a heavy-weight championship fight, with commentators breathlessly discussing the strengths and weaknesses of each candidate, analyzing what each needs to do to "score points" or land the "knockout blow" in the debate. Political pundits and others often claim that any "big punch" landed by a candidate in the debate could be the moment that serves as the "game changer" of the election. As one political strategist claimed, "Debates are always game changers. If you kick somebody's butt in a debate, that matters a lot. It changes votes."[2]

The 2016 campaign was no exception when it came to making similar claims about the importance of presidential debates. One newspaper, for example, discussed Donald Trump's need for a "'game-changing' win" in his second debate against Hillary Clinton in order to "salvage [his] election chances."[3] In 2012, Governor Chris Christie of New Jersey predicted that his party's nominee, Republican Mitt Romney, would get the better of President Barack Obama in their first debate, and as a result, turn the "whole race . . . upside down."[4] Discussion and predictions of such game-changing moments are rooted in presidential debate lore going all the way back to 1960 when Richard Nixon and John Kennedy became the first major-party presidential nominees to debate on television.

But do presidential debates really change votes? Are they the game changers that many often claim them to be? As this chapter will demon-strate, the empirical evidence simply does not support the assertion that presidential debates have much significance in influencing voting behavior or in affecting election outcomes. What presidential debates can do, as the evidence shows, is positively affect voters' knowledge of issues. Put another way, presidential debates may not be game changers, but the effects they do have can add to the larger democratic process.

GAME CHANGERS?

Political historians and observers have identified several presidential debate moments as having been potentially decisive in determining the outcome of the election. The debates of 1960, 1976, 1980, 1988, and 2000 have drawn particular attention. These five have helped to foster the notion that presidential debates are game changers.

1960: Kennedy versus Nixon

Perhaps the most widely discussed game changer in presidential debate history goes back to 1960. Senator John Kennedy and Vice President Richard Nixon were locked in a tight contest for the presidency. Polls from the Gallup Organization showed the contest nearly tied among registered voters before the debates began.[5] When the debates were over, Kennedy had built a small lead over Nixon, which he carried to one of the narrowest victories in presidential election history. According to many accounts of the 1960 election, the debates, particularly the first, were pivotal to Kennedy's success. As a *Time* magazine article recently declared, "It's now common knowledge that without the nation's first televised debate . . . Kennedy would never have been elected president."[6] Another account, making a similar claim, concluded that the Kennedy–Nixon debates "had a major impact on the election's outcome."[7]

Kennedy's success in the debates, according to many, was due to his telegenic appearance. The younger, handsome, and sun-tanned Kennedy answered his debate questions by looking directly into the television camera. The paler looking Nixon, sporting a five o'clock shadow, looked off to the side of his podium to make eye contact with the reporters asking the questions. Nixon's shifting gaze, combined with his less attractive appearance, sent the wrong visual cues to television viewers.[8] A poll from Albert Sindlinger's research firm showed that Kennedy won over the television audience, whereas Nixon won over those who listened to the debate on the radio.[9] Overall, a Gallup poll showed Kennedy moving ahead of Nixon by four points after the debates had concluded.[10] Kennedy edged Nixon in the popular vote by only the slimmest of margins, 49.7 percent to 49.6 percent. Narrow victories for Kennedy in Texas and Illinois were ultimately decisive. Had Kennedy lost those states it would have given Nixon the necessary majority of Electoral College votes. This added to the widespread perception of the debates' significance.

1976: Ford versus Carter

There were no presidential debates for the next three elections (1964, 1968, and 1972), but debates returned in 1976. In an election in which the popular vote separated the two candidates by just two percentage points, Democrat Jimmy Carter won the presidency over incumbent Republican President Gerald Ford. Looking back on the election to explain Carter's narrow victory, some political observers point to a critical moment in one of the debates, a moment many claim may have been the biggest gaffe in presidential debate history.

In the second debate, Max Frankel of *The New York Times* asked Ford about the rise of communism throughout the world, specifically questioning whether U.S. influence was still on equal footing with the Soviet Union in Europe. After a somewhat lengthy answer, Ford concluded with a perplexing assertion, declaring that "there is no Soviet domination of Eastern Europe and there never will be under a Ford administration."[11] Frankel, visibly surprised by Ford's answer, followed up by asking Ford to clarify his comments. Ford repeated his assertion, stating at the outset of his reply, "I don't believe, Mr. Frankel, that the Yugoslavians consider themselves dominated by the Soviet Union. I don't believe that the Romanians consider themselves dominated by the Soviet Union. I don't believe that the Poles consider themselves dominated by the Soviet Union."[12] In the midst of the Cold War, Ford's eyebrow-raising claim of "no Soviet domination of Eastern Europe" led some to question his knowledge of foreign policy.

Postdebate analysis and media coverage focused heavily on Ford's controversial comment. Years later, in an interview with journalist Jim Lehrer, Carter remarked, "This was a very serious mistake that [Ford] made. . . . Certainly it cost him some votes, and as you know, the election was quite close."[13] Another account offered an even stronger assessment, "Why did Gerald Ford lose to Jimmy Carter? . . . President Ford lost because he committed a colossal blunder [of asserting 'no Soviet domination of Eastern Europe'] in the second Ford–Carter debate in San Francisco, October 6, 1976. . . . Ford's debate performance lost the election."[14]

1980: Carter versus Reagan

The 1980 presidential campaign entered the third week of October with President Jimmy Carter holding a narrow three-point lead (45% to 42%) in a Gallup poll of registered voters against former California Governor Ronald Reagan.[15] Carter and Reagan would debate only once, on October 28, 1980. In an otherwise engaging debate, Carter closed his comments by attempting to humanize the serious issue of nuclear proliferation by discussing what his twelve-year-old daughter, Amy, thought about the issue. Carter told a national audience, "I had a discussion with my daughter, Amy, the other day, before I came here, to ask her what the most important issue was. She said she thought nuclear weaponry—and the control of nuclear arms."[16]

After the debate ended, pundits labeled the comment as "bizarre" and late-night television hosts ridiculed Carter for seeming to depend on the advice of a daughter who had yet to reach her teenage years.[17] Reagan, by comparison, more eloquently summarized the case for his candidacy in his closing comments with a simple but memorable line: "Are you better off than you were four years ago?"[18] Carter's small lead evaporated and Reagan would go on to win in a landslide, capturing a ten-point victory in the popular vote and a 489–49 victory in the Electoral College. One account surmised that the debate "all but finished Carter."[19] Another asserted that, "absent the debate . . . Carter would have won reelection."[20]

1988: Bush versus Dukakis

The 1988 presidential debates between Democratic nominee Governor Michael Dukakis of Massachusetts and Republican nominee Vice President George H. W. Bush included one of the most memorable of all debate moments. After a competitive performance from Dukakis in the first debate, followed by a strong showing from Dukakis' running mate Lloyd Bentsen against Republican Dan Quayle, the second Bush–Dukakis debate opened with a memorable question. Panelist Bernard Shaw of CNN asked Dukakis, "Governor, if Kitty Dukakis [the candidate's wife] were raped and murdered, would you favor an irrevocable death penalty for the killer?"[21] Dukakis answered simply and matter-of-factly that he opposed the death penalty and would not apply it even to someone who raped and murdered his wife.

While the substance of Dukakis' response was standard fare for a candidate who opposed the death penalty, Dukakis was criticized for his cold response to the question. To many political observers, the candidate appeared emotionless in answering a question that many thought should have evoked passion. *Time* magazine later described it as "Dukakis' deadly response."[22] One summary described Dukakis as "in robot-mode" when he responded to Shaw and concluded that this debate was one that "contributed decisively to the outcome of [the] election."[23] Dukakis never recovered and lost the election in a landslide, losing the popular vote by seven points, 53 to 46 percent, and the Electoral College vote, 426 to 111.

2000: Bush versus Gore

The 2000 presidential election between Democratic nominee Al Gore and Republican nominee George W. Bush is best remembered for its historically close finish and controversial outcome. In an election that was ultimately decided by the results in the state of Florida, Bush defeated Gore by a mere 537 votes (out of more than six million votes cast in Florida), a margin of victory that was certified only after the U.S. Supreme Court intervened and ordered the state of Florida to end its recount of ballots. Gore's extremely narrow loss led many political pundits to point to various reasons to explain his defeat. This included his performance in the presidential debates.

According to Gallup, Gore took an eight-point lead into the debates with Bush. By the end of three debates, Gore trailed Bush by four points.[24] With such a significant swing before and after the debate period, several political observers cited Gore's performance in his first debate with Bush as the "game-changing" moment.[25] Specifically, Gore was criticized for sighing audibly into his microphone during Bush's debate responses. A number of media analysts described Gore's sighs and general demeanor during the debate as "condescending."[26] Just days after the debate, Gallup showed Gore's eight-point lead was gone.

Gore's numbers continued to decline over the next two debates, moving him from frontrunner status before the debates to underdog status after the debates. This shift prompted some political observers to conclude that Gore "gave away" the election and that his debate performances were one of the major causes.[27] As one account summarized, "Once the television cameras caught that sighing, that constant look on [Gore's] face where he seemed annoyed by the whole idea of having to be there with Bush, it seemed to underscore, as somebody said, [the impression of him] as a teacher's pet who knew all the answers but was annoying and irritating. . . . Then people began to project onto Gore a personality trait of just annoyance and irritation of people in general and it became devastating for him to live that down."[28] Lydia Saad, writing for Gallup, added that "Gore won the popular vote, but he might also have won the Electoral College vote had his 8-point predebate-period lead not slipped away in the last few weeks of the campaign."[29]

Other Memorable Debate Moments

Although the 1960, 1976, 1980, 1988, and 2000 presidential debates stand out as the most frequently mentioned for their game-changing moments, a few other examples deserve honorable mention. In 1984, Ronald Reagan sought reelection and faced former vice president Walter Mondale. Battling charges that his advanced age of seventy-three could potentially impair his decision-making capability, Reagan was asked directly in the second debate about his age. In response, he humorously commented that he was not "going to exploit, for political purposes, [his] opponent's youth and inexperience."[30] Reagan would go on to win 49 of the 50 states against Mondale in one of the most lopsided victories in presidential history, making it difficult to assign any particular debate moment to Reagan's easy reelection win. Still, at least one set of reporters concluded that after Reagan's punch line about his age, "for all practical purposes, the presidential election was over."[31]

In 1992, President George H. W. Bush lost his reelection bid to Democrat Bill Clinton. In a relatively competitive contest that included a serious third-party candidate, Texas billionaire Ross Perot, Bush drew some negative media attention when he glanced at his watch during a town hall debate. In the words of one account, Bush "looked like he was bored, that he didn't care about the debate and that underscored the feeling that he wasn't connected to the problems of the people and the country."[32] The town hall format also played well to Clinton's strengths as he comfortably engaged and connected with members in the audience. While not credited as a game-changing moment, Bush's glance at his watch is still often listed as a notable mistake in the history of presidential debates.[33]

THE EVIDENCE ON PRESIDENTIAL
DEBATES AND VOTING BEHAVIOR

While there are numerous examples of political pundits and political operatives claiming that a specific debate or a particular moment in a debate was the decisive factor in determining the outcome of an election, the overwhelming body of political science research indicates that these claims are dubious. The Gallup Organization has done extensive polling on presidential debates since 1960. Based on data from its daily tracking polls, Gallup identified debates from only two elections, 1960 and 2000, as potentially having had a "meaningful impact on the structure of the presidential races."[34] In other words, in only two cases did the eventual winner of the election go from a deficit position to front-runner as the result of the debates. As noted earlier, Kennedy went from trailing Nixon by one point in the preelection period to leading by four points after their last debate in 1960. However, Kennedy's eventual margin over Nixon in the popular vote, an advantage of less than one-quarter of 1 percent, suggests that the debates may not have had a lasting impact.

In 2000, George W. Bush's predebate to postdebate surge in the polls seems, on the surface, the most likely evidence of debates playing a critical factor in an election outcome. Yet Gallup polls also reveal that voters thought Al Gore was the winner in two of the three presidential debates. This includes the first debate, where 48 to 41 percent of registered voters gave Gore the edge, in spite of his heavy sighing into the microphone.[35]

Other campaigns with game-changing debate moments also fail to survive scrutiny when examining public-opinion data. In 1976, Gerald Ford's much publicized gaffe about "no Soviet domination of Eastern Europe" made headlines, but polls showed no appreciable decline for Ford in polls immediately afterward. In fact the opposite occurred: Ford's polling numbers improved dramatically during the debate period. According to Gallup,

Ford entered the predebate period down fifteen points to Carter, but was positioned only five points down to his challenger in the postdebate period.[36]

In 1980, President Carter's "Amy speech" and Ronald Reagan's strong performance in their debate resulted in voters judging Reagan as the winner. Reagan's ability to turn an otherwise close election into a landslide shortly after the debate provided ample fuel to the argument that the debate was a game changer. However, a careful look at polling data reveals a more complex story. An average of all available polls showed Reagan with a two-point lead immediately before the debate.[37] By the day of the debate, Reagan's numbers had inched up a bit more, suggesting that his campaign was already beginning to generate upward movement in the polls.[38] A number of other events were taking place that may also have been more damaging to Carter than the debate, notably the October release of economic data showing a rise in inflation and his continued inability to negotiate the release of hostages in Iran. The debate seems at best to have merely reinforced the growing momentum in Reagan's favor.[39]

Four years later, Reagan's joke about his age in the second debate with Mondale made headlines—and certainly made people laugh—but it did little to change the dynamics of the race. Reagan entered the second debate with a solid lead and left the second debate with a solid lead. In their first debate, political observers universally agreed that Mondale got the better of Reagan, with some reports describing Reagan's performance as "confused" and most agreeing it was unsteady.[40] Still, Mondale's strong showing failed to revitalize his campaign, prompting one political scientist to conclude that voters "don't easily change their views about who they want to run the country simply on the basis of debating skills."[41]

When examining other more recent and memorable debate moments (Dukakis' failure to show emotion, Bush peering at his watch, Gore's audible sighs) poll numbers again show little to no impact on voter preferences. In fact an analysis from one political scientist shows only a minimal effect, an average of roughly 1 percent absolute change across sixteen presidential debates from 1988 through 2008 (see table 8.1). Another expert on public opinion claimed, "there is no case where we can trace a substantial shift [in public opinion] to the debates."[42] Yet another research team reached a similar conclusion after examining every available presidential election between 1952 and 2008.[43] The only election they identified as displaying a shift during the debate period was in 1976, where evidence shows Ford gaining ground on Carter in spite of Ford's gaffe.[44]

Even after the most decisive debate victory for any presidential candidate ever, a 72 to 20 percent advantage for Mitt Romney over Barack Obama in their first debate[45] in 2012, the effects proved only temporary. Obama lost all of his initial five-point advantage in the predebate period following Romney's strong showing in the first debate. However, Obama

Table 8.1 Incumbent Party Candidates' Poll Standing during Debate Periods

Year	Debate	Predebate	Postdebate	"Bump"	Total Change during Debate Period
1988	First	52.9%	53.2%	0.3%	
	Second	53.7	55.3	1.60	2.4%
1992	First	41.6	41.7	0.2	
	Second	42.8	40.7	-2.0	
	Third	41.7	42.1	0.4	0.5
1996	First	60.3	58.8	-1.5	
	Second	58.6	58.8	0.2	-1.4
2000	First	51.1	50.1	-1.0	
	Second	49.7	48.5	-1.2	
	Third	48.9	47.6	1.4	-3.5
2004	First	52.8	50.5	-2.3	
	Second	50.1	51.0	0.9	
	Third	50.6	50.9	0.3	-2.0
2008	First	48.1	46.8	-1.4	
	Second	46.7	45.7	-0.9	
	Third	45.9	46.2	0.3	-1.9
2012	First	49.0	47.0	-2.0	
	Second	46.0	47.0	1.0	
	Third	45.0	46.0	1.0	-3.0
2016	First	46.0	47.0	1.0	
	Second	46.0	47.0	1.0	
	Third	47.0	50.0	3.0	4.0

Notes: Percentages are standardized to reflect the two-party vote. The numbers reported for the predebate period are based on the polling averages over the six days prior to the debate and the day of the debate. The numbers reported for the postdebate period are based on the polling averages over the seven days following the debate.

Sources: Thomas Holbrook, "Debate Expectations," *Politics by the Numbers*, October 1, 2012, http://politics-by-the-numbers.blogspot.com/2012/10/debate-expectations.html. Data for 2012 from "White House 2012: Daily Tracking," *Gallup*, accessed January 8, 2019, http://pollingreport.com/wh12gent.htm. Data for 2016 from "White House 2016: General Election Trial Heats, Presidential Trial Heat Summary," ABC News/*Washington Post* Poll, accessed January 8, 2019, http://pollingreport.com/wh16gen.htm.

regained his advantage as he went on to capture a four-point victory in the popular vote on Election Day. While it is possible that Obama's rebound may have been due to his stronger performances in the second and third debates, research suggests that debate effects appear to have only a short-term impact. Voters ultimately "come home" and return to initial predebate candidate preferences.[46]

In short, there is little evidence to support the contention that presidential debates have a meaningful impact on how voters cast their ballots.

Even the rare instance of a major gaffe or memorable one liner during a debate will be highly unlikely to transform a presidential election. As one political observer notes, "Super Bowl moments don't happen in debates. If you are looking for a single, magical, transformative moment, you might be let down."[47]

Instead, there is overwhelming evidence to suggest that a myriad of other factors—notably a voter's party affiliation, socioeconomic status, and the state of the economy—play dominant roles in influencing individual voting behavior. The rare voter may change his or her vote based on how a candidate performs in a presidential debate, but it is unlikely that these voters constitute a large enough bloc to affect an election outcome. As one political scientist explains, "When it comes to shifting enough votes to decide the outcome of the election, presidential debates have rarely, if ever, mattered."[48]

WHY PRESIDENTIAL DEBATES RARELY AFFECT VOTING BEHAVIOR

Presidential debates seldom affect voting behavior and election outcomes for several reasons. Perhaps the most straightforward explanation is that debates occur in the final weeks of the election cycle, when most Americans have already formed strong opinions about the candidates. This is especially true when there is an incumbent president running for reelection. In 2012, for instance, voters had a full four years to form an opinion about President Obama. His challenger, Mitt Romney, had begun campaigning for the Republican nomination as early as 2011. With Romney in the public spotlight for many months before his first debate with Obama, most voters had formed strong opinions about him as well. Voters' preexisting views about the candidates often prove difficult to change, even after a commanding debate performance in which one candidate clearly outshines the other. In fact, debates may actually come too late to change a voter's mind in some states because of early voting laws, which allow citizens to cast absentee ballots through the mail or at a designated polling place several weeks before Election Day.

Rather than swaying voters' minds, presidential debates tend to reinforce voters' preexisting views.[49] The debates in 2016 make this point clear. As table 8.2 illustrates, Republicans overwhelmingly favored Trump over Clinton in all three debates, and by margins considerably wider than by independents and Democrats. Likewise, Democrats were more likely than independents and Republicans to see Clinton as the winner in each of the debates. As one political scientist summarizes, "By [debate] time voters have pretty much picked their candidates. . . . People who are political and have a party affiliation are hard to dislodge by the debates. And those

Table 8.2 Perceived Winner of the Clinton-Trump Debates by Party Affiliation

	Clinton	Trump	Both/Neither/No Opinion
First Debate			
All debate watchers	61%	27%	12%
Republicans	28	53	19
Independents	59	30	11
Democrats	92	3	5
Second Debate			
All debate watchers	53%	35%	12%
Republicans	15	71	14
Independents	51	32	17
Democrats	93	3	4
Third Debate			
All debate watchers	60%	31%	9%
Republicans	19	64	17
Independents	58	35	7
Democrats	96	2	2

Source: Lydia Saad, "Clinton Wins Third Debate, Gains Ground as 'Presidential,'" *Gallup*, October 24, 2016, https://news.gallup.com/poll/196643/clinton-wins-third-debate-gains-ground-presidential.aspx.

rooting for their favorite candidate, even if he is doing poorly, aren't necessarily going to change their mind."[50]

Of course, there is a segment of the electorate without fully formed opinions about the candidates when the presidential debate period begins. These persuadable and undecided voters, however, tend to pay the least attention to politics and are thus the least likely to be watching the debates.[51] Of the persuadable and undecided voters who do happen to watch the debates, there is only a small chance that they will view something of significant consequence. A serious gaffe or a highly memorable and one-sided performance by a candidate is the exception rather than the rule in presidential debates.[52]

Finally, it is worth remembering that presidential debates do not occur in a vacuum. It is almost impossible for a voter to avoid exposure to additional information outside of the debates. Voters are likely to see television campaign advertisements, hear radio messages, read campaign materials dropped at their door, or visit a website that offers information about the candidates. Candidates also give speeches on the campaign trail, interviews to reporters, and generally attract almost nonstop news coverage during the final weeks of the campaign. With so much attention focused on the candidates, there is always the possibility of a gaffe or misstep on the campaign trail that could potentially affect the dynamics of the election. Even without a major mistake by a candidate, the sheer volume of information that most voters are exposed to, particularly in the final weeks of the election when the debates occur, makes it difficult to isolate and disentangle the effects a debate may have on public opinion and voting behavior. Any movement in the polls from the pre- to postdebate period is thereby likely the product of more than just the debates themselves.

Yet while the evidence is rather clear that presidential debates rarely, if ever, have a major effect on voting behavior and presidential election outcomes, it would be wrong to dismiss presidential debates as entirely irrelevant. Indeed, research shows presidential debates fulfill an important function in the electoral process. As the next section will discuss, presidential debates can improve voters' knowledge of the candidates and the major issues of the election as well as promote voters' deliberation, all conditions that most agree are important to a healthy democracy.

THE RELEVANCE OF PRESIDENTIAL DEBATES

One of the unique features of a presidential debate is that it allows voters to compare candidates side by side in an unrehearsed setting. Candidates have to address questions and issues in a high-pressure environment, making debates an ideal forum for voters to compare and contrast candidates' issue positions. As two political communication scholars explain, "where in stump speeches candidates tend to indict their opponents, in debate the threat of imminent rebuttal invites a response to charges pending against one's candidacy."[53] The result is that debates are able "to produce a clarity and specificity otherwise absent in campaign discourse."[54] This dynamic makes presidential debates a unique source of political information.

Presidential debates take on added significance because they attract an extremely large audience. This was especially true in 2016, when a record-setting 84 million people tuned in to the first debate. The second and third debates drew somewhat fewer viewers, but still managed to record numbers comparable to those from the previous election cycle.[55] According to a poll from the Gallup Organization, more than two-thirds of Americans reported that they watched the first debate between Barack Obama and Mitt Romney in 2012.[56] The numbers jumped to 76 percent for the second debate, before leveling off slightly at 69 percent for the third debate.[57] Debates in previous presidential election years produced equivalent rates of viewership and listenership.[58] Given that almost any type of learning requires exposure to information, the large audiences that presidential debates attract is no small matter.

Presidential debates also force candidates to simplify complicated political issues and communicate solutions that everyday people can easily understand. This is important because exposure to information alone is not sufficient for voters to acquire knowledge-they must also be able to comprehend the information they receive for learning to occur.[59]

Polling data reveal that large majorities of voters typically report that presidential debates help them make more informed decisions when casting their vote. Surveys suggest that with only one exception (1996), from 1992 through 2016 more than three-fifths of voters reported that presidential debates were "somewhat to very" helpful in their voting decision.[60] Political commercials, by comparison, rated considerably lower, reaching a high of only 38 percent in 1992 and a low of 24 percent in 2012.[61] Presidential debates thereby offer two critical prerequisites for learning: (1) exposure to political information and (2) information with substance that voters can easily process and understand.

Research confirms that individuals watch the debates to help them learn more about the candidates and the issues and that learning indeed occurs.[62] With only few exceptions, studies show an improved ability among voters to answer questions correctly about the candidates and their issue positions, as well as improve their issue awareness and issue knowledge after viewing or listening to a presidential debate.[63] They also were better able to retain political information.[64]

As one would expect, information acquisition is most pronounced among undecided voters who typically have less knowledge about the candidates and issues prior to the debates.[65] In particular, the first debate, when many voters typically have the least amount of information, tends to have the strongest learning effects.[66] Research shows that even those who do not watch or listen to the debates experience a gain in issue awareness, primarily through exposure to media reports and from conversations with friends and family that are common after a presidential debate.[67]

In addition to improving voters' political knowledge, debates can heighten interest in the election.[68] Such heightened interest can help bring more voters to the polls.[69] Likewise, partisan voters often have their political views and convictions reinforced after a presidential debate, which can further boost their level of excitement, and thus their likelihood of voting and becoming otherwise involved.[70]

From the perspective of campaign operatives, presidential debates can play an important role in reinforcing a particular narrative. In 1988, for example, the campaign of George H. W. Bush made efforts to portray Michael Dukakis as an emotionless, technocratic leader. When Dukakis later gave his dry answer to moderator Bernard Shaw's death penalty question during the debate, he strengthened the image that he was emotionless that the Bush campaign had been pushing throughout the election.[71] Likewise, when George H. W. Bush looked at his watch in a town hall meeting in 1992, it reinforced the Clinton campaign's characterization of

Bush as someone out of touch and uninterested in the plight of everyday Americans.[72] In this sense, debates can become important in the battle that campaigns wage over trying to control the public's perceptions of the opposing candidate.

Similarly, campaigns attempt to control the issue agenda in a way that is favorable to their candidate, and debates can reinforce these efforts as well. In fact, there is evidence to suggest that voters often perceive topics covered in a debate as more important than they did before the debate. In one study of the Carter–Ford presidential debate, scholars found that viewers ranked economic and foreign policy issues consistently high. However, after viewing one of the Carter–Ford debates focused entirely on domestic issues, foreign policy issues decreased in importance.[73]

Finally, debates can have significant effects on voters in primary elections. In one study, researchers found that debates held during the 1996 Arizona Republican presidential primary influenced respondents' assessments of the candidates' electability and even changed some voters' preferences.[74] Primary debates, like those that take place during the fall campaign, can also increase issue knowledge.[75]

Taken together, research on presidential debates reveals that they have some important effects. Debates can improve voters' knowledge of the candidates and issues, increase public interest in the election, serve to reinforce a candidate's image and shape the issue agenda, and can even affect voting behavior in primary elections. While presidential debates do not affect general election outcomes and fall short of being the proverbial game changers that they are sometimes touted to be, they most assuredly have some degree of impact on voters and presidential campaigns.

CONCLUSION

Every four years, political pundits trot out the myth that presidential debates can be game-changing events in the upcoming November election. Yet evidence produced from public-opinion polling data suggest otherwise. Presidential debates only minimally affect voting behavior in the November election, and almost never to the extent that they can alter the outcome.

Instead, presidential debates carry out a largely educative role in the electoral process, helping voters with information acquisition. Millions of Americans watch and listen to presidential debates, and they do so for reasons beyond the mere entertainment and spectacle aspect of these events. The public tunes in to presidential debates to learn more about the candidates, and research suggests that this is what occurs. Presidential debates can help voters' deliberation by improving their knowledge of the candidates and issues. They further aid the democratic process by increasing public interest in the election. This increased interest can spur political participation. Presidential debates can also shape the issue agenda, and may even affect voting behavior in presidential primaries. All of this suggests that presidential debates are an important part of American democracy—even if they are not ultimately the game changers that political operatives, pundits, and politicians often make them out to be.

FURTHER READING

Benoit, William L. *Political Election Debates: Informing Voters about Policy and Character*. Lanham, MD: Lexington Books, 2014.

Erikson, Robert S., and Christopher Wlezien. *The Timeline of Presidential Elections: How Campaigns Do (and Do Not) Matter*. Chicago, IL: University of Chicago Press, 2012.

Holbrook, Thomas M. *Do Campaigns Matter?* Thousand Oaks, CA: Sage, 1996.

Jamieson, Kathleen Hall. *Presidential Debates: The Challenge of Creating an Informed Electorate*. New York, NY: Oxford University Press, 1990.

9

Science or Voodoo?

Misconceptions about National Election Polls

I re-word Winston Churchill's famous remarks about democracy and say, "Polls are the worst way of measuring public opinion . . . or of predicting elections—except for all of the others."

—Humphrey Taylor, chairman of the Harris Poll[1]

PUBLIC OPINION POLLS are ubiquitous. Rarely does a day pass without a major newspaper featuring the results of some poll. The frequency of polls only increases during an election season, and this is especially true during a presidential election. However, many people do not understand enough about polling to be able to interpret polls accurately. To make matters worse, media outlets occasionally misrepresent the results of polls. Pollsters themselves also miss the mark from time to time, providing forecasts and predictions that fail to materialize. In one memorable example from the 2016 presidential campaign, *The Huffington Post*, using a forecasting model generated from polling data, confidently predicted that Hillary Clinton would defeat Donald Trump, giving her a 98.2 percent probability of victory and an estimated 323 Electoral College votes. As the publication's senior polling editor Natalie Jackson summarized, "Republican Donald Trump has essentially no path to an Electoral College victory. . . . Clinton should fairly easily hold onto Michigan, Wisconsin and Pennsylvania."[2] Trump, of course, would go to win the election with 304 Electoral College votes, with victories in all three states.

This raises a few questions: Can national election polls and forecasting models be trusted? Are these experts truly able to gauge what Americans believe? One poll conducted in 2000 suggested that only 2 percent of Americans believe that national polls are "always right," while almost 60 percent believe they are right "only some of the time" and 7 percent "hardly ever."[3]

We offer a mixed answer to the question of whether people can trust polls throughout the election cycle. Our objective is less to dispel a particular myth than to give the reader a better understanding of the enterprise of public polling during an election. This understanding is crucial to following news stories throughout the campaign. We offer a set of guidelines on how to read, analyze, and interpret results from polls and forecasting models during a campaign.[4] In the end, the answer to the question of whether to trust a national opinion poll or forecasting model depends on a variety of factors.

THE BASICS OF PUBLIC POLLING

Election polls have a long history in the United States. Since 1824, newspapers have conducted and reported the results of "straws," or informal polls taken to gauge public opinion (which way the wind is blowing the straw).[5] During the nineteenth century, newspapers used polls to give readers a sense of which candidate might be more likely to prevail. However, because most newspapers during this period were partisan publications, they generated polls to advance their partisan agenda by giving the public the impression that their favored candidate was in the lead.

The methodology of early polling was hardly scientific. To conduct a poll, a journalist might ask questions of the passengers aboard a train or interview citizens attending a public gathering.[6] For example, in 1876, the following story ran in the *Chicago Tribune*: "An excursion train containing some 200 people from Dayton, [Ohio], and neighboring towns, arrived last evening via the Pan Handle Road. . . . A vote was taken, resulting as follows: Hayes 65, Tilden 13, neutral 3, Cooper 2."[7]

Straw polls grew in popularity throughout the nineteenth century and, by the early part of the twentieth century, had become a regular feature in newspaper coverage of presidential elections. However, as popular as they were, they were not very useful in predicting the outcome of presidential elections. This was in part because people who did not sympathize with a given paper's partisan leanings would often refuse to return their questionnaires, leading to wildly biased estimates of the vote totals.

Among the many publications that conducted some of the earliest presidential polls was *Literary Digest*, which at the time was the most widely circulated general readership magazine in the nation. Starting in 1916, *Literary Digest* conducted polls predicting the presidential vote. Although the magazine's predicted vote totals were often inaccurate, it correctly predicted the winner in five consecutive elections (1916 through 1932). However, its poll in 1936 showed the incumbent President Franklin Roosevelt losing to his Republican challenger, Alf Landon, in a landslide. The poll projected Landon would receive 57 percent of the vote to Roosevelt's 43 percent.[8] Of course Roosevelt easily won, with 62.5 percent of the vote.

The *Digest*'s well-publicized failure in the 1936 presidential election helped usher in the modern era of scientific polling. Unlike the *Digest*, three enterprising individuals, with backgrounds in market research, correctly predicted the outcome. George Gallup, Elmo Roper, and Archibald Crossley were able to do so by employing more systematic methods of sampling.[9] To understand how Gallup, Roper, and Crossley correctly predicted the winner, and how the *Digest* did not, it is necessary to examine what pollsters do and how they do it.

A poll is an instrument used to measure what a group of people think (or know) about a subject or question. Because asking all the people in a particular group (e.g., registered voters) what they think about a specific topic would be too time consuming or costly to be practical, a pollster asks a smaller group of people. This smaller group is known as a sample. Pollsters estimate what the larger group thinks from a sample.

To understand this process better, imagine trying to predict how a large lecture hall with five hundred students will vote in a presidential election. One approach would be to ask all five hundred students. However, by the time one handed out, collected, and counted all the ballots, the class would be over. Is it reasonable to believe that one could estimate the likely vote outcome by polling only fifty people? Under the right circumstances, the answer is yes.

The reason for this is that polling is based in part on a branch of mathematics known as probability theory, which attempts to quantify how likely it is that a certain event will occur.[10] For example, probability theory (in particular, the central limit theorem) suggests that if one flips a coin one hundred times, it is likely that heads will land face up about fifty times. But to make a sound prediction one first needs a certain number of actual observations. We would need, in other words, to actually flip the coin a certain number of times, say, ten times. Much like with coin flips, probability theory allows pollsters to infer what Americans think based on the actual answers given by approximately 1,500 people, sometimes less.[11]

Yet understanding and applying theories of probability are only one part of the puzzle. To gauge public opinion accurately and to predict election outcomes, we need to ensure that we represent the entirety of the political spectrum in our sample. For example, we know that women are somewhat more likely to vote for Democrats, and men to vote for Republicans. Returning to our lecture hall exercise, we would want to make sure that we include women and men in the sample in roughly similar proportions to their numbers in the whole class. If there was an even divide of men and women in our class (250 women, 250 men), we would want to poll approximately twenty-five women and twenty-five men. Furthermore, we know that people who attend church frequently vote differently than those who do not, that the more affluent cast their ballots differently than those who are less economically well off, and so on. Put simply, to have any confidence that the results from our fifty-person sample would correctly predict the vote of all five hundred students, we would want to ensure that the fifty students who we polled were broadly representative of the entire class.

How is a representative sample identified by a pollster? There are four main strategies for doing this, all of which rely—in some way—on randomly selecting the individuals who take the poll. In the language of survey research, these are known as "probability samples," a reference to the fact that randomness plays a central role in theories of probability.

The first strategy is random sampling. In a simple random sample, there is an equal chance of selecting each person in the larger group, or population. For example, if everyone in our hypothetical class of five hundred had a seat number, we could put slips of paper, numbered one to five hundred, in a basket, shuffle them around, and pick fifty. If conducted fairly (e.g., all sheets of paper are of equal size, folded in half to hide the number, sufficiently shuffled or mixed), the process would provide an equal chance of selection for each student.

A second strategy, a variant of the first, is systematic sampling. Instead of selecting individuals strictly at random, systematic sampling involves moving through a list and selecting names according to a preset strategy. The list itself is assumed to be randomly distributed. For example, in systematic sampling, we could go through our alphabetical class roster and select every tenth name to create a fifty-person sample.

Another technique is stratified sampling. Here, the pollster divides the sampling frame, or the entire group, into strata, or smaller groups. Within each stratum (group), the pollster selects a sample using simple random or systematic sampling. This helps to ensure that the sample sufficiently represents all relevant subgroups. For example, if our class has three hundred men and two hundred women, we would select a sample of thirty men and twenty women.

Multistage cluster sampling follows a similar principle, although here, rather than use subgroup characteristics as the initial basis for sampling, the pollster uses geography instead. For example, a pollster could first select a geographic unit (say, a state), and within that unit select a smaller unit (a county), and within that unit choose an even smaller one (a neighborhood) and then select potential respondents—at random—from the smallest unit. This process reduces costs for the polling firm by concentrating efforts in several small areas. In our class example, we might think about selecting every fifth row of students, then randomly selecting respondents from each.

The important point with respect to sampling, regardless of the technique used, is that the respondents must be representative of the population that the pollster or researcher examines. Probability sampling rests on an assumption that if selected randomly, a sample will be representative of the population. Box 9.1 summarizes these four techniques.

BOX 9.1 | **Techniques for Selecting a Probability Sample**

Random: Individuals are selected from the entire population of interest by chance.

Systematic: Individuals are selected from the entire population of interest according to a set strategy.

Stratified: The population of interest is divided into subgroups, and within each, a certain number of individuals are selected either randomly or systematically.

Multistage cluster: A number of geographic areas are identified, and within each, individuals are selected either randomly or systematically.

This admittedly simplistic explanation of sampling allows us to understand why the *Literary Digest* poll did not correctly predict Roosevelt's victory in 1936. The magazine sent out more than ten million questionnaires and received responses from about 2.3 million people. These totals were more than enough for a reliable prediction of how the American public would vote. However, the magazine used automobile registration and telephone numbers to generate the list of people who would be asked to complete the questionnaire. The problem was that in 1936, people who owned automobiles or had telephones in their home were more likely to have been Republicans (thus, Landon voters) rather than Democrats (Roosevelt supporters). In addition, later research showed that Landon supporters were more likely to return their questionnaires than were those who supported Roosevelt. These two factors produced a biased sample, one not representative of the general population.[12]

In sum, if researchers administer a survey to a sufficiently large and representative sample, and if they fairly word the questions they ask, most polls can be trusted. However, not all polls are created equal. In particular, presidential campaign polls have some common pitfalls worth noting.

PROBLEM OF PSEUDO POLLS

There are many reputable polling firms as well as countless research institutions and university survey centers around the country that conduct scientifically grounded polls. In general, the results of these polls are trustworthy, if one uses a certain amount of discretion in interpreting the results. Yet, because anyone can write and administer a poll, there are some bad polls as well. Which polls should we trust, or more to the point, which should we *not* trust?

"Pseudo polls" are one general category of polls to disregard altogether, especially in understanding the dynamics of a presidential campaign.

Websites (including blogs), local news organizations, talk radio, college newspapers, and others often administer these types of polls. The major problem with pseudo polls is that they typically rely on what some refer to as "convenience," or nonprobability samples. Here, poll administrators simply invite people to participate in the poll and then tabulate the results. The individuals who take the survey are, in other words, self-selected—not randomly selected. For example, cable talk shows sometimes ask their viewers to call a phone number to answer a specific poll question. The results are often heavily skewed toward the opinion of the cable show's host for an obvious reason: only those watching, who are typically fans of the show, respond to the poll. This type of self-selected sample is not representative of the overall public because it excludes the many other Americans who do not watch the show. These nonviewers' opinions are likely to differ significantly from those who do watch the show.

The problems with polls that rely on self-selected samples are thus twofold. First, not everyone has a chance to participate. For example, in the case of Internet polls, the sample includes only those who visit the poll's website. Another problem with this sampling technique is that people who are motivated to respond to the poll usually have more extreme views than the general population.[13] The end result is that the samples in pseudo polls are not representative of the population at large, nor are the views expressed in these polls representative of the views of the population at large.[14]

Although there is no disputing the advantage of a probability sample as compared to a convenience sample, one major challenge confronting survey researchers and pollsters is the problem of low response rates. A report from the Pew Research Center found that the typical telephone survey response rate fell from 36 percent in 1997 to just 6 percent in 2018.[15] This is noteworthy because telephone surveys rely on randomized procedures of contacting potential respondents to ensure a probability sample. However, these exceptionally low response rates raise concerns about nonresponse bias. Put simply, nonresponse bias is error that results when respondents are noticeably different from those who choose not to participate in the poll. If there is reason to suspect that nonrespondents would answer differently than those who did respond to the poll, nonresponse bias can affect data quality and produce misleading or incorrect results.[16]

To address concerns about nonresponse bias, some survey researchers and pollsters have turned to mixed-mode survey designs that employ a combination of sampling and outreach techniques. Mixed-mode data collection has a long history, dating back more than a half century; however, it has increased in popularity as more and more people turn away from taking surveys over the telephone.[17] With roughly 290 million Internet users in the United States,[18] delivery of online surveys and polls has become increasingly popular, with some research showing that carefully executed opt-in Internet panels can produce results as accurate as telephone surveys.[19]

The mixed-mode model does not eliminate telephone contact, but rather combines online and phone delivery—an approach that several reputable firms currently employ, including Survey USA, Rasmussen Reports, and Public Policy Polling. The website FiveThirtyEight.com lists the polling methods and accuracy of various pollsters in the industry (see https://projects.fivethirtyeight.com/pollster-ratings). In viewing this page, one can see that Survey USA's results have been accurate enough to earn a top grade of A as listed on the website. Indeed, "tailored" mixed-mode designs have been shown to produce high-quality results[20] and may reflect the future of where polling is headed, particularly if phone response rates continue to decline any further.

HOW TO DETERMINE LIKELY VOTERS?

A reliable poll of presidential preference should sample only those people who will actually vote. As chapter 2 notes, only approximately 50 to 60 percent of the voting age population casts a ballot in a typical presidential election.[21] How should a polling organization construct a sample of only voters and likely voters? Unfortunately, there is no reliable or accepted way to determine whether an individual will exercise this most basic of political freedoms. Simply asking a person if they are likely to vote will not work. Most people, based on ideas they have about good citizenship, are reluctant to admit they might not vote. So, voter turnout is always lower than the percentage of people who say they are likely to vote. For example, the Pew Research Center conducted a survey prior to the 1996 election asking respondents about their intention to vote. Of those responding, 69 percent said they were "absolutely certain" they would vote, and another 18 percent replied they were "fairly certain." In actuality, voter turnout in 1996 was 49 percent (of the voting age population).[22]

Most polling firms will use at least one, and typically several, screening questions in their attempt to narrow their sample so that it only includes likely voters. The first stage of this screening is almost always to ask whether the respondent is a registered voter. From those who respond in the affirmative, the firm will ask additional questions in an attempt to estimate how likely the individual is to vote. For example, the Pew Research Center asks nine questions to make this determination.[23] Some data analysts go a step further using these individual survey questions and other publicly available data to create a statistical model that assigns a predicted probability of voting to each respondent.[24]

In presidential preference polls, especially those conducted close to the election, how well the polling firm constructs the sample can have a direct effect on the results. For example, a Harris Poll from October 2004 showed President George W. Bush leading Senator John Kerry by two percentage points using one measure of likely voters. But a second poll, employing a different method of measuring registered and likely voters, had Bush ahead by eight points (51% to 43%).[25]

Therefore, it seems prudent to take note of whether the poll bases its results on responses from registered or likely voters. Most major news organizations will include this information somewhere in the story. For example, a late August 2016 poll from Fox News showed Hillary Clinton leading Donald Trump by a margin of six percentage points among *registered* voters. Just a few weeks later in early September, Fox News had Trump ahead of Clinton by one percentage point among *likely* voters.[26]

WHAT ABOUT UNDECIDED VOTERS?

As complicated as it is to ensure that a poll sample includes only those voters most likely to vote, another issue is how to account for the people who say they are undecided. In most presidential campaigns, the number of "undecideds" is as high as 15 percent, and although this percentage drops as the campaign nears its end, it can still be as high as 5 percent in the days prior to Election Day. While it would be a simple matter for a news organization to report the percentage of undecideds in addition to the percentage that favor each candidate, most do not, because it makes for less interesting reading if the poll numbers present an uncertain picture.

One strategy to deal with undecided voters is to have a follow-up question asking the respondent if he or she "leans" toward, or favors, either candidate.[27] While this reduces the number of undecideds, it paints an inaccurate portrait of voter preferences, given that some of these people might change their minds.[28] This was one of the factors responsible for Gallup mistakenly calling the 1948 election for Thomas Dewey (morning newspapers proclaimed that Dewey won, when in fact, Harry Truman was the victor).[29] Another way to reduce the number of undecideds is to present respondents with a secret ballot, but this requires face-to-face interviewing, a rather costly method of polling.

A more common strategy for handling undecideds is assigning them to one candidate or the other based on some formula. One way to do this is to distribute undecided voters in proportion to the candidate's strength. For example, if 46 percent of respondents have expressed a preference for Candidate A, the pollster might allocate 46 percent of the undecided vote to Candidate A. This strategy, however, poses considerable risks given that the closer Election Day looms, the more likely it is that momentum can shift, disproportionately favoring one candidate or the other. There are other formulas for determining the expected breakdown in vote choice among undecideds as well, including using the respondent's past voting record or partisan identification (if any) as a clue for future voting intentions, whether there is an incumbent in the race (undecideds are generally thought to be anti-incumbent), as well as other, more complex solutions.

Additional ways to address this issue are to continue polling as close to Election Day as possible. This reduces the number of undecided voters in the poll. However, this strategy too can result in less-than-perfect results. There is nearly always at least some error in the preelection polls conducted by major polling firms when compared to the actual vote totals. Table 9.1 lists the actual vote margin between the two candidates and the margin taken from the *least* accurate major poll, and the difference between these two figures, from each election cycle from 1980 to 2016.

Yet being off the mark by a few percentage points, but correctly identifying the winner, is a less serious error than the prognostications that confidently predict the wrong winner, as *The Huffington Post* did in the 2016 presidential election. To be fair, numerous others were wrong as

Table 9.1 Actual and Projected Margins from Select Election Polls, 1980–2016

Year	Winner, Actual Vote Margin	Margin from Least Accurate Projection	Difference
1980	Reagan +10	Reagan +1 (CBS/*New York Times*)	9
1984	Reagan +18	Reagan +10 (Roper)/+25 (*USA Today*)	8/7
1988	Bush +8	Bush +12 (Gallup)	4
1992	Clinton +8	Clinton +12 (Gallup/CNN/*USA Today*)	4
1996	Clinton +8	Clinton +18 (CBS/*New York Times*)	10
2000	Bush and Gore (even)	Bush +7 (Hotline)	7
2004	Bush +2.4	Bush +6 (*Newsweek*)	3.6
2008	Obama +7.3	Obama +13 (CBS News)	5.7
2012	Obama +4	Obama +3 (Pew)	1
2016	Trump −2	Clinton +6 (Monmouth)	4

Sources: Data from 1980 through 2000 adapted from Robert S. Erikson and Kent L. Tedin, *American Public Opinion: Its Origins, Content, and Impact*, 7th ed. (New York: Longman, 2005), 44. Data for 2004 from Robert S. Erikson and Kent L. Tedin, *American Public Opinion: Its Origins, Content, and Impact*, updated 7th ed. (New York: Longman, 2007), 51. Data for 2008 from "White House 2008: General Election Trial Heats, Presidential Trial Heat Summary," PollingReport.com, accessed June 1, 2009, http://www.pollingreport.com/wh08gen.htm. Data for 2012 from "White House 2012: Presidential Trial Heat Summary," PollingReport.com, accessed May 20, 2015, http://www.pollingreport.com/wh12gen.htm. Data for 2016 from "General Election: Trump vs. Clinton vs. Johnson vs. Stein," RealClearPolitics.com, accessed March 14, 2019, https://www.realclearpolitics.com/epolls/2016/president/us/general_election_trump_vs_clinton_vs_johnson_vs_stein-5952.html.

well, including the *New York Times* (which gave Clinton an 85 percent probability of winning) and Nate Silver's FiveThirtyEight forecasting model (which gave Clinton a 71.4 percent probability of winning). At first blush, these failed predictions would appear to be an indictment on the entire polling industry. But such a conclusion would be unfair. As a report from the American Association for Public Opinion Research (AAPOR) concluded, national polls in the 2016 presidential election were generally correct and accurate by historical standards.[30] The final national polls taken just before the November general election gave Clinton an average lead of three percentage points over Trump,[31] and Clinton won the popular vote by two percentage points.

So, what went wrong in 2016? Polling in the Upper Midwest underestimated Trump's support. Specifically, polls in Pennsylvania, Michigan, and Wisconsin—states that had supported the Democratic presidential nominee in six consecutive elections dating back to 1992—showed leads for Clinton that ultimately did not hold on Election Day. The AAPOR Committee found that a large percentage of voters, as high as 13 percent in Wisconsin and Pennsylvania, remained undecided until the final days of the election. These late-deciding voters went disproportionately for Trump, by some thirty percentage points in Wisconsin and by seventeen percentage points in Pennsylvania.[32] These errors contributed to the failure of several prominent forecasting models, which had previously produced remarkably accurate results in the 2008 and the 2012 presidential elections.[33] In the absence of reliable polling data in three highly competitive states that totaled a combined 46 Electoral College votes, an election that appeared to be clearly headed in the direction of a Clinton victory broke instead for Trump. As Professor Gary Smith reminds us in his book *Standard Deviations*, "Garbage in, garbage out is a snappy reminder of the fact that . . . [i]f a computer's calculations are based on bad data, the output is not gospel, but garbage."[34]

PROBLEM OF TIMING: PHASES OF THE CAMPAIGN

Polls taken and released during certain periods of time during the campaign can be misleading, giving a false impression of a candidate's strength or weakness. We should, in other words, interpret them cautiously. This is especially true with respect to polls taken during the preprimary phase of the campaign, immediately after each party's convention, and after the presidential debates.

Preprimary polls, or those taken before the Iowa caucuses and New Hampshire primary, have in the past been a fairly good predictor of who will win the party nomination. From 1980 to 2000, all but one candidate (Gary Hart in 1988) who was leading in the Gallup poll of party identifiers immediately prior to the Iowa caucuses won their party's nomination.[35] This said, there is considerable fluctuation in these poll numbers before January of the election year.

For example, in 2003, several candidates, including Joe Lieberman, Dick Gephardt, Wesley Clark, and the eventual presumed front-runner, Howard Dean, led in these preprimary polls.[36] John Kerry, however, was the eventual winner of the Democratic nomination. In fact, in 2008, neither of the two candidates who led in the final poll before Iowa (Hillary Clinton and Rudy Giuliani) went on to secure their party's nomination. During the 2012 Republican presidential primary, former Texas Governor Rick Perry led the Republican presidential field throughout August and September 2011, while former House Speaker Newt Gingrich surged into the lead for parts of November and December 2011. Both candidates lost to the party's eventual nominee, Mitt Romney.

These "trial heat" polls do not measure actual preferences as much as they track name recognition or simple familiarity with the name of the individual.[37] In addition, these polls are sensitive to the news cycle. Before Wesley Clark's formal entrance into the race on September 17, 2003, most polls showed other Democratic candidates leading the field. Yet, in the month following his announcement to enter the race, Clark consistently ranked in the top tier of candidates. One can only assume this was at least partly the result of the media coverage generated by his announcement, because he won only one Democratic primary.[38]

Republican Senator Fred Thompson, who also starred in the television series *Law & Order* for five seasons, announced his candidacy in early September 2007 and polled between 15 and 20 percent throughout the rest of the year. He did not, however, win a single primary. The same was true for Republican Ben Carson, who led the Republican field in early November 2015 by six percentage points, according to an NBC/*Wall Street Journal* poll.[39] Carson, however, ultimately finished in fourth place in the Iowa caucuses, and his campaign sputtered to an end by early March. While polls taken just prior to the Iowa caucuses and the New Hampshire primary are a good indicator of who will be the eventual nominee, polls taken much earlier than November or December of the year prior to the election are not very reliable.

In a similar way, polls taken immediately after each candidate's party convention (or a candidate debate) typically do not measure actual candidate strength. Although there are exceptions (e.g., 1984, 1996), it is quite common for each nominee's approval numbers to go up five to ten percentage points after the convention. In 2016, this postconvention "bump" or "bounce" was somewhat smaller, averaging about four percentage points for both Donald Trump and Hillary Clinton.[40] Typically, challengers benefit more than incumbents do from the postconvention bounce because they are less well known to the general public. Still, convention bounces for either candidate usually dissipate fairly quickly, as was the case with Al Gore in 2000 and John McCain in 2008. We should note that in a small number of cases the postconvention bounce can be a prelude to a strong fall campaign, as happened for Bill Clinton in 1992.[41] In short, one should treat polls taken just after the conventions with caution.

Polls following presidential debates are similarly volatile. This is partly a function of the fact that firms must conduct these postdebate polls quickly, using smaller than normal samples (about 600 people). In addition, postdebate polls are sensitive to media coverage of the debate.[42] Often different organizations report somewhat contradictory—or at least differing—results. For example, after the first presidential debate in 2016 (on September 26), a CNN poll had Hillary Clinton winning one debate by a margin of thirty-five percentage points (62% to 27%), while a Public Policy Polling survey gave Clinton the advantage by only eleven percentage points (51% to 40%).[43] However, polls that employed an online methodology, such as one from Fox News and another from *Time*, showed Trump winning the debate by fifteen percentage points (50% to 35%) and four percentage points (52% to 48%), respectively.[44]

Neither candidate showed any major gains in election polls after the debate. A Reuters poll, for example, showed a two-point gain for Trump from the predebate to postdebate period, whereas a Fox News poll reported a two-point postdebate bounce for Clinton.[45] A UPI/CVoter poll showed almost no change, revealing only a half-percentage point shift toward Clinton and a six-tenths of a percentage point drop for Trump.[46] These postdebate polls from the 2016 election are consistent with previous ones from other presidential elections, which consistently show that the candidate who "wins" the debates rarely makes any long-lasting gains that translate into additional votes on Election Day (see also chapter 8).[47]

In short, preprimary, postconvention, and postdebate polls should be treated with caution. Results from these polls are often fleeting—a snapshot of what may be happening at a particular period in the election cycle, but ultimately not a good predictor of what the final election outcome will be. Moreover, as suggested earlier, there is often considerable variation in candidate strength as Election Day approaches. The closer a poll is conducted to Election Day, the more likely it is to be accurate.

SAMPLES, DATA, AND REPORTING

Although there are times when the pollsters and forecasters get it wrong, as happened in the critical states of Wisconsin, Michigan, and Pennsylvania in 2016, most polls that receive coverage from major news organizations are well designed and administered. Yet, sometimes news organizations do not fully explain the results. For example, some stories might not indicate whether their sample consisted of registered or likely voters. More commonly, press accounts may misrepresent what a poll actually means, especially with respect to the margin separating the candidates. This leads to a discussion of the margin of error of polls.

As previously discussed, it is possible to infer what a population thinks by relying on the responses of a properly constructed probability sample. Nonetheless, it is important to remember that the theory driving this inference is one of probability, not certainty. If we flip a coin ten times, it is probable that heads will land face up about five times. However, common sense suggests that it will not be exactly five times every time we do this. Indeed, an outcome of exactly five heads and five tails will occur only about 25 percent of the time.[48] So, it would be wrong to conclude that there was something wrong with the coin if, say, there were six heads and four tails in those first ten tosses. There is random variation or "noise" in almost all data collection.

This error, due to random variation, occurs not just with coin flips, but for polls as well. This is referred to this as a poll's margin of error (or sampling error).[49] This number, which is often noted in the poll's methodology section, is expressed in plus or minus terms ($\pm$). As with coin flips, error due to random chance decreases as we do more testing. In other words, as more people take part in a poll, the results will tend to be more accurate. A nationwide poll of fifty people, for example, would have significantly more random variation ($\pm14\%$) than a poll of one thousand people ($\pm3\%$).

For example, a CBS News election poll on the eve of the 2016 presidential election showed Hillary Clinton leading Donald Trump, 45 percent to 41 percent, with a margin of error of ±3 percentage points.[50] Translated, this meant that as few as 42 percent (45 −3) supported Clinton and as many as 44 percent (41 +3) supported Trump, or as many as 48 percent (45 +3) supported Clinton and as few as 38 percent (41 −3) supported Trump.

This is important to understand because headlines and news stories sometimes misrepresent what is actually happening in election polls with respect to the margin of error.[51] Although this specific story qualified its claims, one Harris Poll report from October 2000 claimed that "Bush Leads Gore by Five Points," 48 to 43 percent. But with the survey's margin of error (3%) factored in, Bush could have had as little as 45 percent, and Gore as much as 46 percent.[52] CBS News reported in 2000 that Gore won the last presidential debate by five percentage points over Bush (45% to 40%), but the margin of error for this poll was 4 percent—almost as much as the difference between the two.[53] Margin of error matters, especially if the two candidates are in a competitive race, which is usually the case in presidential elections.

The media often report the poll numbers of various subgroups in preelection presidential polls as well. In these polls, a reliable sample size is sometimes a problem. A national poll based on responses from one thousand individuals would have a 3 percent margin of error associated with it. If there was a split in the sample according to gender, there would be a subsample of approximately 490 men. The margin of error would be greater for this subsample. If there was a split in the sample for men according to their party identification, the sample would split further into three more categories: one each for Republicans, Democrats, and independents. The sample would continue to grow smaller with further divisions along race, income, or other socioeconomic characteristics. With each division, the sample becomes smaller and therefore associated with a greater margin of error. As such, one should treat group analyses of presidential polling data with caution given that subgroups have higher margins of error associated with them.[54]

APPLYING NATIONAL POLLING RESULTS
TO A STATE-BY-STATE CONTEST

Before the 2000 presidential election, the winner of the nation's popular vote was also the winner of the Electoral College vote in every election of the twentieth century. With such a strong correlation, it seemed a more than reasonable assumption that by polling likely voters nationally, the results would be accurate in predicting the winner of the election. However, the presidential elections of 2000 and 2016 bucked historical trends by producing a winner of the popular vote (Al Gore in 2000 and Hillary Clinton in 2016) that was different from the winner of the Electoral College vote (George W. Bush in 2000 and Donald Trump in 2016). These two elections highlight the potential folly of using national polls to predict the winner of the presidential election.

The Electoral College allocates votes on a state-by-state basis, dependent (in all but two states) on the winner of the popular vote in that state. These rules suggest that state polling results will yield greater insights about which candidate is more likely to win than what we can glean from the results that come from national polls. In particular, polls are important to follow in a few key "battleground" states (states that could realistically swing to either candidate). Watching state polls allows one a more nuanced—and accurate—view of how each candidate is doing and, more important, where each candidate is doing well or poorly.

Of course, as noted earlier, these state-level polls can create havoc when the numbers are wrong, as they were in the battleground states of Wisconsin, Michigan, and Pennsylvania in 2016. As Nate Silver concluded in the aftermath of the 2016 election, "Clinton underperformed her polls significantly throughout the Midwest . . . by 4 points in Michigan . . . by 5 points in Pennsylvania and by 6 points in . . . Wisconsin. [These three states] flipped to Trump and cost her the election."[55] Nonetheless, the overall track record of state-level polls has been generally good and helped produce extremely accurate forecasting predictions in the 2008 and 2012 presidential elections.

CONCLUSION

So, is polling an art, a science, or some form of modern voodoo? As our discussion has made clear, polling is a science, but hardly an exact science (table 9.1 was a good illustration of this point). One objective of this chapter was to provide the tools to become better consumers of preelection presidential polls. Box 9.2 summarizes the various points made throughout the chapter in short-question form. While it is not necessary to study every poll intensively, moving mentally through this checklist is a helpful way to understand what the polls are really telling us.

BOX 9.2	Interpreting Preelection Polls: A Checklist

- Who conducted the poll? A reputable firm or university research team?
- Is the poll based on a representative sample of the population?
- Is the poll based on responses from registered or likely voters?
- How has the poll dealt with undecided voters?
- Is the poll focused on too narrow a phase of the campaign, and if so, does the accompanying story account for that?
- Is the sample (or the subsamples) large enough to base inferences on?
- Does the accompanying story or headline properly account for the poll's margin of error?
- In a close presidential race, does the story accompanying the poll account for the fact that certain state races will be more important in determining the Electoral College winner?

FURTHER READING

Asher, Herbert. *Polling and the Public: What Every Citizen Should Know*. 9th ed. Washington, DC: CQ Press, 2017.

Erikson, Robert S., and Tedin, Kent L. *American Public Opinion: Its Origins, Content, and Impact*. 9th ed. New York, NY: Routledge, 2015.

Silver, Nate. *The Signal and the Noise: Why So Many Predictions Fail, But Some Don't*. New York, NY: Penguin Press, 2012.

Traugott, Michael W., and Lavrakas, Paul J. *The Voter's Guide to Election Polls*. 5th ed. Lanham, MD: Rowman & Littlefield, 2016.

10

May the Best Person Win?

The Illusion of Competitive Congressional Elections

> If a group of planners sat down and tried to design a pair of assemblies with the goal of serving members' reelection needs year in and year out, they would be hard pressed to improve on what exists [in the U.S. Congress].
>
> —David R. Mayhew[1]

DEMOCRATIC THEORY SPECIFIES that citizens elect most of their leaders in free, fair, and regular elections.[2] The notion that these elections should be competitive is implicit. There would be little reason to hold an election if the outcome was a foregone conclusion. Interestingly, and perhaps not surprisingly, most Americans believe that congressional elections are competitive. According to one poll on the subject, 71 percent of registered voters anticipated a "close contest" in their district's U.S. House election.[3]

A significantly smaller percentage of congressional races, however, are actually competitive. This chapter examines this lack of electoral competitiveness in congressional elections. We begin by showing that congressional elections have become less competitive in recent years, especially elections to the House of Representatives. In particular, we illustrate that incumbents rarely lose in their bids for reelection. As Ronald Reagan once quipped, there was more turnover in the former Soviet Union's presidium than in the U.S. Congress.[4] In addition to winning, incumbents are doing so by greater margins.

Following this we examine the advantages incumbents have in their bids for reelection. First, there are various institutional factors associated with the job that provide incumbents with an advantage. These include an organizational base for their campaign in the form of offices and staffers, a greater ability to communicate easily with voters and potential voters, as well as being in a position to solve problems constituents might be having with the federal bureaucracy. In addition, certain legislative norms in

Congress help members enhance their reputations. Incumbents also have greater access to interest groups and political action committees (PACs) to help finance their campaigns. This greater ability to raise funds contributes to a "scare-off" effect, which helps depress the entrance of adequately funded quality challengers. Finally, recent trends in congressional redistricting, greater name recognition, and voter loyalty advantages incumbents as well.

In the final section of the chapter, we shift to a discussion of how incumbents can lose. Here, we focus on the fact that the scare-off effect does not always work, how presidential politics affects congressional elections, and the occasional effect of "national tides" on what are essentially local elections. We conclude that while American elections generally satisfy the conditions for a democracy, the lack of competitiveness in congressional elections poses some problems for a healthy democratic system.

BACKGROUND

For much of our nation's early history, it was quite common for a U.S. House representative to serve only one or two terms (senators were not directly elected until after the ratification of the Seventeenth Amendment in 1913). There were a relatively high number of incumbents who did not seek reelection each election cycle. Three general reasons help explain this.

First, in earlier times, the notion of a "career" in Congress was not desirable for most ambitious professionals. Mediocre salaries, hot and humid summers in Washington, DC, long stretches of time away from home, and the rather limited responsibilities of the federal government all combined to make the job of a U.S. Congressman less attractive than it is today. Second, even those who wished to stay in Washington for multiple terms were hard pressed to do so. Most congressional elections were highly contested, close races. Third, many members were prevented from running for more than one or two terms. In many states, especially non-Southern states, party organizations had informal term limits that prevented members from seeking the nomination more than one or two times (during this time, political parties controlled the nomination process).[5]

However, as the century progressed, the percentage of House incumbents running for reelection increased, and the percentage of those retiring—voluntarily or otherwise—decreased. Table 10.1 shows that over time, considerably more House incumbents ran for reelection and a much smaller percentage opted to retire. Another way to look at this would be to track the number of first-term members (freshmen) in the House or the average number of terms served by House members over time.[6] As table 10.2 indicates, the percentage of freshmen in the House dropped more than thirty percentage points (from 51.3 to 20.4), and the average number of terms that members served more than doubled (from 1.9 to 4.3) in the century after 1850. Together, tables 10.1 and 10.2 display a pattern of steadily increasing tenure in the House from the mid-1800s forward.

The pattern of increased numbers of incumbents running for and winning elections accelerated in the post–World War II era (see table 10.3). Since 1946, the percentage of House incumbents who sought reelection topped 90 percent in twenty-eight of thirty-seven elections, and the percentage of those seeking reelection dipped below 85 percent only once. This occurred in 1992, in the aftermath of a major check-writing scandal, when only 84.6 percent of House incumbents sought reelection. In addition, during the post–Second World War era, very few of those seeking reelection lost in either the primary or general elections. Only once, in 1992, did more

Table 10.1   House Incumbents Running for Reelection and Retirement Rates, by Decade (1850–1910)

Decade	Number Running for Reelection	Percentage Retiring
1850s	60	27.1%
1870s	64	22.8%
1880s	66	20.0%
1890s	73	17.3%
1900s	80	11.2%

Sources: Samuel Kernell, "Toward Understanding 19th Century Congressional Careers: Ambition, Competition, and Rotation," American Journal of Political Science 21 (1977): 684, table 2; and John B. Gilmour and Paul Rothstein, "A Dynamic Model of Loss, Retirement, and Tenure in the U.S. House of Representatives," The Journal of Politics 58 (1996): 54–68, 57, table 1. Data for the 1860s is not included because Southern states did not hold elections to Congress during the Civil War years.

Table 10.2   Percentage of First-Term Members and Mean Tenure, House of Representatives, by Decade (1851–1949)

Decade	Percentage First-Term Members	Mean Number Terms
1850s	51.3	1.88
1870s	49.1	2.09
1880s	39.0	2.47
1890s	39.7	2.54
1900s	23.8	3.43
1910s	26.2	3.55
1920s	19.6	3.99
1930s	25.6	3.92
1940s	20.4	4.34

Source: Nelson W. Polsby, "The Institutionalization of the U.S. House of Representatives," The American Political Science Review 62 (1968): 146, tables 1 and 2.

Table 10.3   Reelection Rates for House Incumbents, 1946–2018

Year	Number of Incumbents Seeking Reelection (%)		Sought Reelection, Defeated in Primary (%)		Won Primary, Defeated in General Election (%)		Percentage Running Reelected
1946	398	(91.5)	18	(4.5)	52	(13.1)	82.4
1948	400	(92.0)	15	(3.8)	68	(17.0)	79.3
1950	400	(92.0)	6	(1.5)	32	(8.0)	90.5
1952	389	(89.4)	9	(2.3)	26	(6.7)	91.0
1954	407	(93.6)	6	(1.5)	22	(5.4)	93.1
1956	411	(94.5)	6	(1.5)	16	(3.9)	94.6
1958	396	(91.0)	3	(0.8)	37	(9.3)	89.9
1960	405	(93.1)	5	(1.2)	25	(6.2)	92.6
1962	402	(92.4)	12	(3.0)	22	(5.5)	91.5
1964	397	(91.3)	8	(2.0)	45	(11.3)	86.6
1966	411	(94.5)	8	(1.9)	41	(10.0)	88.1
1968	409	(94.0)	4	(1.0)	9	(2.2)	96.8
1970	401	(92.2)	10	(2.5)	12	(3.0)	94.5
1972	393	(90.3)	11	(2.8)	13	(3.3)	93.6
1974	391	(89.9)	8	(2.0)	40	(10.2)	87.7
1976	384	(88.3)	3	(0.8)	13	(3.4)	95.8
1978	382	(87.8)	5	(1.3)	19	(5.0)	93.7
1980	398	(91.5)	6	(1.5)	31	(7.8)	90.7
1982	393	(90.3)	10	(2.5)	29	(7.4)	90.1
1984	411	(94.5)	3	(0.7)	16	(3.9)	95.4
1986	394	(90.6)	3	(0.8)	6	(1.5)	97.7
1988	409	(94.0)	1	(0.2)	6	(1.5)	98.3
1990	406	(93.3)	1	(0.2)	15	(3.7)	96.0
1992	368	(84.6)	19	(5.2)	24	(6.5)	88.3
1994	387	(89.0)	4	(1.0)	34	(8.8)	90.2
1996	384	(88.3)	2	(0.5)	21	(5.5)	94.0
1998	402	(92.4)	1	(0.2)	6	(1.5)	98.3
2000	403	(92.6)	3	(0.7)	6	(1.5)	97.8
2002	398	(91.5)	8	(2.0)	8	(2.0)	96.2
2004	404	(92.9)	2	(0.5)	7	(1.7)	92.9
2006	403	(92.6)	2	(0.5)	22	(5.5)	94.0
2008	399	(91.7)	4	(1.0)	19	(4.8)	94.2
2010	397	(91.3)	4	(1.0)	54	(13.6)	85.4
2012	391	(89.9)	13	(3.3)	27	(6.9)	89.8
2014	392	(90.1)	5	(1.3)	13	(3.3)	95.4
2016	392	(90.1)	4	(1.0)	8	(2.0)	96.9
2018	376	(86.4)	4	(1.0)	30	(8.1)	91.0

Source: Norman J. Ornstein, Thomas E. Mann, Raffaela Wakeman, Andrew Rugg, Molly Reynolds, Curtlyn Kramer, Nick Zeppos, et al., 2017, "Vital Statistics on Congress," The Brookings Institution, https://www.brookings.edu/multi-chapter-report/vital-statistics-on-congress/.

than 5 percent of incumbents who sought reelection *not* win their party's primary, and the percentage defeated in the general election topped 10 percent just once (the 2010 elections) since 1976.

Table 10.4 Reelection Rates for Senate Incumbents, 1946–2018

Year	Number of Races	Sought Reelection (%)		Sought Reelection, Defeated in Primary (%)		Won Primary, Defeated in General Election (%)		Percentage Running Reelected
1946	37	30	(81.1)	6	(20.0)	7	(23.3)	56.7
1948	33	25	(75.8)	2	(8.0)	8	(32.0)	60.0
1950	36	32	(88.9)	5	(15.6)	5	(15.6)	68.8
1952	35	29	(82.9)	1	(3.4)	10	(34.5)	62.1
1954	38	32	(84.2)	2	(6.3)	5	(15.6)	78.1
1956	35	30	(85.7)	0	-	4	(13.3)	86.7
1958	36	27	(75.0)	0	-	10	(37.0)	63.0
1960	35	29	(82.9)	0	-	2	(6.9)	93.1
1962	39	35	(89.7)	1	(2.9)	5	(14.3)	82.9
1964	35	32	(91.4)	0	-	4	(12.5)	87.5
1966	35	32	(91.4)	3	(9.4)	1	(3.1)	87.5
1968	34	27	(79.4)	4	(14.8)	4	(14.8)	70.4
1970	35	31	(88.6)	1	(3.2)	6	(19.4)	77.4
1972	34	27	(79.4)	2	(7.4)	5	(18.5)	74.1
1974	34	27	(79.4)	2	(7.4)	2	(7.4)	85.2
1976	33	25	(75.8)	0	-	9	(36.0)	64.0
1978	35	25	(71.4)	3	(12.0)	7	(28.0)	60.0
1980	34	29	(85.3)	4	(13.8)	9	(31.0)	55.2
1982	33	30	(90.9)	0	-	2	(6.7)	93.3
1984	33	29	(87.9)	0	-	3	(10.3)	89.7
1986	34	28	(82.4)	0	-	7	(25.0)	75.0
1988	33	27	(81.8)	0	-	4	(14.8)	85.2
1990	35	32	(91.4)	0	-	1	(3.1)	96.9
1992	36	28	(77.8)	1	(3.6)	4	(14.3)	82.1
1994	35	26	(74.3)	0	-	2	(7.7)	92.3
1996	34	21	(61.8)	1	(4.8)	1	(4.8)	90.5
1998	34	29	(85.3)	0	-	3	(10.3)	89.7
2000	34	29	(85.3)	0	-	6	(20.7)	79.3
2002	34	27	(79.4)	1	(3.7)	2	(7.4)	88.9
2004	34	26	(76.5)	0	-	1	(3.8)	96.2
2006	34	28	(82.4)	1	(3.6)	6	(21.4)	78.6
2008	35	30	(85.7)	0	-	5	(16.7)	83.3
2010	37	25	(67.6)	3	(12.0)	2	(8.0)	84.0
2012	33	23	(69.7)	1	(4.3)	1	(4.3)	91.3
2014	36	29	(80.6)	0	-	5	(17.2)	79.3
2016	34	29	(85.3)	0	-	2	(6.9)	93.1
2018	33	32	(97.0)	0	-	5	(15.6)	84.4

Source: Norman J. Ornstein, Thomas E. Mann, Raffaela Wakeman, Andrew Rugg, Molly Reynolds, Curtlyn Kramer, Nick Zeppos, et al., 2017, "Vital Statistics on Congress," The Brookings Institution, https://www.brookings.edu/multi-chapter-report/vital-statistics-on-congress/.

In fact, it is often the case that incumbents face no major-party opposition at all in the general election. In 1998, almost one in four incumbents (94, or 23.4%) had no major-party opposition. In 2018, this number fell to a "mere" 41 (9.4%). These races are by definition uncompetitive. While the House returns a very high percentage of incumbents, the Senate is slightly more competitive. Since 1946, Senate incumbents have sought reelection at a rate of 75 percent or higher in all but five elections (1978, 1994, 1996, 2010, and 2012; see table 10.4). Very few senators ever lose their primary bids. Of those who gained their party nomination and stood in the general election, in only two elections (1952 and 1958) did the number of defeated incumbent senators reach ten. In the recent 2018 election, 84 percent of incumbent senators seeking reelection were successful. While there is more variation in Senate reelection rates overall than in House races, the general trend of elections becoming less competitive is similar.

Congressional incumbents not only are winning but they are also doing so by larger margins. In 1974, political scientist David Mayhew noted that fewer elections in the postwar era could be classified as competitive. Mayhew dubbed this trend "the case of the vanishing marginals," a reference to the fact that close races in the House were becoming rare.[7] (Senate races tend to be more competitive for reasons we will discuss shortly.)

As figure 10.1 shows, this trend has become more pronounced over time, especially in the House. The figure represents the percentage of House races in which the winner received more than 60 percent of the vote (traditionally defined as an uncompetitive election).[8] To be fair, it is worth noting that

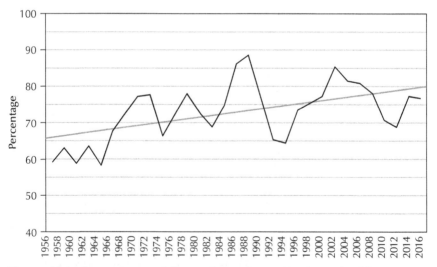

Figure 10.1 Percentage of House Incumbents Reelected with at Least 60 Percent of the Major Party Vote, 1956–2016.
Source: Norman J. Ornstein, Thomas E. Mann, Raffaela Wakeman, Andrew Rugg, Molly Reynolds, Curtlyn Kramer, Nick Zeppos, et al., 2017, "Vital Statistics on Congress," The Brookings Institution, https://www.brookings.edu/multi-chapter-report/vital-statistics-on-congress/.

open-seat elections to Congress are in fact quite competitive. Still, incumbency reelection rates and their margins of victory are impossible to ignore.

Why are congressional elections so noncompetitive? There are several contributing factors, most of which revolve around the various advantages incumbents enjoy by virtue of being the current officeholder. This is the subject of the next section.

THE ELECTORAL ADVANTAGES OF INCUMBENCY

Our discussion of the advantages of incumbency is divided into several sections. The first section deals with various institutional factors, or perks of the office. These advantages include a large staff working for members of Congress, as well as office space, computers, and so on. In addition, members of Congress have and use various ways to communicate with their constituents at taxpayers' or at little expense. Incumbents also aggressively solve bureaucratic problems for members of their district in hopes that voters will return those favors on Election Day. Finally, there are certain norms guiding legislative activity itself that favor incumbents, allowing them to build and present their record in a favorable light.

In addition to these institutional advantages, there are other aspects of incumbency that give incumbents an edge over challengers. One is an overwhelming edge in raising campaign funds, which can sometimes scare off quality challengers.[9] Congressional redistricting efforts have helped incumbents in recent years as well. Finally, the criteria that people use to make their voting decisions favor incumbents. Together, these factors provide the current officeholder with an enormous edge in his or her bid for reelection.

Office and Staff

Institutional advantages are those associated with doing the job of a member of Congress. Congressional office comes with various perks, often referred to (e.g., in American government textbooks) as "in kind" advantages, some of which aid in the reelection efforts of members. One advantage is the fact that each member of Congress has a staff that also serves as the nucleus of a permanent campaign organization, and the number of these staffers has grown dramatically in the past century.

The number of employees in the House of Representatives has increased approximately sevenfold since 1930. In 1950, the House employed slightly fewer than 2,000 staffers. By 1990, that number exceeded 7,500. Individually, the average member has fifteen employees (staffers) but is allowed eighteen full-time and four part-time employees.[10] In 1955, there were approximately 1,000 staffers in the Senate and by 1990, 4,000. However, individually they average thirty to thirty-five staffers per senator, from as few as thirteen to as many as seventy-one. There are no limits to the number of staffers a senator may employ.[11] Beyond serving as an unofficial nucleus for their campaign organization, staffers are also used for casework in in the member's district, especially if it looks to be a tight race.

Members of Congress are also given allowances for "travel, telecommunications, district office rental, office equipment, stationery, computer services, and mail."[12] Some House and Senate members have as many as five or six offices in their districts or states.[13] All of this comes at the expense of the taxpayer. While staffers technically cannot be used for the campaign, the member's press secretary is especially important in helping to generate favorable news about the congressperson at the local level.[14] In addition, staffers help with constituency service, which creates a favorable impression that may translate into votes on Election Day.

Direct Communications

Members of Congress take full advantage of what is known as the "franking" privilege. This is the right of members of Congress to send letters to their constituents informing them about what is happening in Washington, at government expense. The rationale for this is straightforward. The health of a representative democracy depends in part on an informed citizenry, and central to this is knowing what our representative is doing in government. In fact, the precedent for this practice dates back to 1660 in the British House of Commons and was granted by the Continental Congress to members in 1775. Subsequently, the first U.S. Congress passed a law granting its members the privilege in 1789.[15]

One widely circulated account suggests that new members are urged to "use the frank,"[16] and by all accounts, they do so. Members of Congress send mass newsletters to all constituents as well as more narrowly tailored messages to different segments of their electorate. Often recipients are invited in these messages to send their thoughts to their member of Congress. Estimates suggest that from the mid-1960s to 1990, the volume of franked mail has at least tripled and perhaps quadrupled. Importantly, the amount of franked mail is higher during election years.[17]

In 1990, Congress enacted new regulations limiting the amount of franked mail to one piece per address per state for a senator and three pieces per address per House district. Other regulations, such as prohibiting personal photographs of or references to the member and integrating franking costs into the members' office expenses were added. However, at minimum, these communications keep the incumbent's name fresh in voters' minds and present a favorable image of him or her.

Casework in the District

It is not unusual for an ordinary citizen to need assistance from time to time navigating or circumventing the bureaucracy that makes up modern government. Citizens might contact their member of Congress for any number of reasons, which could include, for example, help with an expired passport only days before a planned trip or a tax problem with the Internal Revenue Service. Here, the member would be acting in a capacity analogous to that of an ombud, a government-appointed individual who looks after the rights and needs of citizens in their dealing with government. Originally a Scandinavian concept, ombuds are found in virtually all modern bureaucracies (including some larger corporations). Members of Congress take this type of work—referred to as casework—very seriously.

Each member of Congress receives thousands of such requests each year. While it is impossible for members to handle each request personally, much of the staff work handled in district offices is devoted to resolving citizens' problems and answering requests. This is an extremely effective way to win the loyalty and votes of constituents. A favor done for a constituent makes it more likely that he or she will repay the kindness come election time—and perhaps even tell others. This type of interpersonal, word-of-mouth advertising is invaluable.[18]

Favorable Local Media

Incumbents have certain advantages with various media that make it easier to boost name recognition among their constituents as well as communicate and cultivate a favorable view among supporters and potential supporters. First, all members of Congress have their own websites, which allow interested parties to learn about what they are doing in Washington.[19] The government pays for these websites, and members use them to publicize their achievements, downplay their shortcomings, and invite visitors to send comments and feedback.

Second, both parties in each House of Congress, as well as the chambers themselves, have state-of-the-art audiovisual studios. Here, members can produce short statements to the press, interviews, and other types of programming. This allows incumbents to feed the local media, which is always looking for story material, especially on 90- or 120-minute evening newscasts.[20] Some members are regular guests on various local programs; others have their own local programs (e.g., a call-in show). Almost all produce press releases on a fairly regular basis that local news organizations print or air unedited, presenting them as news.

The link with local media outlets is important because studies show that local news organizations are rarely as confrontational as the national press.[21] When these outlets feature members in a thirty-second spot answering a few questions, the questions are rarely difficult and the answers rarely challenged. This is in part because the news organizations in question (typically the electronic media) are in need of material and want to make sure they have access in the future, so they work at not offending the member. In addition, local reporters are often less well prepared for the interview or versed in national politics in general. The result is generally favorable coverage in local media, which is especially helpful for members of the House, who mainly run on local issues.[22]

Legislative Norms

In a representative democracy, an assumption exists that there is a link between what people want and what elected officials work to accomplish. Members of Congress understand that this is what people expect. Therefore, it is not surprising that their legislative activity is geared toward working—or at least appearing to work—for the people in their district. With so many decentralized committees and subcommittees in Congress, new members have almost no trouble seeking out and receiving an assignment on a committee that deals with policy concerns important to their district. For example, if the legislator is from Washington state, he or she might seek assignment on the Merchant Marine and Fisheries Committee; if from the Midwest, on agriculture. Because the details of most policy is worked out in committees, this allows the legislator to go back to the district and claim to be doing something for the district.[23]

Another legislative norm is that a member is not required or expected to vote with his or her party if that vote will damage them electorally. Weak party discipline allows members to protect themselves if the party's position contradicts what constituents expect. Finally, most members cooperate with other members when it comes to distributive legislation. If there is "pork" (government projects that benefit a specific locale) to be spread around, everyone gets a piece to take home to the district. Finally, members will often support another member's bill with the expectation of reciprocity in the future. This reciprocity is referred to as "logrolling," and it allows members to claim credit for legislation that is popular in their home district.

Financial Advantages

Congressional elections cost a great deal of money. In 2018, all congressional elections combined cost a total of approximately $5.7 billion.[24] Unlike other incumbent advantages, financial aspects of congressional campaigns are easy to quantify, and a good deal has been written on this subject.[25] Until recently, the United States has had one of the most transparent campaign finance systems in the world.[26] This provided a detailed understanding of the financial advantage incumbents have over their challengers.

Most incumbents start their campaigns with money left over from the previous campaign. This is referred to as their "war chest," and the amount of money accumulated in them can be substantial. Press accounts, for example, have already taken notice of several congressional incumbents "building cash-on-hand advantages" before their races "heat up" heading into the 2020 election.[27] Even with cash-on-hand advantages, incumbents continue to raise enormous sums of money. They do this because reelection is never a certainty.[28]

Beyond having a head start in the money race, incumbents can raise money more easily than most challengers. This is especially true when soliciting funds from Washington-based PACs, which disproportionately give money to incumbents.[29] One reason for this is that PACs know that incumbents are more likely to win, and they want to ensure future congressional access by backing the winning candidate. Incumbents also have financial backing from congressional party campaign committees, as well as access to money from state party organizations. In addition, individual donors who give large sums of money are more likely to give to incumbents.[30] The point is that most campaign dollars go to incumbents, making it difficult for challengers to raise the resources necessary to be competitive.

Lack of Quality Challengers

Another reason why incumbents enjoy high reelection rates is the lack of quality challengers. A quality challenger is an individual who can mount a viable campaign and possesses a combination of characteristics that can convince voters that he or she is qualified to be their representative. These qualities include, but are not limited to, having previously held public office (either elective or otherwise); being a celebrity (show business, sports, etc.); or being a prominent local business, religious, or community leader. At minimum, a quality challenger usually enjoys some name recognition in the community (district or state) and has enough connections to support the fundraising efforts necessary to challenge a congressional incumbent.[31]

Most challengers in congressional elections are amateurs, or lesser-quality candidates. They lack some, or all, of the various characteristics, background, and experience mentioned earlier. Importantly, experienced politicians or prominent leaders—potential quality challengers—have enough political savvy to know that the chances of defeating an incumbent member of Congress are slim. Generally, open-seat races are more likely to attract quality candidates, leaving most incumbents to face off against relative amateurs. As previously noted, fundraising efforts by incumbents further deter quality candidates. Raising money early, as well as being active in the district, goes a long way toward deterring potential challengers. This is the so-called scare-off effect.[32] While it is clear that anything can happen in a campaign, most challengers pose little threat to incumbents.[33]

Congressional Redistricting

House district boundaries in every state are redrawn every ten years following the census. This ensures that districts within each state contain approximately equal numbers of people. Few voters know about or pay much attention to this process. Redistricting is a very contentious exercise because it almost always gives an advantage to a certain party or group.

To illustrate how districting could advantage one group over others, imagine a state with twelve equal geographic divisions (e.g., counties), with each division containing equal numbers of straight partisan voters. In other words, all voters in each geographic division vote the party line in every election. The top box in figure 10.2 represents this scenario, as well as which geographic divisions belong to which party (D = Democrat, R = Republican). Each party can claim six of these geographic divisions, meaning that support for each party is evenly split. From this state, four congressional districts, each containing roughly equal numbers of voters and three of these geographic divisions, are drawn. The examples below the "Partisan Distribution" box show three of the ways in which these districts may be drawn.

In "Districting Plan #1," Democrats and Republicans will each win in two districts. However, if district lines are drawn slightly differently, as shown in "Districting Plan #2," Republicans win in only one district, while Democrats win in three. "Districting Plan #3" gives the Republicans the advantage.[34]

Drawing district lines to maximize the electoral advantage of a group, party, or faction is known as gerrymandering. The term, first used in 1812, characterized the salamander-like redistricting plan drawn by Massachusetts Governor Elbridge Gerry. Partisan gerrymandering, or redistricting that favors a specific party, enjoys a long history in the United States. While not an exact science, since the 1990s gerrymandering has evolved into a practice

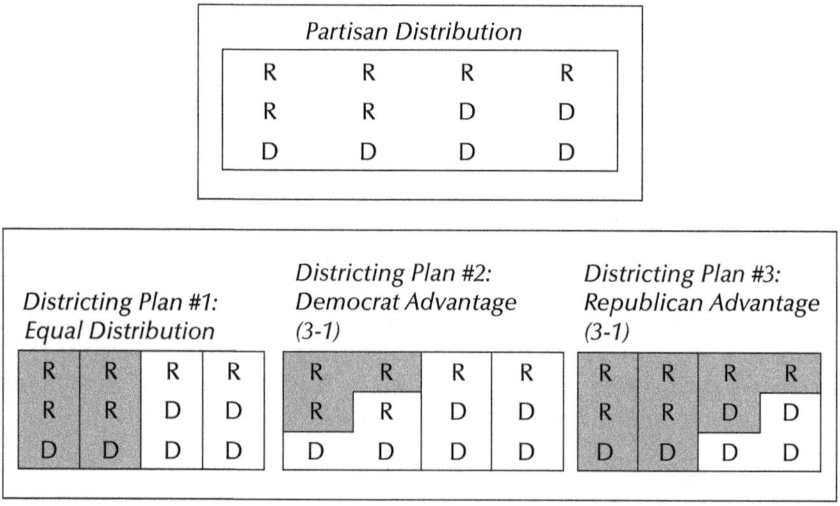

Figure 10.2   Example: Partisan Effects of Districting.
Source: Originally published by Michael D. Robbins, "Gerrymander and the Need for Redistricting Reform," October 25, 2006 (no longer available).

of incumbent-based, or "sweetheart," gerrymandering. This is largely a bipartisan effort where district lines are drawn to ensure that there is a high concentration of each party's supporters in "their" respective districts. Thus, the status quo (incumbents of each party) is protected. While some recent research suggests that the effect is minimal, many claim that incumbent-based districts lead to a decline in the number of competitive elections, at least in the House, as more districts are "packed" on a partisan basis.[35]

A "Sorting" of the Electorate

In addition to partisan congressional redistricting plans, incumbents are also helped by the fact that congressional districts are more likely to be comprised of politically like-minded individuals. In other words, many congressional districts are not very politically diverse. This makes it more likely that incumbents, already advantaged by partisan districting plans, will win.

Several works have noted that geographic divisions in the United States capture significant political differences within the electorate.[36] Perhaps the most extensive work on the politics of geography (or the "politics of place") comes from Bill Bishop's *The Big Sort*. Bishop's work shows that most counties in the United States have become increasingly partisan. According to Bishop, as Americans have clustered into like-minded communities that share the same political and cultural values, divisions across different communities have grown.[37] For example, in the nationally competitive presidential election of 1976, approximately 27 percent of the public resided in a county where either Republican Gerald Ford or Democrat Jimmy Carter won by a landslide (more than twenty percentage points). In the elections of 2004 and 2008, that percentage increased to 48 percent. By 2016, the percentage of people living in a landslide county increased even further to 60 percent.[38]

Even at the state level, landslide results have become more common. In 1976, there was an average winning margin of ten percentage points in the fifty states and the District of Columbia. This increased to fifteen percentage points in 2000 and to eighteen percentage points in 2016. Conversely, there were only seventeen states where the presidential contest was decided by ten points or less in 2016 compared to thirty-one states in 1976. Political scientist Alan Abramowitz has concluded that "the divide between the red states and blue states is deeper than at any time in the past 60 years."[39] This divide is evident within states as well. Republicans consistently capture better than 20 percent more of the vote for president than Democrats in rural areas. Put simply, Democrats hold the advantage in urban areas, Republicans in rural areas. Differences in the vote separating urban and rural areas in the 2016 election were "as stark as American politics has produced since the years just before and after 1920."[40] These aggregate patterns suggest that communities are growing more politically polarized, which in the end, typically advantages the partisan incumbent who represents the district.

Voting Behavior

To round out our discussion, we should also note something about voting behavior, or how people vote. A few aspects of voting in congressional elections are important with respect to incumbent advantages. First, the electorate usually knows the incumbent better than the challenger. While people do not always cast their votes for the better-known candidate, the converse of this is probably a fair assumption: people are less likely to vote for an unknown candidate.[41] This is especially true in midterm elections where interest and voter turnout is lower than in presidential election years. Generally, lower turnout advantages incumbents.

Another factor that favors incumbents is the party loyalty of voters. Ticket splitting, or casting one's vote for the presidential candidate of one party while voting for the congressional candidate of the other party, increased consistently throughout the middle part of the past century. This trend seems to have reversed itself. In 1972, 192 districts split their votes in this way. Only 86 did so in 2000. By 2016, just eight percent of districts voted for one party for the House and the other party for president.[42] In short, voters, who are packed into increasingly partisan-leaning districts are voting to support their party. But since recent redistricting efforts have generally protected incumbents, "their party" is more likely to be the party of the incumbent.

Finally, it should be noted that members of Congress pay special attention throughout their careers, and especially during the campaign, to the way in which they present themselves. Here, the landmark study of Richard Fenno is informative.[43] Fenno followed and observed a number of House members, concluding that they self-consciously adopted a style or persona that was compatible with the culture of their district. He labeled this their "home style." For example, a House member from rural Georgia would be hard pressed to win an election if he traveled the district in a three-piece Brooks Brothers suit. In a district like this, a candidate would likely present himself as a common member of the local community, hoping to establish a connection with the majority of voters. This example is a bit exaggerated, but according to Fenno's work, not by much. And it seems to pay off.

CONCLUSION: CAN INCUMBENTS LOSE?

Challengers clearly face uphill battles in congressional elections. However, there are some factors that make it more likely that a challenger can be competitive. First, the scare-off effect does not always work.[44] Incumbents sometimes show signs of weakness or are weakened by circumstance. This can be the result of any number of factors including unfavorable redistricting, a small war chest, press criticism, or scandal. All of these factors can make incumbents look vulnerable, attracting quality challengers to the fray.

Or, more simply, any of these factors can actually make an incumbent more vulnerable, giving challengers a better chance to win.

Second, presidential politics sometimes influence congressional elections. The two most obvious ways in which this occurs are either the "coattail" effects of a popular presidential candidate or the historic tendency for a president's party to lose seats in midterm elections. In the first case, an extremely popular presidential candidate can increase the popularity—and thus the chances for victory—of the congressional candidates in her party. This happened, for example, in 1980 when Ronald Reagan's popularity helped the Republicans win control of the Senate for the first time since 1954. Barack Obama's popularity helped many Democratic candidates in 2008. Alternatively, it is also historically the case that the president's party loses seats in the midterm elections (see table 10.5).

Some midterm elections bring greater losses than others, but in most, a fairly significant number of the president's party loses. Incumbents inevitably suffer some of these losses. In 2006, Republicans lost their majorities in both the U.S. House and Senate, in part because of their association with President George W. Bush, whose popularity gradually and steadily dropped following his reelection in 2004. Democrats, with Barack Obama in the White House, lost sixty-three seats in the House and six in the Senate in

Table 10.5 Midterm Losses for Presidential Party

Year	President (Party)	House	Senate*
1946	Franklin Roosevelt and Harry Truman (Dem.)	45	12
1950	Harry Truman (Dem.)	29	6
1954	Dwight Eisenhower (Rep.)	18	1
1958	Dwight Eisenhower (Rep.)	48	13
1962	John Kennedy (Dem.)	4	(3)
1966	Lyndon Johnson (Dem.)	47	4
1970	Richard Nixon (Rep.)	12	(2)
1974	Richard Nixon and Gerald Ford (Rep.)	48	5
1978	Jimmy Carter (Dem.)	15	3
1982	Ronald Reagan (Rep.)	26	(1)
1986	Ronald Reagan (Rep.)	5	8
1990	Gorge H. W. Bush (Rep.)	8	1
1994	Bill Clinton (Dem.)	52	8
2006	George W. Bush (Rep.)	30	6
2010	Barack Obama (Dem.)	63	6
2014	Barack Obama (Dem.)	13	9
2018	Donald Trump (Rep.)	40	(2)

Source: Gerhard Peters, "Seats in Congress Gained/Lost by the President's Party in Mid-Term Elections," *The American Presidency Project*, ed. John T. Woolley and Gerhard Peters, Santa Barbara, CA: University of California, 1999–2015, http://www.presidency.ucsb.edu/data/mid-term_elections.php.
*Numbers in parentheses were gains for the presidential party.

2010, followed by further losses in 2014. Republicans, with Donald Trump in the Oval Office, lost forty seats in 2018.

A final factor is the occasional effect of what scholars refer to as "national tides" on congressional elections. Local elections generally favor incumbents. Congressional elections are primarily local affairs, more so in the House than in the Senate. However, national political factors sometimes influence congressional elections, favoring one party over the other. This was the case, for example, in 1974, when an anti-Watergate sentiment swept the country, and the Democrats made large gains. In 1980, anti-Carter sentiment and a national recession helped produce a significant number of victories for Republicans. Anti-incumbent and anti-congressional feelings in 1992 (surrounding various congressional scandals and the Clarence Thomas hearings) helped 110 newcomers win election to Congress. Republicans won both houses of Congress for the first time in more than four decades in 1994, partly as the result of an anti-Congress and anti-Clinton mood prevailing in the country. In 1998, anti-impeachment sentiment helped the Democrats reverse historical trends and gain seats, and in 2002, national security concerns helped Republicans do the same. In all of these cases, a prevailing mood in the country overcame local concerns to help oust a significant number of incumbents.

In short, incumbents rarely lose, although challengers can sometimes capitalize on national conditions that might be in their favor. The word "campaign" was originally used to refer to military operations and adopted for political use later. To use this metaphor, challengers face an overwhelming disadvantage given that their opponents have been gearing up for battle for months, are already on the field, and have an arsenal in place.

We are not the first observers to note that congressional elections have become less competitive over the course of the last century.[45] However, many Americans do not realize or appreciate how uncompetitive congressional elections have become. While the high rate of incumbent victories might, to some degree, equate to voter satisfaction, it more likely reflects the numerous advantages that incumbents have. This has undoubtedly increased the number of uncompetitive congressional contests, which, as noted earlier, has consequences for democracy.

FURTHER READING

Fenno, Richard F., Jr. *Home Style: House Members in Their Districts*. New York, NY: Longman, 2003.

Herrnson, Paul S. *Congressional Elections: Campaigning at Home and in Washington*. 7th ed. Washington, DC: CQ Press, 2016.

Jacobson, Gary C., and Jamie L. Carson. *The Politics of Congressional Elections*. 9th ed. Lanham, MD: Rowman & Littlefield, 2016.

Mayhew, David R. *Congress: The Electoral Connection*. New Haven, CT: Yale University, 1974.

11

The American People Have Spoken . . . or Have They?

The Myth of the Presidential Mandate

IN THE LATE HOURS OF November 8, 2016, the nation's major news networks announced that Republican presidential candidate Donald Trump had defeated his Democratic opponent, Hillary Clinton, to win the presidency. Almost immediately afterward, journalists and pundits from around the nation began to weigh in on a familiar question: Did the results of the election reflect a mandate from the American people? Trump supporters were quick to claim that this was precisely what his victory signified. Former New York City Mayor Rudy Giuliani, for example, claimed that Trump "definitely" had a mandate from the American people.[1]

Donald Trump's signature campaign issue in 2016 was the wall he proposed building along the U.S.–Mexico border. However, rather than focus on this, supporters claimed that his victory represented voters' rejection of politics as usual. Spokesperson Kellyanne Conway claimed that the president-elect's election was, in effect, "a repudiation of some of the things we've had."[2] House Speaker Paul Ryan went further, suggesting that Trump had "a clear mandate, and mission . . . to make America great again."[3]

In 2012, progressive liberal writers and politicians were no less willing to make similar claims about President Barack Obama's victory over Mitt Romney. Joan Walsh of *Salon*, for example, declared, "President Obama's reelection represents a victory for the Democratic ideal of activist government and a *mandate* for more of it."[4] David Weigel of *Slate* followed just a few hours later with an article bearing the headline, "Yes, There Is a Mandate for Higher Taxes."[5]

Presidential elections are not the only ones about which we hear politicians and others claiming to have won a mandate. In midterm elections, a decisive victory for one party or the other also gives rise to talk of a mandate. Republican congressional leaders made such claims following their sweeping midterm election wins in 1994, 2010, and 2014, while Democratic congressional leaders made similar claims following their landslide victories in 2006 and 2018.

Yet despite the frequency of these claims, the overwhelming consensus among political scientists is that elections, even ones that produce a landslide winner, rarely if ever reflect a strong and uniform desire from the American public for sweeping policy change. Instead, research shows rather clearly that most people base their voting calculation on a variety of different factors. Issues and policies are just one of many considerations. Several other complications, discussed later in this chapter, also exist that make it exceptionally difficult to connect election outcomes to voters' policy preferences.

In fact, there is ample anecdotal evidence to illustrate how the frequent misinterpretation of a "mandate" has led to failed policy proposals, from Bill Clinton's efforts to reform the health-care system to George W. Bush's proposal to amend the Social Security Act. Numerous other examples exist, all of which reinforce the larger point of this chapter: mandates are almost always illusionary. In this chapter, we review the prevalence of the mandate claim in more detail and then define in a more concrete fashion what a mandate entails. We then discuss why genuine mandates are much less common than the claims themselves. Finally, we conclude the chapter with an explanation for why politicians and others so often claim to have won a mandate in spite of evidence that shows elections so rarely produce them.

THE PREVALENCE OF THE MANDATE CLAIM

Mandate claims have a long history, dating back as far as the presidency of Andrew Jackson.[6] Before Jackson, mandate claims from victorious presidential candidates were virtually nonexistent because they were inconsistent with early conceptions of presidential power and influence. The prevailing thought in the late eighteenth and early nineteenth centuries was that the executive branch was secondary to Congress when it came to domestic policymaking.[7]

But Jackson, who served as the nation's chief executive from 1829 to 1837, argued that because the president of the United States was the only public figure to run in a nationwide election, a victory in this contest carried special meaning. The winning presidential candidate had won not only the right to serve as president of the United States but could also rightfully claim to be the one true representative of the people nationwide. Members of Congress, after all, represented only the local interests of their constituents. The policies that winning presidential candidates promised during the election therefore best reflected the general will, allowing the president to command a dominant role in policymaking. Such an interpretation allowed Jackson to justify actions he undertook as president to eliminate the Second Bank of the United States. In Jackson's words, "the President is the direct representative of the American people, but the Secretaries are not."[8]

In the years following Jackson's presidency, several other presidents made similar claims. President James Polk remarked that the president represented "the whole people of the United States."[9] Woodrow Wilson not only agreed but further argued that the president, as the only representative of the whole nation, held a special place in the government that entitled the chief executive to take a dominant role over Congress in policymaking.[10] Likewise, Franklin Roosevelt, following his victory over Herbert Hoover in 1932, claimed his election to the presidency represented a "mandate for direct, vigorous action."[11]

Two decades after Roosevelt's assertion, President Dwight Eisenhower referenced the "summons to governmental responsibility issued by the American people" following his victory to the White House.[12] In 1980, Vice President-Elect George H. W. Bush triumphantly announced that President-Elect Ronald Reagan and he had won a "mandate for change."[13] Reporting on Reagan's inauguration in 1981, Hedrick Smith of *The New York Times* observed, "some Republicans believe an irresistible conservative tide has swept the nation . . . they say, the mood of the country and Congress has shifted irreversibly to the right."[14]

Presidential mandate claims have been just as frequent in recent years. One study that systematically examined President George W. Bush's communications in early 2005 reported that nearly one-quarter of his public statements included mandate claims.[15] In 2012, President Obama also could not resist the temptation to claim a mandate after his reelection. In the days following his victory, the president remarked that his win represented a mandate to increase taxes on the wealthiest Americans to help reduce the federal deficit, claiming this was "a central question of the election."[16] Obama then added that it was time for Congress to get behind his plan because it "reflect[ed] the will of the American people."[17]

Not surprisingly, presidents who are landslide winners make common use of mandate rhetoric. Perhaps more interesting, however, is that presidents who win narrow victories use mandate rhetoric almost as frequently. For instance, the frequency of mandate rhetoric by Franklin Roosevelt following his decisive win over Alf Landon in 1936 was roughly the same as that used by Jimmy Carter following his razor-thin victory over Gerald Ford in 1976.[18]

Numerous examples also exist of members of Congress and their supporters claiming a mandate after a convincing victory in midterm elections. The 1994 congressional elections shifted control of both the U.S. House and U.S. Senate from the Democratic Party to the Republican Party for the first time in four decades. Afterward, House Speaker Newt Gingrich quickly declared a "mandate" for conservative principles and for the Republican Party's "Contract with America," which outlined a series of policies that Republican candidates promised to support if elected.[19] Like Gingrich, some reporters also saw the election as signifying a major change in policy direction. Robert Samuelson of *The Washington Post* observed, "In the mid-1960s, Congress enacted a major tax cut, approved the Civil Rights Act of 1964, and created Medicare and Medicaid. Government was to be society's problem solver. The new Congress is best seen as ending this era."[20]

A little more than a decade later in 2006, the Republicans lost their House majority in a landslide to Democrats. Incoming speaker Nancy Pelosi sounded the familiar mandate theme. In a victory speech to supporters she commented, "tonight is a great victory for the American people. Today the American people voted for change, and they voted for Democrats to take our country in a new direction."[21] Just four years later, Republicans reversed the tide and regained control of the U.S. House in an election that saw the party net a remarkable sixty-three seats. The incoming Republican leadership, led by John Boehner and Eric Cantor, declared in their victory celebration that Republicans had won a "mandate" to cut the size of government.[22]

In 2014, congressional Republicans expanded their majority in the U.S. House and took control of the U.S. Senate for the first time in eight years. Conservative media commentators wasted no time in declaring that the election represented a public repudiation of President Obama's policies. Andrew McCarthy of the *National Review* wrote, "November was all about Obama's liberty-strangling, crony-coddling, financially reckless agenda. Voters emphatically defeated these policies. The American people want them stopped. That is what they sent Republicans to Washington to do. That is the mandate from the midterms."[23] Not to be outdone, radio host Rush Limbaugh remarked that the Republicans' 2014 success marked "one of the most important, biggest mandates [to stop a president's policies] I can recall a party ever having."[24]

More recently, those on the left of the political spectrum interpreted landslide victories by the Democrats in the House of Representatives in 2018 as a repudiation of President Trump himself, his policies, and his policy proposals. One writer dramatically claimed that "a people's wave" had delivered a "clear rebuke of Trump" and gave the party a "mandate to chart [a] bold progressive course."[25] Long-term House member Maxine Waters (D-CA) similarly claimed a "mandate from the American public."[26] Ironically, by December, the president's border wall proposal had helped trigger a partial government shutdown.

All of these examples serve to illustrate the fact that mandate claims have been ubiquitous in election after election for nearly two centuries. But what exactly is a mandate? We turn to that question next.

DEFINING A MANDATE

While the use of the term "mandate" has a long history, not everyone agrees on its meaning. To President Kennedy, a mandate required no more than a simple victory on Election Day. Kennedy's speechwriter, Theodore Sorensen, recounted that the former president saw his own narrow victory over Richard Nixon in 1960 as a mandate. According to Sorensen, Kennedy explained that every election "has a winner and a loser" and that "a margin of only one vote would still be a mandate."[27]

Yet Kennedy's definition would defy the conventional understanding of the word's meaning. Most political scientists and political pundits usually understand a mandate as requiring a relatively large electoral victory by a presidential candidate and even his party in Congress.[28] In 2012, for instance, Barack Obama's reelection failed to sweep his party back into control of the U.S. House of Representatives. House Speaker John Boehner, a Republican, made clear that this tempered any claims of a mandate by the president. Commenting a few days before Election Night, Boehner commented to a reporter, "Listen, our majority is going to get reelected. We'll have as much of a mandate as he [President Obama] will."[29]

Some argue further that a mandate requires more than simply a large electoral victory for the entire party, but an *unexpectedly* large electoral victory.[30] By exceeding expectations, the winning candidate and party can claim that the public has "sent a message." To the winners, this message has inescapable policy implications, as campaign promises ultimately become a central part of the legislative agenda for governing.

Another common element in defining a mandate is that the winning candidates and their party must provide a clear and unified set of policy proposals.[31] In a midterm election, a mandate requires a "nationalized" election in which congressional candidates do not run on their own individualized set of local issues, but instead make the national party's legislative agenda central to their campaigns. The Republicans' "Contract with America" in 1994 was a good example of this. For presidential candidates, a policy mandate requires that they offer specific legislative proposals rather than campaigning on more general principles for governing. When this occurs, the victors can claim that the election results reflect, at least in some measure, popular support for their policy proposals. As one team of political scientists concluded, "no election can be a mandate for policy change without a clear policy message."[32] In fact, the policy message in question must also be unique, and pledge a new and different policy direction, such as Ronald Reagan's pledge in 1980 to increase defense spending significantly and to reduce the size of the federal government.

In addition to candidates offering a clear and unified set of policy proposals during the election, a mandate further requires that voters possess a minimum of knowledge in certain areas.[33] Most notably, voters must be familiar with the major political issues central to the election to be able to form opinions about the policies that the candidates and parties propose. Voters must also possess accurate knowledge of where the candidates and the parties stand on those issues. If voters are largely ignorant of the major issues concerning public policy or if they struggle to connect candidates and parties to their respective policy proposals, election outcomes become a very poor instrument to gauge public support for the policy initiatives of the winning candidates and their party.

Not only must the public be informed about the issues, and the candidates' and parties' positions on these issues, they must also cast their vote on the basis of these issues and policies.[34] An electorate focused on the personal characteristics of the candidates, such as the high marks for honesty that Jimmy Carter received from the public in the 1976 presidential election[35] (which came two years after Richard Nixon's resignation for the Watergate scandal), would fail to qualify as an election that reflected a policy mandate. Even when issues are the central concern of voters, candidates must do more than simply offer policy proposals. Candidates need to propose policies that a large segment of the public desires for a mandate to exist.[36] If voter turnout is low, this can complicate claims of a mandate because it becomes more difficult to know if the policy preferences of voters are consistent with the policy preferences of nonvoters.

This matter is of particular relevance in midterm elections when voter turnout is considerably lower than in presidential elections. The opinions of nonvoters in midterm elections, who may become voters in the presidential election two years later, can quickly become relevant and problematic to the victorious party if their policy proposals are unpopular with this segment of the electorate.

Finally, a policy mandate requires that public opinion be stable on the issues and the policies that candidates and parties campaign on during the election.[37] If public opinion is fleeting, voters' support at election time for a set of policy proposals can quickly dissipate when the time comes for the winning candidates and party to govern. The absence of stable opinion thereby complicates any claims by the president or the party of the congressional majority of a policy mandate.

A number of conditions therefore must be met in order for a president or the majority party in Congress to make credible claims of a mandate for the adoption of sweeping policy changes. To summarize, these conditions would include the following:

- A large electoral victory, especially if unexpectedly large.
- The winners (candidates and/or party) have provided a clear and unified set of policy proposals.
- Voters possess enough knowledge about the political issues central to the election, and also know where the candidates and the parties stand on those issues.
- Voters must cast their vote on the basis of these issues.
- Public opinion on the issue(s) must be somewhat stable.
- Voter turnout in the election must be relatively high.

Taken together, this set of conditions is a fairly high hurdle to clear before a legitimate mandate can be claimed.

WHY MANDATE CLAIMS ARE USUALLY WRONG

Despite frequent claims of a mandate by politicians, pundits, and political commentators, few elections ever genuinely produce them. The fact is that election results are only rarely expressions of voter preferences on issues and public policies. Many voters do *not* begin their decision-making process by examining the issues first and then aligning themselves with the candidate who shares their positions on those issues. Instead, scholarship suggests that the process of deciding for whom to vote works quite differently.[38]

Most voters look first to the most basic of cues, a candidate's party affiliation.[39] From there, voters consider a range of other criteria that include retrospective evaluations of the performance of the party in power to the legislative record of the candidates to the personal attributes of those running for office.[40] The issue positions of the candidates are a consideration for some voters, but research on voting behavior shows that the casual direction in this case may run in reverse. In other words, rather than a voter considering their issue positions and then lining this information up with the candidate who most shares their views on the issues, voters more commonly select the candidate and then simply adopt the issue positions of their preferred candidate.[41]

The lack of a firm connection to issues for many voters in most elections severely complicates interpretations of what policies the public wants after an election, even when there is a landslide winner. This is made all the more difficult in a country such as the United States, which has a large and heterogeneous population. In 1984, for example, Ronald Reagan soundly defeated his Democratic opponent, Walter Mondale, by an eighteen-point margin in the popular vote, 59 to 41 percent. However, exit polls showed voters were more likely to agree with Mondale on a host of major issues ranging from defense spending to environmental protection to civil rights.[42] Quite obviously, these issues were not paramount to many voters in their voting decision.

In addition, presidential candidates often express positions on a wide range of policies. In the case of an issue-oriented voter, agreement on one or even many issues with a candidate does not necessarily translate into support for all of the candidate's issue positions. A voter, for instance, who is strongly opposed to illegal immigration, may decide to vote for Donald Trump, based on that issue alone. Yet, that same voter might also disagree sharply with Trump's positions on abortion and gay marriage. A vote for a presidential candidate may therefore translate into public support on some issues, but not on others.

In midterm elections, the process is even more difficult to disentangle. Congressional candidates in the same party often do not run on the same set of issues or agree on the policies of how best to address those issues. This is especially common in a candidate-centered system like the one in the United States, in which candidates rather than political parties take on the dominant responsibilities associated with waging a campaign for public office.[43] For example, local preferences might dictate that a Southern Democrat oppose gun control policy; however, a Northeastern Democrat might take the opposite position and support gun control legislation given the policy's popularity in that candidate's home state or district. Even in cases like the 1994 election, when congressional Republicans lined up nationally behind their "Contract with America," polls still showed only limited public knowledge of many of the policies outlined in it.[44] Given these difficulties, election outcomes correctly have been called a very "blunt instrument" for which to measure public support on issues and policies.[45]

Of course, the availability of exit poll data offers some improved ability to understand whether an issue or set of issues dominated a particular election. Yet even exit poll results must be read and interpreted carefully to determine whether a mandate exists, and if so, for what policies. A 2012 exit poll showed, for example, that economic issues were the top priority of voters (59%) and that 70 percent of Obama voters agreed with the president's position that income tax rates should be increased on those earning $250,000 a year or more. A superficial analysis of those figures might suggest to some that Obama won a mandate for higher taxes on the wealthy. But a deeper analysis raises questions about that conclusion. For starters, three in ten Obama supporters disagreed with the president on his position. When combined with those who supported Obama's opponent, Mitt Romney, and who also disagreed with a policy for higher taxes on the wealthy, overall support for Obama's tax plan comes in at 47 percent compared to the 48 percent who opposed it (with the remainder undecided).[46] This is hardly a result that appears to reflect a strong public consensus.

Republican claims that Trump's victory was a clear mandate for tougher immigration policies or support for an expanded border wall that would separate the United States and Mexico were even more problematic. For example, 2016 exit polls suggested that a full 71 percent of voters supported the idea that illegal immigrants should be given a clear path to citizenship, while only 25 percent were in favor of immediate deportation. And while 86 percent of those who voted for Trump favored building the wall, only 41 percent of all voters did so, as opposed to the 54 percent of voters who were against such a policy.[47] These numbers fall well short of a mandate.

Indeed, more often than not on the issues of most importance and controversy, exit polls fail to show any clear public consensus on matters of public policy. One reason for this is that recent presidential elections have been rather competitive. Since 2000, the largest difference in the popular vote in a presidential election was a seven-point advantage for Barack Obama over John McCain in 2008. Prior to 2000, the winning presidential candidate registered an advantage of more than seven points in five of six elections from 1980 to 1996. With such a divided electorate in recent elections, interpreting and claiming a genuine mandate is a daunting task.

Taken together, a mandate claim in an election is usually just that—a claim. The many conditions necessary for a genuine mandate rarely, if ever, occur. Even during landslide elections, public opinion almost never unifies around a single issue or set of issues. This raises a final question: If elections so rarely produce mandates, why are mandate claims so common?

REASONS FOR CLAIMING A MANDATE

The main reason for the prevalence of mandate claims is that they can serve as a potentially useful part of a larger legislative strategy for the president and congressional leaders. Both rightfully understand that a successful legislative strategy involves shaping press coverage and public opinion. Creating the perception and promoting the idea of an electoral mandate can have obvious benefits.

For starters, the perception of a mandate provides the winning president or majority party in Congress with enhanced credibility for their legislative proposals. If the policies of the president or the majority party in Congress are consistent with the wishes of the American people, as mandates presume, then those who oppose the policies are not merely offering respectful dissent, but are acting contrary to the public will. If that perception takes hold, opposition itself becomes more challenging because the losing side does not want to be tagged as being "out of touch" with the

American people. Moreover, in the immediate aftermath of the election, the party on the losing side must reflect on why its candidates fared poorly in the election. In this environment, the perception of a mandate takes on added significance as the minority party must be concerned with the risk of losing even more electoral support in the next election for opposing policies that have genuine popular backing. Because reelection concerns are always at the forefront of the strategic calculus of most elected officials, the perception of a mandate can dampen opposition, empowering the winners of the election to exploit these circumstances by gaining a window of opportunity to enact their policies more easily.[48]

Mandate claims further shape political discourse. In the election of 1980, Ronald Reagan's convincing victory over Jimmy Carter failed to show in exit polls that there was a genuine change in the public's policy attitudes.[49] Nonetheless, widespread claims of a Reagan mandate (with some even calling Reagan's victory a "revolution") appears to have influenced the national policy discussion, shifting it from the question of how much the federal government would *spend* on social programs to how much the federal government would *cut* on social programs.[50] Nearly a half century earlier, Franklin Roosevelt's victory over Herbert Hoover in 1932, and the resulting belief that he had won a mandate, shifted national political discussion away from whether the federal government should act to combat the Great Depression to how much involvement the federal government should have in that regard.[51] Such a shift in the national political discourse presents obvious advantages for the president or majority party in Congress. Indeed, in the case of Roosevelt's first term in office, the belief in a Roosevelt mandate seems to have registered with legislators. In 1933, Congress passed all fifteen of Roosevelt's major legislative proposals, with several Republicans even crossing party lines in support.[52]

Mandate claims can also be a function of the imperfect and incomplete information that often comes out of an election campaign.[53] The outcome itself, as previously noted, can have a multitude of potential causes. This leaves the winning presidential candidate and the majority party in Congress with the task of trying to figure out what those causes were and if those causes carried with them popular support for policies promised on the campaign trail. An obvious way to begin to discern this is for the winning side to float the claim of a mandate—much like a trial balloon—and then gauge public response afterward. The public's reaction to any mandate claims, whether favorable or unfavorable, provides helpful information to the president and majority party in Congress about how to pursue a legislative strategy going forward. A favorable reaction, for instance, might indicate a larger ideological change in the electorate, one conducive to an aggressive legislative strategy. A negative reaction might suggest that the election outcome was simply the result of idiosyncratic factors. In this case, a more cautious legislative strategy would make sense. In short, mandate claims can help a president and congressional leaders acquire needed information in an environment often dominated by uncertainty concerning the message the public has sent in an election.

Finally, claims of a mandate from presidents may reflect a need for those holding the office to assert their authority.[54] In a political period dominated by partisan polarization in Congress, the prestige and respect for the office of the president has declined in recent years.[55] With less informal power than in the past, recent presidents, dealing with a polarized Congress, have been more inclined to use mandate rhetoric as a means to compensate for these changes in the institutional environment. This development and the other aforementioned explanations all provide valuable incentives for elected officials to claim a mandate, even when a legitimate one may not exist.

CONCLUSION

Two seemingly paradoxical occurrences are a common part of the modern postelection environment: (1) the leaders and supporters of the winning party will claim an electoral mandate, even though (2) the conditions necessary for a legitimate mandate are rarely present. As this chapter discussed, the persistent claims of electoral mandates are the product of numerous incentives that exist for the president and congressional leaders to make such claims. The persistence of such rhetoric, however vacuous, can nonetheless often have significant consequences when presidents and congressional leaders begin to believe their own mandate claims.

Presidents, in particular, have a long history of "over-reach."[56] Indeed, all three of our most recent past presidents can attest to this. Bill Clinton witnessed the loss of the Democratic Party's majority status in the U.S. House and U.S. Senate by the Newt Gingrich–led Republicans in the 1994 election after public backlash to Clinton's efforts to reform the health-care system. Early in his second term as president, George W. Bush, believing he had a mandate, pushed to reform Social Security through a partial privatization plan. Even with Republican majorities in the House and Senate, those efforts quickly fell flat as public opinion polls showed little support for Bush's initiative.

Barack Obama interpreted his 2008 victory as a mandate for "fundamental change"[57] to reform the nation's health-care system. Despite his comfortable election victory and the fact that he was able to see his health-care reform legislation become law, public opinion polls showed the new law was unpopular with the public.[58] In fact what ultimately became known as "Obamacare" likely contributed to the Democratic Party's historic losses in the 2010 election.[59]

In 2016, Donald Trump and supporters claimed a broad mandate. One analyst opined, "Trump was handed a considerable mandate from a vast swath of America on Tuesday. They clearly want real change in the national government."[60] Kellyanne Conway claimed that Trump had a mandate "to carry out the will of the people on issues ranging from Obamacare to national security."[61] But such vague assertions do not easily translate into policy change. We have seen, for example, that most Americans do not support President Trump's signature proposal to build an expanded border wall.[62]

Political scientists largely agree that mandate claims have little merit. While such claims are likely to continue, political scientist Robert Dahl has urged us to ignore them. Writing several decades ago, he concluded, "Perhaps the most we can hope for is that commentators on public affairs in the media and in academic pursuits will dismiss claims to a mandate with the scorn they usually deserve."[63] This chapter echoes Dahl's sentiment that "no elected leader, including the president, is uniquely privileged to say what an election means."[64]

The good news is that mandates, whether real or not, are unnecessary for a democracy to function. Elections do not have to "mean" anything. The simple fact that a transition of power has occurred with ballots rather than bullets (i.e., nonviolently) should be cause enough for celebration.

FURTHER READING

Azari, Julia R. *Delivering the People's Message: The Changing Politics of the Presidential Mandate*. Ithaca, NY: Cornell University Press, 2014.

Conley, Patricia Heidotting. *Presidential Mandates: How Elections Shape the National Agenda*. Chicago, IL: University of Chicago Press, 2001.

Grossback, Lawrence J., David A. M. Peterson, and James A. Stimson. 2006. *Mandate Politics*. New York, NY: Cambridge University Press.

Notes

PREFACE

1. Paul F. Boller Jr., *Presidential Campaigns: From George Washington to George W. Bush* (New York, NY: Oxford University Press, 2004).

CHAPTER 1

1. We wish to acknowledge the contributions to this chapter made by Bruce Keith et al., *The Myth of the Independent Voter* (Berkeley, CA: University of California Press, 1992), and the contributors to the volume. William G. Mayer, ed., *The Swing Voter in American Politics* (Washington, DC: Brookings Institution, 2008).

2. Henry Olsen, "Tipping the Scales: How Small Groups in Each Party May Outweigh the Rest in the 2018 Midterm Elections," Voter Study Group, August 2018, https://www.voterstudygroup.org/publication/tipping-the-scales. See also Linda Killian, "Yes, Independent Swing Voters Are Real. And May Decide Who Wins Elections," *The Daily Beast*, updated April 14, 2017, http://www.thedailyb east.com/articles/2014/11/03/how-swing-voters-keep-washington-divided.html.

3. See for example, Linda Killian, *The Swing Vote: The Untapped Power of Independents* (New York: St. Martin's Press, 2011); Marcia Ford, *We the Purple: Faith, Politics, and the Independent Voter* (Colorado Springs, CO: Tyndale House, 2008); and Mark Satin, *Radical Middle: The Politics We Need Now* (Boulder, CO: Westview Press, 2004).

4. For recent examples, see Michelle Diggles, "Unaffiliated: The Rise of Independents from 2008 to 2016," *Third Way*, July 5, 2016, https://www.thirdway .org/memo/unaffiliated-the-rise-of-independents-from-2008-to-2016; Renata Sago, Ben Markus, and Jude Joffe-Block, "Sick of Political Parties, Unaffiliated Voters are Changing Politics," *NPR*, February 28, 2016, https://www.npr.org/2016/02/28 /467961962/sick-of-political-parties-unaffiliated-voters-are-changing-politics.

5. Steven Shepard, "Could Undecided Voters Swing the Election?" *Politico*, August 29, 2016, https://www.politico.com/story/2016/08/undecided-voters-clin ton-trump-sanders-227456; J. T. Young, "Winning the 2016 Election Means

Winning Independents," *Forbes*, April 27, 2015, https://www.forbes.com/sites/r ealspin/2015/04/27/2016-election-a-partisan-fight-for-nonpartisan-voters/#49a8f9 e30102.

6. CNN Politics, "Exit Polls," *CNN.Com*, updated November 23, 2016, https ://www.cnn.com/election/2016/results/exit-polls.

7. Kate Dailey, "The American Independent: A Voter on the Rise," *BBC News*, January 11, 2012, http://www.bbc.com/news/magazine-16480070; "Pew Poll Notes Rise in Independent Voters," *NPR*, May 21, 2009, http://www.npr.org/templates/s tory/story.php?storyId=104406480; John P. Avlon, "Independent Voters Burgeon-ing," *New York Sun*, April 28, 2006, www.nysun.com/article/31852; Rhodes Cook, "Moving On: More Voters Are Steering Away from Party Labels," *Washington Post*, June 27, 2004, B1.

8. George C. Edwards III, Martin P. Wattenberg, and Robert L. Lineberry, *Government in America: People, Politics, and Policy, Study Edition, Brief Version* (New York, NY: Longman, 2002), emphasis in original. Among others, see also "The Election: Turbulence and Tranquility," in *The Elections of 1996*, ed. Michael Nelson (Washington, DC: CQ Press, 1997), 63–64.

9. David Broder, *The Party's Over: The Failure of Politics in America* (New York, NY: Harper, 1972).

10. Paul Allen Beck and Marjorie Random Hershey, *Party Politics in America*, 9th ed. (New York, NY: Longman, 2001), 118. To be fair, some parties', cam-paigns', and elections' texts have not been taken with the notion of growing numbers of independents. See, for example, Nelson Polsby and Aaron Wildavsky, *Presidential Elections*, 10th ed. (Chatham, NJ: Chatham House, 2000), 18; William J. Keefe and Marc J. Hetherington, *Parties, Politics, and Public Policy in America*, 9th ed. (Washington, DC: CQ Press, 2003), 173–76.

11. Jeffrey M. Jones, "Americans Continue to Embrace Political Independence," *Gallup*, January 7, 2019, https://news.gallup.com/poll/245801/americans-continue-embrace-political-independence.aspx.

12. See Russell J. Dalton, *The Apartisan American: Dealignment and the Trans-formation of Electoral Politics* (Thousand Oaks, CA: CQ Press, 2013); and Russell J. Dalton, *Citizen Politics: Public Opinion and Political Parties in Advanced Indus-trial Democracies*, 3rd ed. (New York, NY: Chatham House, 2002), 183–86.

13. For the classic formulation of this theory, see Martin P. Wattenberg, *The Decline of American Political Parties, 1952–1996* (Cambridge, MA: Harvard Uni-versity Press, 1998); and Dalton, *The Apartisan American*.

14. See "The Origins of ANES," www.electionstudies.org/overview/origins.htm.

15. See "About ANES, 2006–2009," www.electionstudies.org/overview/overvie w.htm.

16. For those inclined to investigate further, this question is variable VCF0301 in the 2004 NES Cumulative Data File data set. See "Party Identification 7-Point Scale 1952–2004," www.electionstudies.org/nesguide/toptable/tab2a_1.htm.

17. Angus Campbell, Gerald Gurin, and Warren E. Miller, *The Voter Decides* (Evanston, IL: Row, Peterson, 1954); Angus Campbell, Philip E. Converse, War-ren E. Miller, and Donald E. Stokes, *The American Voter* (New York, NY: Wiley, 1960).

18. Anthony Downs, *An Economic Theory of Democracy* (New York, NY: Harper, 1957), suggested that citizens select candidates or parties based on proximity to their own preferences. V. O. Key Jr., *The Responsible Electorate: Rationality in Presidential Voting 1936–1960* (Cambridge, MA: Belknap, 1966), argued that voters are more rational than *The American Voter* suggests. Samuel L. Popkin, *The Reasoning Voter: Communication and Persuasion in Presidential Campaigns* (Chicago, IL: University of Chicago Press, 1991), updates Key's theory with particular attention to the effects of the media. Morris P. Fiorina argued in *Retrospective Voting in American National Elections* (New Haven, CT: Yale University Press, 1981) that citizens base their voting choices on the past performance of politicians and parties.

19. See Paul Allen Beck, "A Socialization Theory of Partisan Realignment," in *The Politics of Future Citizens*, ed. Richard G. Niemi (San Francisco, CA: Jossey-Bass, 1974); Philip E. Converse, *The Dynamics of Party Support: Cohort-Analyzing Party Identification* (Beverly Hills, CA: Sage, 1976); Paul R. Abramson, "Developing Party Identification: A Further Examination of Life-Cycle, Generational, and Period Effects," *American Journal of Political Science* 23 (1979): 78–96; and Paul Allen Beck and M. Kent Jennings, "Family Traditions, Political Periods, and the Development of Partisan Orientations," *Journal of Politics* 53 (1991): 742–63.

20. Barry C. Burden and Casey A. Klofstad, "Affect and Cognition in Party Identification," *Political Psychology* 26 (2005): 869–86.

21. Martin P. Wattenberg, "Turnout Decline in the U.S. and Other Advanced Industrial Democracies," *Center for the Study of Democracy* (1998), www.democ.uci.edu/publications/papersseriespre2001/marty.html.

22. David Shribman, "Hunting The Elusive Swing Vote," *Globe and Mail*, September 6, 2008, A23.

23. Carl M. Cannon and Carol Kaufmann, "Meet the 2008 Supervoters," *ReadersDigest.com*, www.rd.com/your-america-inspiring-people-and-stories/2008-swing-voters-at-the-ballots--election-/article98943.html.

24. Al From and Victoria Lynch, "Who Are the Swing Voters? Key Groups That Decide National Elections," Democratic Leadership Council Political Study, September 2008, www.dlc.org/print.cfm?contentid=254754.

25. Chris Wilson, "Are You a Swing Voter? A Slate Interactive Calculator," Slate.com, October 27, 2008, www.slate.com/id/2203144.

26. Doug Sosnik, "Swing Voters Hold the Key to 2020. Here's Who They Are," *Washington Post*, June 18, 2019, https://www.washingtonpost.com/opinions/2019/06/18/swing-voters-hold-key-heres-who-they-are/.

27. Daron R. Shaw, "Swing Voting and U.S. Presidential Elections," in *The Swing Voter in American Politics*, ed. William G. Mayer (Washington, DC: Brookings Institution, 2008), 77.

28. Mayer, *The Swing Voter*.

29. For a summary of several different fad categorizations of swing voters, see Christopher Beam, "One-Armed Vegetarian Live-In Boyfriends: The Quest for This Year's Sexy Swing Demographic," *Slate*, July 16, 2008, http://www.slate.com/articles/news_and_politics/politics/2008/07/onearmed_vegetarian_livein_boyfriends.html.

30. Shaw, "Swing Voting," 77.

31. Quoted in William G. Mayer and Ruy Teixeira, "Conclusion: The State of the Discussion," in *The Swing Voter in American Politics*, ed. William G. Mayer (Washington, DC: Brookings Institution, 2008), 134.

32. Philip Converse, "Information Flow and the Stability of Partisan Attitudes," *Public Opinion* Quarterly 26 (1962): 578–99.

33. Key Jr., *The Responsible Electorate*.

34. Rasmussen Reports, "Election 2016: White House Watch," n.d., http://www .rasmussenreports.com/public_content/politics/questions/pt_survey_questions/octo ber_2016/questions_election_2016_white_house_watch. See also Jeffrey M. Jones, "Swing Voters in the Gallup Poll, 1944 to 2004," in *The Swing Voter in American Politics*, ed. William G. Mayer (Washington, DC: Brookings Institution, 2008), 35.

35. Mayer, *The Swing Voter*.

36. See Adam Clymer and Ken Winneg, "Swing Voters? Hah! The Not Very 'Persuadables' and the Not Really 'Undecideds' in 2004," in *The Swing Voter in American Politics*, ed. William G. Mayer (Washington, DC: Brookings Institution, 2008) for Annenberg's question wording.

37. In both of these cases the identification of swing voters was made by using what are known in the NES data set as candidate "thermometer" scores, which measure how warmly (positively) an individual feels toward candidates. See William G. Mayer, "What Exactly Is a Swing Voter? Definition and Measurement," in *The Swing Voter in American Politics*, ed. William G. Mayer (Washington, DC: Brookings Institution, 2008); James Campbell, "Do Swing Voters Swing Elections?" in *The Swing Voter in American Politics*, ed. William G. Mayer (Washington, DC: Brookings Institution, 2008).

38. Shaw, "Swing Voting."

39. Clymer and Winneg, "Swing Voters?"; Michael Dimock, April Clark, and Juliana Menasce Horowitz, "Campaign Dynamics and the Swing Vote in the 2004 Election," in *The Swing Voter in American Politics*, ed. William G. Mayer (Washington, DC: Brookings Institution, 2008); Jones, "Swing Voters in the Gallup Poll."

40. Clymer and Winneg, "Swing Voters?"; see Andrew Gelman, Sharad Goe, Douglas Rivers, and David Rothschild, "The Mythical Swing Voter," *Quarterly Journal of Political Science* 11 (2016): 103–30, for a more recent analysis.

41. Dimock et al., "Campaign Dynamics and the Swing Vote"; Jones, "Swing Voters in the Gallup Poll"; Campbell, "Do Swing Voters Swing Elections?"

42. Shaw, "Swing Voting."

43. Dimock et al., "Campaign Dynamics and the Swing Vote"; Jones, "Swing Voters in the Gallup Poll."

44. Campbell, "Do Swing Voters Swing Elections?"

45. Robert J. Dinkin, *Campaigning in America: A History of Election Practices* (New York, NY: Greenwood, 1989), 74.

46. Allan Peskin, *Garfield* (Kent, OH: Kent State University Press, 1978), 504.

47. Paul R. Abramson, John H. Aldrich, and David W. Rohde, *Change and Continuity in the 2004 Elections* (Washington, DC: CQ Press, 2006), 100–1.

48. Costas Panagopoulos, *Political Campaigns: Concepts, Context, and Consequences* (New York, NY: Oxford University, 2017), 152.

49. Peter L. Francia, *The Future of Organized Labor in American Politics* (New York, NY: Columbia University Press, 2006).

50. Evan Thomas, *Election 2004: How Bush Won and What You Can Expect in the Future* (New York, NY: Public Affairs, 2004), 168.

51. Stephen J. Wayne, *The Road to the White House 2004: The Politics of Presidential Elections* (Belmont, CA: Wadsworth, 2004), 216–217.

52. Wayne, *Road to the White House.*

53. William Saletan, "Conclusion," in *Divided States of America: The Slash and Burn Politics of the 2004 Presidential Election*, ed. Larry J. Sabato (New York, NY: Longman, 2006), 269–78.

54. Saletan, "Conclusion."

55. Alec MacGillis, "Obama Camp Relying Heavily on Ground Effort," *Washington Post*, October 12, 2008, A4.

56. James W. Ceaser, Andrew E. Busch, and John J. Pitney Jr., *After Hope and Change: The 2012 Elections and American Politics* (Lanham, MD: Rowman & Littlefield, 2013).

57. CNN Politics, "Exit Polls."

58. Jens Manuel Krogstad and Mark Hugo Lopez, "Black Voter Turnout Fell in 2016, Even As a Record Number of Americans Cast Ballots," *Pew Research Center*, May 12, 2017, http://www.pewresearch.org/fact-tank/2017/05/12/black-voter-turnout-fell-in-2016-even-as-a-record-number-of-americans-cast-ballots/.

59. James W. Ceaser, Andrew E. Busch, and John J. Pitney Jr., *Defying the Odds: The 2016 Elections and American Politics* (Lanham, MD: Rowman & Littlefield, 2017), 119.

CHAPTER 2

1. John Nichols, "What to Do About Record Low Voter Turnout? Call a Holiday!" *The Nation*, November 17, 2014, http://www.thenation.com/blog/190769/what-do-about-record-low-voter-turnout-call-holiday#.

2. We wish to acknowledge the contribution to this chapter made by Michael P. McDonald and Samuel Popkin, "The Myth of the Vanishing Voter," *American Political Science Review* 95 (2001): 963–74.

3. Horace Cooper, "Voter Fraud Is Real: Why the Voting Rights Act Should Be Used to Fight Election Fraud," The National Center for Public Policy Research, August 1, 2012, http://www.nationalcenter.org/NPA636.html.

4. "Judge Strikes Photo ID Requirement for PA Voters," *WPXI News*, January 17, 2014, http://www.wpxi.com/news/news/local/judge-strikes-photo-id-requirement-pa-voters/ncr7m/.

5. Jason D. Mycoff, Michael W. Wagner, and David C. Wilson, "The Empirical Effects of Voter-ID Laws: Present or Absent?" *PS: Political Science and Politics* 42 (2009): 121–26. See also Benjamin Highton, "Voter Identification Laws and Turnout in the United States," *Annual Review of Political Science* 20 (2017): 149–67.

6. See, for example, Morris P. Fiorina, Paul E. Peterson, and Bertram Johnson, *The New American Democracy*, 3rd ed. (New York, NY: Longman, 2003), 164–65.

7. Editorial Board, "The Worst Voter Turnout in 72 Years," *The New York Times*, November 11, 2014, http://www.nytimes.com/2014/11/12/opinion/the-worst-voter-turnout-in-72-years.html.

8. See Bryan Mercurio, "Democracy in Decline: Can Internet Voting Save the Electoral Process?" *John Marshall Journal of Computer & Information Law* 22 (2004), papers.ssrn.com/sol3/papers.cfm?abstract_id=590441.

9. Ruy A. Teixeira, *Why Americans Don't Vote: Turnout Decline in the United States, 1960–1984* (Westport, CT: Greenwood, 1987); Ruy A. Teixeira, *The Disappearing American Voter* (Washington, DC: Brookings Institution, 1992); Frances Fox Piven and Richard A. Cloward, *Why Americans Don't Vote* (New York, NY: Pantheon, 1988); Frances Fox Piven and Richard A. Cloward, *Why Americans Still Don't Vote: And Why Politicians Want It That Way* (Boston, MA: Beacon, 2000); Mark Lawrence Kornbluh, *Why America Stopped Voting: The Decline of Participatory Democracy and the Emergence of Modern American Politics* (New York, NY: New York University, 2000); Martin P. Wattenberg, *Where Have All the Voters Gone?* (Cambridge, MA: Harvard University Press, 2002); Lisa Hill, "Low Voter Turnout in the United States: Is Compulsory Voting a Viable Solution?" *Journal of Theoretical Politics* 18 (2006): 207–32; Arend Lijphart, "Unequal Participation: Democracy's Unresolved Dilemma," *American Political Science Review* 91 (1997): 1–14.

10. Walter Dean Burnham, "The Turnout Problem," in *Elections American Style*, ed. A. James Reichley (Washington, DC: Brookings Institution, 1987).

11. "About the Project," *Vanishing Voter Project*, www.vanishingvoter.org/about.shtml.

12. Donald P. Green and Ron Shachar, "Habit Formation and Political Behaviour: Evidence of Consuetude in Voter Turnout," *British Journal of Political Science* 30 (2000): 561–73.

13. Eric Plutzer, "Becoming a Habitual Voter: Inertia, Resources, and Growth in Young Adulthood," *American Political Science Review* 96 (2002): 41–56.

14. Robert D. Putnam, *Bowling Alone: The Collapse and Revival of American Community* (New York: Simon & Schuster, 2000), 204.

15. Richard Timpone, "Structure, Behavior, and Voter Turnout in the United Stares," *American Political Science Review* 92 (1998): 145–72.

16. John P. Katosh and Michael W. Traugott, "Costs and Values in the Calculus of Voting," *American Journal of Political Science* 26 (1982): 361–76. For more information about trust in government, see Joseph S. Nye Jr., Philip D. Zelikow, and David C. King, eds., *Why People Don't Trust Government* (Cambridge, MA: Harvard University Press, 1997).

17. Steven J. Rosenstone and John Mark Hanson, *Mobilization, Participation, and Democracy in America* (New York, NY: Macmillan, 1993); Cornelius P. Cotter, James L. Gibson, John F. Bibby, and Robert J. Huckshorn, *Party Organizations in American Politics* (New York, NY: Praeger, 1984).

18. William H. Flanigan and Nancy H. Zingale, *Political Behavior of the American Electorate*, 11th ed. (Washington, DC: CQ Press, 2005).

19. Some of the landmark works in this area are by Sidney Verba, Kay Lehman Schlozman, and Henry E. Brady, *Voice and Equality* (Cambridge, MA: Harvard

University Press, 1995); Raymond E. Wolfinger and Steven J. Rosenstone, *Who Votes?* (New Haven, CT: Yale University Press, 1980); Sidney Verba and Norman H. Nie, *Participation in America: Political Democracy and Social Equality* (New York, NY: Harper & Row, 1972). See also Jan E. Leighley and Jonathan Nagler, *Who Votes Now? Demographics, Issues, Inequality, and Turnout in the United States* (Princeton, NJ: Princeton University Press, 2014).

20. Martin P. Wattenberg, *Is Voting for Young People?* (New York, NY: Pearson Longman, 2007); Mark Bauerlein, *The Dumbest Generation: How the Digital Age Stupefies Young Americans and Jeopardizes Our Future (Or, Don't Trust Anyone Under 30)* (New York, NY: Tarcher Penguin, 2008).

21. Statistics reported in this section are derived by a method similar to deriving VEP statistics. See Mark Hugo Lopez, Emily Kirby, and Jared Sagoff, "The Youth Vote 2004, with a Historical Look at Youth Voting Patterns, 1972–2004," Working Paper 35, Center for Information and Research on Civic Learning and Engagement, July 2005.

22. Jody C Baumgartner and Peter L. Francia, *Conventional Wisdom and American Elections: Exploding Myths, Exploring Misconceptions*, 1st ed. (Lanham, MD: Rowman & Littlefield, 2008), chap. 1.

23. This section draws heavily on David Lee Hill, *American Voter Turnout: An Institutional Approach* (Boulder, CO: Westview, 2006).

24. For a more complete treatment of this subject, see Mark N. Franklin, *Voter Turnout and the Dynamics of Electoral Competition in Established Democracies since 1945* (New York, NY: Cambridge University Press, 2004).

25. In almost all elections in the United States, the Australian ballot is used, which lists each office separately. Another balloting system is used in parliamentary elections, where citizens are presented with a list of party candidates, from which they choose one party list.

26. Jeffrey A. Karp and Susan A. Banducci, "Political Efficacy and Participation in Twenty-Seven Democracies: How Electoral Systems Shape Political Behavior," *British Journal of Political Science* 38 (2008): 311–34. See also G. Bingham Powell, "American Voter Turnout in Comparative Perspective," *American Political Science Review* 80 (1986): 17–43; Robert Jackman, "Political Institutions and Voter Turnout in the Industrial Democracies," *American Political Science Review* 81 (1987): 405–24.

27. Anthony Downs, *An Economic Theory of Democracy* (New York: Harper & Row, 1957).

28. "History of AVR & Implementation Dates," Brennan Center for Justice, June 19, 2019, https://www.brennancenter.org/analysis/history-avr-implementation-dates.

29. "Same Day Registration," National Conference of State Legislatures, June 28, 2019, http://www.ncsl.org/research/elections-and-campaigns/same-day-registration.aspx.

30. State-by-State Time Off to Vote Laws, Findlaw.com, http://www.fndlaw.com/voting-rights-law.html.

31. For information on the effects of early voting, see Robert M. Stein and Patricia A. Garcia-Monet, "Voting Early but Not Often," *Social Science Quarterly*

78 (1997): 657–71; Paul Gronke, Eva Galanes-Rosenbaum, and Peter A. Miller, "Early Voting and Turnout," *PS: Politics & Political Science* 40, no. 4 (October 2007): 639–45. For information on the effects of motor voter laws, see Daniel P. Franklin and Eric E. Grier, "Effects of Motor Voter Legislation: Voter Turnout, Registration, and Partisan Advantage in the 1992 Presidential Election," *American Politics Research* 25 (1997): 104–17; Stephen Knack, "Does 'Motor Voter' Work? Evidence from State-Level Data," *Journal of Politics* 57 (1995): 796–811; Michael D. Martinez and David Hill, "Did Motor Voter Work?" *American Politics Research* 27 (1999): 296–315.

32. Flanigan and Zingale, *Political Behavior of the American Electorate.*

33. Peter W. Wielhouwer and Brad Lockerbie, "Party Contacting and Political Participation, 1952–90," *American Journal of Political Science* 38 (1994): 211–29; Costas Panagopoulos and Peter L. Francia, "Grassroots Mobilization in the 2008 Presidential Election," *Journal of Political Marketing* 8 (2009): 315–33.

34. Diana Burgess, Beth Haney, Mark Snyder, John L. Sullivan, and John E. Transue, "Rocking the Vote: Using Personalized Messages to Motivate Voting among Young Adults," *Public Opinion Quarterly* 64 (2000): 29–52.

35. Alan Gerber and Donald Green, "The Effects of Canvassing, Telephone Calls, and Direct Mail on Voter Turnout: A Field Experiment," *American Political Science Review* 94 (2000): 653–63.

36. McDonald and Popkin, "The Myth of the Vanishing Voter."

37. J. Gregory Robison, "Accuracy and Coverage Evaluation: Demographic Analysis Results," U.S. Census Bureau, March 2, 2001, https://www.census.gov/dmd/www/pdf/Fr4.pdf.

38. Philip E. Converse, "Change in the American Electorate," in *The Human Meaning of Social Change*, ed. Angus Campbell and Philip E. Converse (New York, NY: Russell Sage, 1972).

39. For an excellent review of voter fraud in the 1800s, see Peter H. Argersinger, "New Perspectives on Election Fraud in the Gilded Age," *Political Science Quarterly* 100 (Winter 1985–1986): 669–87.

40. McDonald and Popkin, "The Myth of the Vanishing Voter," 964.

41. Jerrold G. Rusk, "The Effect of the Australian Ballot Reform on Split Ticket Voting: 1876–1908," *American Political Science Review* 64 (1970): 1220–38.

42. Russell J. Dalton, *Citizen Politics: Public Opinion and Political Parties in Advanced Industrial Democracies*, 3rd ed. (New York, NY: Chatham House, 2002).

43. "2014 November General Election Turnout Rates," *United States Elections Project*, last updated September 5, 2018, http://www.electproject.org/2014g. See also Jose A. DelReal, "Voter Turnout in 2014 Was the Lowest Since WWII," *The Washington Post*, November 10, 2014, http://www.washingtonpost.com/blogs/post-politics/wp/2014/11/10/voter-turnout-in-2014-was-the-lowest-since-wwii.

44. Editorial Board, "The Worst Voter Turnout in 72 Years."

45. Grace Segers, "Record Voter Turnout in 2018 Midterm Elections," *CBS News*, November 7, 2018, https://www.cbsnews.com/news/record-voter-turnout-in-2018-midterm-elections/.

46. See James W. Caeser and Andrew E. Busch, *The Perfect Tie: The True Story of the 2000 Presidential Election* (Lanham, MD: Rowman & Littlefield, 2001);

James W. Caeser and Andrew E. Busch, *Red Over Blue: The 2004 Elections and American Politics* (Lanham, MD: Rowman & Littlefield, 2005); James W. Caeser and Andrew E. Busch, *Epic Journey: The 2008 Elections and American Politics* (Lanham, MD: Rowman & Littlefield, 2009).

47. Adam Liptak, "Voting Problems in Ohio Set Off an Alarm," *The New York Times*, November 7, 2004, http://www.nytimes.com/2004/11/07/politics/campaig n/07elect.html. See also Adam Cohen, "No One Should Have to Stand in Line for 10 Hours to Vote," *The New York Times*, August 25, 2008, http://www.nytimes.c om/2008/08/26/opinion/26tue4.html.

48. "Thousands of Voter Registration Forms Faked, Officials Say," *CNN*, October 10, 2008, http://www.cnn.com/2008/POLITICS/10/09/acorn.fraud.claims.

49. See Hans Von Spakovsky, "Here Comes the 2014 Voter Fraud," *The Wall Street Journal*, October 27, 2014, http://www.wsj.com/articles/hans-von-spakovsk y-here-comes-the-2014-voter-fraud-1414450805; John Fund, "Voter Fraud: We've Got Proof, It's Easy," *The National Review*, January 12, 2014, http://www.nati onalreview.com/article/368234/voter-fraud-weve-got-proof-its-easy-john-fund.

50. Kevin Drum, "The Dog That Voted and Other Election Fraud Yarns," *Mother Jones*, http://www.motherjones.com/politics/2012/07/voter-suppression-kev in-drum; Jonathan Weiler, "The Last Refuge of Scoundrels—Republicans and Voter Suppression," *The Huffington Post*, November 5, 2012, www.huffngtonpost.com/ jonathan-weiler/the-last-refuge-of-scound_b_2079941.html.

51. However, see Jesse T. Richman, Gulshan A. Chatta, and David C. Earnest, "Do Non-Citizens Vote in U.S. Elections," *Electoral Studies* 36 (2014): 149–57, who found that the number of noncitizens who have managed to vote in some states over the years was sufficient to potentially alter electoral outcomes.

52. Eric Lipton and Ian Urbana, "In 5-Year Effort, Scant Evidence of Voter Fraud," *The New York Times*, April 12, 2007, http://www.nytimes.com/2007/04 /12/washington/12fraud.html; Lorraine C. Minnite, "The Politics of Voter Fraud," Project Vote, March 5, 2007, http://www.projectvote.org/images/publications/Pol icy%20Reports%20and%20Guides/Politics_of_Voter_ Fraud_Final.pdf; Philip Bump, "The Fix: The Disconnect Between Voter ID Laws and Voter Fraud," *Washington Post*, October 13, 2014, http://www.washingtonpost.com/blogs/the-fx/wp/2014/10/13/the-disconnect-between-voter-id-laws-and-voter-fraud/; Jane Mayer, "The Voter-Fraud Myth," *The New Yorker*, October 29, 2012, http:// www.newyorker.com/magazine/2012/10/29/the-voter-fraud-myth; Sarah Childress, "Why Voter ID Laws Aren't Really about Fraud," *Frontline*, October 20, 2014, http://www.pbs.org/wgbh/pages/frontline/government-elections-politics/ why-voter-id-laws-arent-really-about-fraud/; Natasha Khan and Corbin Carson, "Comprehensive Database of U.S. Voter Fraud Uncovers No Evidence That Photo ID Is Needed," *News21*, August 12, 2012, http://votingrights.news21.com/article/ election-fraud/.

53. Justin Levitt, "The Truth About Voter Fraud," Brennan Center for Justice, 2007, http://www.brennancenter.org/sites/default/fles/analysis/The%20Truth%2 0About%20Voter%20Fraud.pdf.

54. Levitt, "The Truth About Voter Fraud."

55. Susan Myrick, "110 Year Olds Vote Strong in NC," *Civitas Review*, http:// civitasreview.com/elections-campaigns/110-year-olds-vote-strong-in-nc.

56. "Are There Really 112 Year Old Voters on the State's Voter Rolls," North Carolina State Board of Elections, http://www.wral.com/asset/news/state/nccapito l/2012/10/31/11722418/SBOE_Response_to_Civitas_Report.pdf.

57. See http://www.eac.gov/assets/1/AssetManager/Exhibit%20M.PDF.

58. "Suppressing the Vote," *The Daily Show with Jon Stewart*, October 23, 2013, http://thedailyshow.cc.com/videos/dxhtvk/suppressing-the-vote.

59. Manny Fernandez, "Party Predictions Differ in Texas on Impact of New Voter ID Law," *The New York Times*, February 5, 2014, http://www.nytimes.c om/2014/02/06/us/party-predictions-differ-in-texas-on-impact-of-new-voter-id-law .html; Larry Elder, "The 'Voter ID Is Racist' Con," October 25, 2018, https ://www.realclearpolitics.com/articles/2018/10/25/the_voter_id_is_racist_con_1384 48.html.

60. Lonna Rae Atkeson, Lisa Ann Bryant, Thad E. Hall, Kyle Saunders, and Michael R. Alvarez, "A New Barrier to Participation: Heterogeneous Application of Voter Identification Policies," *Electoral Studies* 29 (2010): 66–73; United States Government Accountability Office, "Issues Related to State Voter Identification Laws," GAO-14-634, September 2014, http://www.gao.gov/assets/670/665966.pdf; Richard Sobel and Robert Ellis Smith, "Voter-ID Laws Discourage Participation, Particularly among Minorities, and Trigger a Constitutional Remedy in Lost Rep-resentation," *PS: Political Science & Politics* 42, no. 1 (2009): 107–10; Zoltan Hajnal, Nazita Lajevardi, and Lindsay Nielson, "Voter Identification Laws and the Suppression of Minority Votes," *The Journal of Politics* 79, no. 2 (2017): 363–79.

61. R. Michael Alvarez, Delia Bailey, and Jonathan N. Katz, "The Effect of Voter Identification Laws on Turnout," *SSRN Electronic Journal* (2008): 1–28.

62. Jason D. Mycoff, Michael W. Wagner, and David C. Wilson, "The Effect of Voter Identification Laws on Aggregate and Individual Level Turnout" (paper prepared for presentation at the annual meeting of the American Political Science Association, Chicago, Illinois, August 2007); John R. Lott Jr., "Evidence of Voter Fraud and the Impact that Regulations to Reduce Fraud have on Voter Participation Rates," Brennan Center for Justice, August 18, 2006, http://www.brennancen-ter .org/sites/default/fles/legal-work/3386f09ec84f302074_hum6bqnxj.pdf; Stephen Ansolabehere, "Effects of Identification Requirements on Voting: Evidence from the Experiences of Voters on Election Day," *PS: Politics & Political Science* 42, no. 1 (January 2009): 127–30.

63. Justin Grimmer, Eitan Hersh, Marc Meredith, Jonathan Mummolo, and Clayton Nall, "Obstacles to Estimating Voter ID Laws' Effect on Turnout," *Journal of Politics* 80, no. 3 (2018): 1045–51; Robert S. Erikson and Lorraine C. Minnite, "Modeling Problems in the Voter Identification—Voter Turnout Debate," *Election Law Journal* 8, no. 2 (2009): 85–101.

64. Barry C. Burden, "Voter Turnout and National Election Studies," *Political Analysis* 8, no. 4 (2000): 389–98.

65. John Sides, "Do Voter Identification Laws Depress Turnout?" *The Mon-key Cage*, http://themonkeycage.org/2011/10/03/do-voter-identifcation-laws-depres s-turnout-redux.

CHAPTER 3

1. William J. Keefe and Marc J. Hetherington, *Parties, Politics, and Public Policy in America*, 9th ed. (Washington, DC: CQ Press, 2003), 49.

2. Alexander Cockburn and Jeffrey St. Clair, eds., *Dime's Worth of Difference: Beyond the Lesser of Two Evils* (Oakland, CA: AK Press, 2004).

3. Eric Boehlert, "Nader's Nadir," *Salon*, February 22, 2004, archive.salon.com/news/feature/2004/02/21/nader/index_np.html.

4. Eric Alterman, "Bush's Useful Idiot," *Nation*, September 16, 2004, www.the-nation.com/doc/20041004/alterman.

5. "Party Images," *Gallup*, https://news.gallup.com/poll/24655/party-images.aspx.

6. RJ Reinhart, "Majority in U.S. Still Say a Third Party Is Needed," *Gallup*, October 26, 2018, https://news.gallup.com/poll/244094/majority-say-third-party-needed.aspx.

7. See http://avalon.law.yale.edu/18th_century/washing.asp.

8. Reinhart, "Majority in U.S. Still Say a Third Party Is Needed."

9. Jeffrey M. Jones, "Americans Continue to Say a Third Political Party Is Needed," *Gallup*, September 24, 2014, https://news.gallup.com/poll/177284/americans-continue-say-third-political-party-needed.aspx.

10. Evans Lynn, as quoted in Allison Hammond, "Many Students Would Welcome a Third Major Political Party," *USA Today*, October 19, 2013, http://www.usatoday.com/story/news/nation/2013/10/19/millennials-want-political-reorganization/3013343/.

11. Great Britain's Labour Party and Germany's Social Democratic Party, however, have recently received significant attention for adopting what some call "third way" positions that defy traditional left-wing policy prescriptions. See Knut Roder, *Social Democracy and Labour Market Policy: Developments in Britain and Germany* (New York, NY: Routledge, 2003).

12. Alan Ware, *Political Parties and Party Systems* (New York, NY: Oxford University Press, 1996).

13. Jamie Coomarasamy, "Marine and Jean-Marie Le Pen Fight Over French National Front," *BBC*, May 22, 2015, http://www.bbc.com/news/world-europe-32809900.

14. Alan I. Abramowitz, *The Polarized Public: Why Government Is So Dysfunctional* (New York, NY: Pearson, 2013).

15. Keith T. Poole and Howard Rosenthal, *Ideology and Congress*, 2nd ed. (New Brunswick, NJ: Transaction Publishers, 2007); Sean M. Theriault, *Party Polarization in Congress* (New York, NY: Cambridge University Press, 2008).

16. V. O. Key Jr., *Politics, Parties, and Pressure Groups*, 5th ed. (New York, NY: Crowell, 1964).

17. Louis Hartz, *The Liberal Tradition in America* (New York, NY: Harcourt, Brace, and World, 1955).

18. Morris P. Fiorina, Samuel J. Abrams, and Jeremy C. Pope, *Culture War? The Myth of a Polarized America* (New York, NY: Longman, 2005).

19. Fiorina, Abrams, and Pope, *Culture War?*

20. Duncan Black, "On the Rationale of Group Decision-Making," *Journal of Political Economy* 56 (1948): 23–34; Anthony Downs, *An Economic Theory of Democracy* (New York, NY: Harper and Row, 1957).

21. "City Council Election Methods," *FairVote: The Center for Voting and Democracy*, www.fairvote.org/media/documents/City_Council_Manual.pdf.

22. Individual electors in Maine and Nebraska are awarded based on the winner of the presidential vote in each House district. In practice, all typically end up being allocated to the winner of the popular vote. See Stephen J. Wayne, *The Road to the White House 2004: The Politics of Presidential Elections* (Belmont, CA: Wadsworth, 2004), 323.

23. Examples include stipulating that a party must receive a minimum percentage of votes (say, 5%) to receive any seats, or accounting for partial seats.

24. Maurice Duverger, *Political Parties: Their Organization and Activity in the Modern State*, trans. Barbara North and Robert North, 2nd ed. (New York, NY: Wiley, 1965). See also Arend Lijphart, *Electoral Systems and Party Systems: A Study of Twenty-Seven Democracies, 1945–1990* (Oxford, UK: Oxford University Press, 1994).

25. The Republicans and Democrats are unlikely to try to align with each other. Why? According to the "minimal winning coalition" rule posited by William Riker, parties or groups have no incentive to build a majority that is larger than necessary to win. See William H. Riker, *The Theory of Political Coalitions* (New Haven, CT: Yale University Press, 1962).

26. David A. Lieb, "AP: GOP Won More Seats in 2018 than Suggested by Vote Share," Associated Press, March 21, 2019, https://www.apnews.com/9fd72a4c1c57 42aead977ee27815d776.

27. That is, any individual contribution total of $250 or less is matched dollar for dollar, while a $251 donation or higher would receive no more than a $250 match.

28. For more information, see the website of the Federal Election Commission at https://www.fec.gov/introduction-campaign-finance/understanding-ways-suppor t-federal-candidates/presidential-elections/public-funding-presidential-elections/.

29. Marilyn W. Thompson, "Green Party's Jill Stein Gets a Financial Boost, Thanks to Taxpayers," *The Washington Post*, September 20, 2016, https://www .washingtonpost.com/politics/green-partys-jill-stein-gets-a-financial-boost-thanks-to-taxpayers/2016/09/20/dffa8950-7e99-11e6-8d0c-fb6c00c90481_story.html.

30. For more information, see the website of the Federal Election Commission at https://www.fec.gov/introduction-campaign-finance/understanding-ways-suppor t-federal-candidates/presidential-elections/public-funding-presidential-elections/.

31. "Presidential Election Campaign Fund," *Federal Election Commission*, April 9, 2014, http://www.fec.gov/press/bkgnd/fund.shtml.

32. Clifford W. Brown, Lynda W. Powell, and Clyde Wilcox, *Serious Money: Fundraising and Contributing in Presidential Nomination Campaigns* (New York, NY: Cambridge University Press, 1995).

33. See James D. Hunter, *Culture Wars* (New York, NY: Basic Books, 1991), for one of the first treatments of the culture war phenomenon.

34. Judith Parris, *The Convention Problem: Issues in Reform of Presidential Nominating Procedures* (Washington, DC: Brookings Institution, 1972).

35. Larry Smith, "The Party Platforms as Institutional Discourse: The Democrats and Republicans of 1988," *Presidential Studies Quarterly* 22 (1992): 531.

36. "Republicans: Convention Notes," *Time*, August 26, 1996, 21.

37. Poole and Rosenthal, *Ideology and Congress.*

38. Mathew I. Pinzur, "Nader Mounts Attack at UNF on Major 'Look-Alike' Parties," *Florida Times-Union*, October 13, 2000, A09.

39. See Jacob S. Hacker and Paul Pierson, *Off Center: The Republican Revolution and the Erosion of American Democracy* (New Haven, CT: Yale University Press, 2006). See also Geoffrey Layman, *The Great Divide: Religious and Cultural Conflict in American Party Politics* (New York, NY: Columbia University Press, 2001).

40. Thomas E. Mann, "Redistricting Reform: What Is Desirable? Possible?" in *Party Lines: Competition, Partisanship, and Congressional Redistricting*, ed. Thomas E. Mann and Bruce E. Cain (Washington, DC: Brookings Institution Press, 2005), 92–114.

41. Keith T. Poole, "The Decline and Rise of Party Polarization in Congress during the Twentieth Century," *Extensions* (Fall 2005): 9.

42. For more information, see the website of the Green Party at http://www.gp.org.

43. For more information, see the website of the Libertarian Party at http://www.lp.org.

CHAPTER 4

1. "Americans Views on Money and Politics," *The New York Times,* June 2, 2015, https://www.nytimes.com/interactive/2015/06/02/us/politics/money-in-politics-poll.html.

2. Betsy Cooper, Daniel Cox, Rachel Lienesch, and Robert P. Jones, "The Divide Over America's Future: 1950 or 2050? Findings from the 2016 American Values Survey," *PRRI*, October 25, 2016, https://www.prri.org/research/poll-1950s-2050-divided-nations-direction-post-election.

3. Bradley Jones, "Most Americans Want to Limit Campaign Spending, Say Big Donors Have Greater Political Influence," *The Pew Research Center*, May 8, 2018, https://www.pewresearch.org/fact-tank/2018/05/08/most-americans-want-to-limit-campaign-spending-say-big-donors-have-greater-political-influence.

4. See, for example, Suzy Khimm, "What Occupy DC Wants: Less Corporate Money in Politics," *The Washington Post*, October 4, 2011, https://www.washingtonpost.com/blogs/ezra-klein/post/what-occupy-dc-wants-less-corporate-money-in-politics/2011/10/03/gIQAgUj4IL_blog.html?utm_term=.6507cb76ebbd. See also "Udall Introduces Constitutional Amendment to Overturn Citizens United and Get Big Money Out of Politics," Press release, January 24, 2017, https://www.tomudall.senate.gov/news/press-releases/udall-introduces-constitutional-amendment-to-overturn-citizens-united-and-get-big-money-out-of-politics.

5. Quoted in Melvin I. Urofsky, *Money and Free Speech: Campaign Finance Reform and the Courts* (Lawrence, KS: University of Kansas Press, 2005), 3.

6. Anthony Corrado, "A History of Federal Campaign Finance Law," in *Campaign Finance Reform: A Sourcebook*, ed. Anthony Corrado, Thomas E. Mann, Daniel R. Ortiz, Trevor Potter, and Frank J. Sorauf (Washington, DC: Brookings, 1997), 27.

7. For more information, see Document 2.4, The Federal Corrupt Practices Act of 1925, in *Campaign Finance Reform: A Sourcebook*, ed. Anthony Corrado, Thomas E. Mann, Daniel R. Ortiz, Trevor Potter, and Frank J. Sorauf (Washington, DC: Brookings, 1997), 42–46.

8. Robert E. Mutch, *Buying the Vote: A History of Campaign Finance Reform* (New York, NY: Oxford University Press, 2014). For more on the Watergate scandal, see Stanley I. Kutler, *The Wars of Watergate: The Last Crisis of Richard Nixon* (New York, NY: W.W. Norton, 1990).

9. David B. Magleby and Eric A. Smith, "Party Soft Money in the 2000 Congressional Elections," in *The Other Campaign: Soft Money and Issue Advocacy in the 2000 Congressional Elections*, ed. David B. Magleby (Lanham, MD: Rowman & Littlefield, 2003), 33.

10. See, for example, William Greider, "The Hard Fight against Soft Money," *Rolling Stone*, June 26, 1997, http://www.rollingstone.com/politics/news/the-hard-fght-against-soft-money-19970626; and Alexander Keyssar, "The Right to Vote and Election 2000," in *The Unfinished Election of 2000*, ed. Jack N. Rakove (New York, NY: Basic Books, 2001), 98.

11. Ted Nance, *Gangs of America: The Rise of Corporate Power and the Disabling of Democracy* (San Francisco, CA: Berrett-Koehler, 2003), 150.

12. Specifically, any broadcast, cable, or satellite communication received by 50,000 or more people.

13. *McConnell v. Federal Election Commission*, 540 U.S. 93 (2003). Quotation in *McConnell v. Federal Election Commission* was accessed from http://www.law.cornell.edu/supct/html/02-1674.ZS.html.

14. *McConnell v. Federal Election Commission*.

15. *Federal Election Commission v. Wisconsin Right to Life, Inc.*, 551 U.S. 449 (2007).

16. Conor M. Dowling and Michael G. Miller, *Super PAC! Money, Elections, and Voters after Citizens United* (New York, NY: Routledge, 2014), 11.

17. Robert Barnes, "'Hillary: The Movie' to Get Supreme Court Screening," *The Washington Post*, March 15, 2009, http://www.washingtonpost.com/wp-dyn/content/article/2009/03/14/AR2009031401603.html.

18. Likewise, in 1990, the U.S. Supreme Court ruled in *Austin v. Michigan Chamber of Commerce* that corporations could not use their general treasuries for independent expenditures in federal elections.

19. For a more detailed summary, see Dowling and Miller, *Super PAC!*, 19.

20. *Citizens United v. Federal Election Commission*, 558 U.S. 08-205 (2010). Justice Kennedy's quotation in *Citizens United v. Federal Election Commission* was accessed from http://www.law.cornell.edu/supct/html/08-205.ZO.html.

21. Fred Wertheimer, "Pro & Con: Is the Supreme Court's Ruling on Campaigns Bad for Democracy? Yes, Turning Clock Back 100 Years, Decision Will Corrupt Government," *Atlanta Journal Constitution*, January 27, 2010, http://www.ajc .com/ opinion/pro-s-ruling-on-285259.html.

22. Keith Olbermann, "Olbermann: U.S. Government for Sale," *MSNBC*, January 21, 2010, http://www.msnbc.msn.com/id/34981476/ns/msnbc_tv-count down_ with_keith_olbermann/print/0/displaymode/1098/.

23. Celestine Bohlen, "American Democracy is Drowning in Money," *The New York Times*, September 20, 2017, https://www.nytimes.com/2017/09/20/opinion/de mocracy-drowning-cash.html.

24. Karl Evers-Hillstrom, Raymond Arke, and Luke Robinson, "A Look at the Impact of Citizens United on Its 9th Anniversary," *The Center for Responsive Politics*, January 21, 2019, https://www.opensecrets.org/news/2019/01/citizens-unite d. See also "Blue Wave of Money Propels 2018 Election to Record-Breaking $5.2 Billion in Spending," *Center for Responsive Politics*, October 29, 2018, https://ww w.opensecrets.org/news/2018/10/2018-midterm-record-breaking-5-2-billion.

25. Anne Caprara, "Campaign Planning and Management: The Key Elements of Campaigns," in *Campaigns and Elections American Style: The Changing Landscape of Political Campaigns*, ed. Candice J. Nelson and James A. Thurber (New York, NY: Routledge, 2019). See also Jody C Baumgartner, *Modern Presidential Electioneering: An Organizational and Comparative Approach* (Westport, CT: Praeger, 2000).

26. Percentages from Travis Ridout, in Maggie Koerth-Baker, "How Money Affects Elections," *FiveThirtyEight*, September 10, 2018, https://fivethirtyeight.c om/features/money-and-elections-a-complicated-love-story. For additional information on campaign spending, including advertising, see "Expenditures," The Center for Responsive Politics, https://www.opensecrets.org/expends.

27. Koerth-Baker, "How Money Affects Elections."

28. Ted Brader, "Striking a Responsive Chord: How Political Ads Motivate and Persuade Voters by Appealing to Emotions," *American Journal of Political Science* 49 (2005): 388–405.

29. Jamie L. Carson, "Strategy, Selection, and Candidate Competition in U.S. House and Senate Elections," *Journal of Politics* 67 (2005): 1–28. See also Janet M. Box-Steffensmeier, "A Dynamic Analysis of the Role of War Chests in Campaign Strategy," *American Journal of Political Science* 40 (1996): 352–71.

30. Robert Biersack, Paul S. Herrnson, and Clyde Wilcox, "Seeds for Success: Early Money in Congressional Elections," *Legislative Studies Quarterly* 18 (1993): 535–51.

31. Peter L. Francia, John C. Green, Paul S. Herrnson, Lynda W. Powell, and Clyde Wilcox, *The Financiers of Congressional Elections: Investors, Ideologues, and Intimates* (New York, NY: Columbia University Press, 2003). For further discussion about the role of campaign contributions and access, see Joshua L. Kalla and David E. Broockman, "Campaign Contributions Facilitate Access to Congressional Officials: A Randomized Field Experiment," *American Journal of Political Science* 60 (2015): 545–58.

32. Francia et al., *The Financiers of Congressional Elections*.

33. Quoted in Paul West, "Elizabeth Dole Drops Presidential Candidacy; GOP Run is 'Futile,' She Says, Noting Huge Bush Campaign Funds," *The Baltimore Sun*, October 21, 1999, https://www.baltimoresun.com/news/bs-xpm-1999-10-21-991 0210047-story.html.

34. West, "Elizabeth Dole Drops Presidential Candidacy."

35. Marty Cohen, David Karol, Hans Noel, and John Zaller, *The Party Decides: Presidential Nominations Before and After Reform* (Chicago, IL: University of Chicago Press, 2008), 309. See also David A. Breaux and Anthony Gierzynski, "'It's Money That Matters': Campaign Expenditures and State Legislative Primaries," *Legislative Studies Quarterly* 16 (1991): 429–43.

36. Donald P. Green and Alan S. Gerber, *Get Out the Vote! How to Increase Voter Turnout* (Washington, DC: Brookings Institution Press, 2004).

37. Paul S. Herrnson, *Congressional Elections: Campaigning at Home and in Washington* (Washington, DC: CQ Press, 2016), chap. 9. See also Nicholas R. Seabrook, "Money and State Legislative Elections: The Conditional Impact of Political Context," *American Politics Research* 38 (2010): 399–424.

38. Cindy D. Kam and Elizabeth J. Zechmeister, "Name Recognition and Candidate Support," *American Journal of Political Science* 57 (2013): 971–86.

39. Gary C. Jacobson, "The Effects of Campaign Spending in Congressional Elections," *American Political Science Review* 72 (1978): 769–83. See also Alan I. Abramowitz, "Incumbency Campaign Spending and the Decline of Competition in U.S. House Elections," *Journal of Politics* 43 (1991): 34–56.

40. Steven D. Levitt, "Using Repeat Challengers to Estimate the Effect of Campaign Spending on Election Outcomes in the U.S. House," *Journal of Political Economy* 102 (1994): 777–98.

41. Quoted in The Associated Press, "Money in Elections Doesn't Mean What You Think It Does," *WTOP*, October 29, 2018, https://awsstage.wtop.com/nati onal/2018/10/money-in-elections-doesnt-mean-what-you-think-it-does/.

42. Michael M. Franz and Travis N. Ridout, "Does Political Advertising Persuade?" *Political Behavior* 29 (2007): 465–91.

43. Box-Steffensmeier, "Role of War Chests in Campaign Strategy."

44. Alan S. Gerber, "Does Campaign Spending Work? Field Experiments Provide Evidence and Suggest New Theory," *American Behavioral Scientist* 47 (2004): 541–74.

45. Herrnson, *Congressional Elections*. See also Alan I. Abramowitz, "The Rise of Negative Partisanship and the Nationalization of U.S. Elections in the 21st Century," *Election Studies* 41 (2016): 12–22.

46. For a more complete discussion on the effects of economic conditions on elections, see Richard Nadeau and Michael S. Lewis-Beck, "National Economic Voting in U.S. Presidential Elections," *Journal of Politics* 63 (2001): 159–81. See also Robert S. Erikson, "Economic Conditions and the Presidential Vote," *American Political Science Review* 83 (1989): 567–73.

47. James E. Campbell and Joe A. Summers, "Presidential Coattails in Senate Elections," *American Political Science Review* 84 (1990): 513–24. See also James E. Campbell, "Presidential Coattails and Midterm Losses in State Legislative Elections," *American Political Science Review* 80 (1986): 45–63.

48. Jane Mayer, *Dark Money: The Hidden History of Billionaires Behind the Rise of the Radical Right* (New York, NY: Anchor Books, 2016).

49. Martin Gilens, *Affluence and Influence: Economic Inequality and Political Power in America* (Princeton, NJ: Princeton University Press, 2016). See also Lynda W. Powell, *The Influence of Campaign Contributions in State Legislatures* (Ann Arbor, MI: University of Michigan Press, 2012).

50. For a review of the literature, see Richard A. Smith, "Interest Group Influence in the U.S. Congress," *Legislative Studies Quarterly* 20 (1995): 89–139. See also Douglas D. Roscoe and Shannon Jenkins, "A Meta-Analysis of Campaign Contributions' Impact on Roll-Call Voting," *Social Science Quarterly* 86 (2005): 52–68.

51. See, for example, John R. Wright, "Contributions, Lobbying, and Committee Voting in the U.S. House of Representatives," *American Political Science Review* 84 (1990): 417–38.

52. Smith, "Interest Group Influence in the U.S. Congress," 91.

53. "2016 Republican Party Platform on Campaign Finance is a Far Cry from the Teddy Roosevelt Days," *Campaign Legal Center*, July 19, 2016, https://campaignlegal.org/update/2016-republican-platform-campaign-finance-far-cry-teddy-roosevelt-days.

54. "Most Expensive Midterm Ever: Cost of 2018 Election Surpasses $5.7 Billion," *Center for Responsive Politics*, February 6, 2019, https://www.opensecrets.org/news/2019/02/cost-of-2018-election-5pnt7bil.

CHAPTER 5

1. Herman Cain, "Let the Veepstakes Begin," Townhall.com, February 26, 2007, www.townhall.com/columnists/HermanCain/2007/02/26/let_the_veepstakes_begin; Rick Klein, "Never Too Early for the Veepstakes Race," *ABC News Online*, June 12, 2007, abcnews.go.com/Politics/story?id=3270446&page=1; Matt Mackowiak, "Veepstakes: The Contenders," PoliticalInsider.com, February 5, 2007, politicalinsider.com/2007/02/veepstakes_the_contenders.html; Larry Sabato, "The Outrage of Early Vice Presidential Speculation," *Sabato's Crystal Ball* V, no. 9 (March 29, 2007), www.centerforpolitics.org/crystalball/article.php?id=LJS2007032901.

2. Jody C Baumgartner, "The Veepstakes: Forecasting Vice Presidential Selection in 2008," *PS: Politics and Political Science* 41 (October 2000): 765–72.

3. James Harding, "Voters Weigh up Kerry by the Company He Keeps: Speculation on the Democrat's Likely Running Mate Is Rife," *Financial Times*, May 20, 2004, search.ft.com/nonFtArticle?id=040520000684.

4. For a recent example of the "ticket balance" claim, see John Feehery, "Picking a Vice President," *The Hill*, March 12, 2012, http://thehill.com/opinion/columnists/ john-feehery/215591-picking-a-vice-president.

5. Jody C Baumgartner, *The American Vice Presidency Reconsidered* (Westport, CT: Praeger, 2006), 1.

6. Jody C Baumgartner, "The Second Best Choice? Vice Presidential Candidate Qualifications in the Traditional and Modern Eras," *White House Studies* 6 (2006): 179–95.

7. James Bryce, *The American Commonwealth*, vol. 2 (New York, NY: Macmillan, 1893), 46.

8. Baumgartner, *The American Vice Presidency Reconsidered*, 21–22.

9. Baumgartner, "The Second Best Choice?"

10. Bryce, *The American Commonwealth*.

11. Baumgartner, *The American Vice Presidency Reconsidered*, 18–19.

12. Baumgartner, *The American Vice Presidency Reconsidered*, 18–19.

13. Baumgartner, *The American Vice Presidency Reconsidered*, 18–19.

14. Robert L. Dudley and Ronald B. Rapoport, "Vice Presidential Candidates and the Home State Advantage: Playing Second Banana at Home and on the Road," *American Journal of Political Science* 33 (1989): 537–40.

15. Baumgartner, *The American Vice Presidency Reconsidered*, 55–56.

16. Birch Bayh, *One Heartbeat Away: Presidential Disability And Succession* (Indianapolis, IN: Bobbs-Merrill, 1968); Michael Nelson, *A Heartbeat Away* (New York, NY: Twentieth Century Fund, 1988).

17. Joel K. Goldstein, *The Modern American Vice Presidency: The Transformation of a Political Institution* (Princeton, NJ: Princeton University, 1982); Paul C. Light, *Vice-Presidential Power: Advice and Influence in the White House* (Baltimore, MD: Johns Hopkins University, 1984); Baumgartner, *The American Vice Presidency Reconsidered*.

18. Baumgartner, "The Veepstakes."

19. Baumgartner, *The American Vice Presidency Reconsidered*, 62–63.

20. Light, *Vice-Presidential Power*.

21. Baumgartner, *The American Vice Presidency Reconsidered*, 59.

22. Tom Hamburger, "Obama Advisor Jim Johnson Resigns Amid Criticism," *Los Angeles Times*, June 12, 2008, articles.latimes.com/2008/jun/12/nation/na-johnson12; J. Taylor Rushing, "McCain Picks Former Reagan Official To Head VP Search," *The Hill*, May 23, 2008, thehill.com/campaign-2008/mccain-selects-former-reagan-offcial-to-head-vp-search-2008-05-23.html.

23. See, for example, Lee Sigelman and Paul J. Wahlbeck, "The 'Veepstakes': Strategic Choice in Presidential Running Mate Selection," *American Political Science Review* 91 (1997): 855–64; Robert P. Watson and Richard M. Yon, "Vice Presidential Selection in the Modern Era," *White House Studies* 6 (2006): 163–78; Baumgartner, "The Second Best Choice"; Mark Hiller and Douglas Kriner, "Institutional Change and the Dynamics of Vice Presidential Selection," *Presidential Studies Quarterly* 38 (2008): 401–21; Jody C Baumgartner, "The Post-Palin Calculus: The 2012 Republican Veepstakes," *PS: Politics and Political Science* 45 (2012): 605–9. This discussion draws heavily on Baumgartner, "The Veepstakes."

24. Jody C Baumgartner, "Vice Presidential Selection in the Convention Era: Experience or Electoral Advantage?" *Congress and the Presidency* 39 (2012): 297–315.

25. Baumgartner, "The Veepstakes."

26. Baumgartner, *The American Vice Presidency Reconsidered*, 78.

27. Vice presidential candidates who carried their home state from 1980 to 2016 are Mike Pence (2016), Tim Kaine (2016), Joe Biden (2008 and 2012), Sarah Palin

(2008), Dick Cheney (2000 and 2004), Joe Lieberman (2000), Al Gore (1992 and 1996), Dan Quayle (1988 and 1992), George H. W. Bush (1980 and 1984), and Walter Mondale (1980). Vice presidential candidates who failed to win their home state from 1980 to 2016 are Paul Ryan (2012), John Edwards (2004), Jack Kemp (1996), Lloyd Bentsen (1988), and Geraldine Ferraro (1984).

28. Baumgartner, "The Veepstakes," 765–66.
29. Baumgartner, "The Veepstakes," 765–66.
30. Baumgartner, "The Veepstakes," 765–66.
31. Baumgartner, "The Veepstakes," 765–66.
32. Baumgartner, "The Veepstakes," 765–66.
33. Baumgartner, "The Veepstakes," 765–66.
34. Baumgartner, "The Second Best Choice?"
35. Baumgartner, *The American Vice Presidency Reconsidered*.
36. Nelson W. Polsby and Aaron Wildavsky, *Presidential Elections: Strategies and Structures in American Politics*, 11th ed. (Lanham, MD: Rowman & Littlefield, 2004), 132.
37. David S. Broder and Bob Woodward, *The Man Who Would Be President: Dan Quayle* (New York, NY: Simon & Schuster, 1992).
38. Baumgartner, *The American Vice Presidency Reconsidered*.
39. Baumgartner, *The Vice Presidency*, 2.
40. Nelson, "The Election," 68.
41. See, for example, Matthew Continetti, "Five Myths About Sarah Palin," *The Washington Post*, October 17, 2010, http://www.washingtonpost.com/wp-dyn/content/article/2010/10/14/AR2010101404794.html.
42. Baumgartner, *The Vice Presidency*, 115.
43. For a summary of these studies, see Jonathan Chait, "Did Palin Hurt McCain?" *The New Republic*, October 15, 2010, http://www.newrepublic.com/blog/jonathan-chait/78407/did-palin-hurt-mccain.
44. From Baumgartner, *The Vice Presidency*, 115; see Danny M. Atkinson, "The Electoral Significance of the Vice Presidency," *Presidential Studies Quarterly* 12, no. 3 (1992): 330–36; David W. Romero, "Requiem for a Lightweight: Vice Presidential Candidate Evaluations and the Presidential Vote," *Presidential Studies Quarterly* 31, no. 3 (2001): 454–63; Thomas M. Holbrook, "The Behavioral Consequences of Vice-Presidential Debates: Does the Undercard Have Any Punch?" *American Politics Quarterly* 22, no. 4 (1994): 469–82; Brian J. Brox and Madison L. Cassels, "The Contemporary Effects of Vice-Presidential Nominees: Sarah Palin and the 2008 Presidential Campaign," *Journal of Political Marketing* 8 (2009): 349–63; Edward M. Burmila and Josh M. Ryan, "Reconsidering the 'Palin Effect' in the 2008 Presidential Election," *Political Research Quarterly* 66 (2013): 952–59; Jonathan Knuckey, "Comments on Reconsidering the 'Palin Effect'," *Political Research Quarterly* 66 (2013): 960–63; and Jonathan Knuckey, "The 'Palin Effect' in the 2008 U.S. Presidential Election," *Political Research Quarterly* 20 (2008): 1–15.
45. Marie D. Natoli, *American Prince, American Pauper: The Contemporary Vice Presidency in Perspective* (Westport, CT: Greenwood Press, 1985), 43.

CHAPTER 6

1. Fox News, "Why 2016 Will Be Most Negative, Nasty Presidential Campaign in Modern American History," Fox News.com, January 14, 2016, https://www.fox news.com/opinion/why-2016-will-be-most-negative-nasty-presidential-campaign -in-modern-american-history.

2. Joseph Cummins, "This Is the Dirtiest Presidential Race Since '72," *Politico*, February 17, 2016, https://www.politico.com/magazine/story/2016/02/2016-electio ns-nastiest-presidential-election-since-1972-213644.

3. Adam Eley, "Is This the Nastiest US Election Campaign?" BBC.com, November 8, 2016, https://www.bbc.com/news/av/election-us-2016-37904916/i s-this-the-nastiest-us-election-campaign.

4. Nancy Cordes, "Negative Presidential Campaign Ads Going to New Extremes," *CBS News*, August 10, 2012, http://www.cbsnews.com/news/negative-presidential-campaign-ads-going-to-new-extremes/.

5. Nicole Greenstein, "Negative Ads: A Shift in Tone for the 2012 Campaign," *Time*, July 17, 2012, http://swampland.time.com/2012/07/17/negative-ads-a-shi ft-in-tone-for-the-2012-campaign/.

6. Craig Crawford, "Memorable Moments 2008," *Huffington Post*, November 3, 2008, www.huffingtonpost.com/craig-crawford/memorable-moments-2008 _b_140442.html.

7. Michael Musto, "The McCain Campaign is the Ugliest Ever," *The Village Voice*, October 24, 2008, blogs.villagevoice.com/dailymusto/archives/2008/10/the_ mccain_camp.php.

8. "Cindy McCain: Obama Has 'Waged the Dirtiest Campaign in American History,'" *ABC News*, October 7, 2008, blogs.abcnews.com/politicalpunch/20 08/10/ cindy-mccain-ob.html.

9. "Most Scurrilous Campaign in History?" *MSNBC*, October 15, 2008, first read.msnbc.msn.com/archive/2008/10/15/1548251.aspx.

10. Kathleen Hall Jamieson, *Dirty Politics: Deception, Distraction, and Democracy* (New York, NY: Oxford University Press, 1992), 43.

11. Jamieson, *Dirty Politics*, 43.

12. See, for example, Stephen Ansolabehere, Shanto Iyengar, Adam Simon, and Nicholas Valentino, "Does Attack Advertising Demobilize the Electorate?" *American Political Science Review* 88 (1994): 829–38; William G. Mayer, "In Defense of Negative Campaigning," *Political Science Quarterly* 111 (1996): 437–55; Richard R. Lau and Gerald M. Pomper, *Negative Campaigning: An Analysis of U.S. Senate Elections* (Lanham, MD: Rowman & Littlefield, 2004); David Mark, *Going Dirty: The Art of Negative Campaigning* (Lanham, MD: Rowman & Littlefield, 2006).

13. Mark, *Going Dirty*, chap. 1.

14. Ansolabehere et al., "Does Attack Advertising Demobilize the Electorate?"; Stephen Ansolabehere and Shanto Iyengar, *Going Negative* (New York, NY: Free Press, 1995); Stephen Ansolabehere, Shanto Iyengar, and Adam Simon, "The Case of Negative Advertising and Turnout," *American Political Science Review* 93 (1999): 901–33.

15. Gina M. Garramone, Charles T. Atkin, Bruce E. Pinkleton, and Richard T. Cole, "Effects of Negative Political Advertising on the Political Process," *Journal of*

Broadcasting and Electronic Media 34 (1990): 299–311; Craig L. Brians and Martin P. Wattenberg, "Campaign Issue Knowledge and Salience: Comparing Reception from TV Commercials, TV News, and Newspapers," *American Journal of Political Science* 40 (1996): 172–93; Mayer, "In Defense of Negative Campaigning"; Steven E. Finkel and John Geer, "A Spot Check: Casting Doubt on the Demobilizing Effect of Attack Advertising," *American Journal of Political Science* 42 (1998): 573–95; Kim Fridkin Kahn and Patrick J. Kenney, "Do Negative Campaigns Mobilize or Suppress Turnout? Clarifying the Relationship between Negativity and Participation," *American Political Science Review* 93 (1999): 877–89.

16. Aaron Burr, who became the vice president after the election of 1800, later shot and killed Alexander Hamilton in a duel, at least in part because of the political attacks and opposition he endured from Hamilton. See Buckner F. Melton Jr., *Aaron Burr: Conspiracy to Treason* (New York, NY: John Wiley & Sons, 2002), 23–24.

17. Paul F. Boller Jr., *Presidential Campaigns: From George Washington to George W. Bush* (New York, NY: Oxford University Press, 2004), 11. See also Charles O. Lerche Jr., "Jefferson and the Election of 1800: A Case Study in the Political Smear," *The William and Mary Quarterly* 5 (1948): 467–91.

18. Victor Kamber, *Poison Politics: Are Negative Campaigns Destroying Democracy?* (New York, NY: Basic Books, 1997), 15.

19. Boller, *Presidential Campaigns*, 12.

20. Jamieson, *Dirty Politics*, 31.

21. Boller, *Presidential Campaigns*, 12.

22. Kerwin C. Swint, *Mudslingers: The Top 25 Negative Political Campaigns of All Time* (Westport, CT: Praeger, 2006), 184.

23. Swint, *Mudslingers*, 185.

24. For more information about the election of 1800, see Susan Dunn, *Jefferson's Second Revolution: The Election Crisis of 1800 and the Triumph of Republicanism* (New York, NY: Houghton Mifflin, 2004). For more information about election results and totals for the election of 1800 and others covered in this chapter, see Jerrold G. Rusk, *A Statistical History of the American Electorate* (Washington, DC: CQ Press, 2001).

25. According to Kerwin Swint, in *Mudslingers*, the election of 1800 ranks as the fourth dirtiest campaign in U.S. history.

26. Totals from Rusk, *Statistical History of the American Electorate*.

27. Swint, *Mudslingers*, 213.

28. Jeffrey A. Jenkins and Brian R. Sala, "The Spatial Theory of Voting and the Presidential Election of 1824," *American Journal of Political Science* 42 (1998): 1157–79.

29. Boller, *Presidential Campaigns*, 44.

30. Boller, *Presidential Campaigns*, 44.

31. Swint, *Mudslingers*, 217.

32. Norma Basch, "Marriage, Morals, and Politics in the Election of 1828," *The Journal of American History* 80 (1993): 890–918. See also Boller, *Presidential Campaigns*, 45.

33. Boller, *Presidential Campaigns*, 46.

34. Basch, "Marriage, Morals, and Politics in the Election of 1828."

35. Boller, *Presidential Campaigns*, 46.

36. In *Mudslingers*, Kerwin Swint labeled the 1828 election as the most negative presidential campaign in history and the second most negative of all time (with only the George Wallace–Albert Brewer election for governor of Alabama in 1970 coming in higher).

37. Swint, *Mudslingers*, 194.

38. Boller, *Presidential Campaigns*, 118–19.

39. Ward Hill Lamon, *Recollections of Abraham Lincoln, 1847–1865* (Chicago: A.C. McClurg, 1895), 143–48; Boller, *Presidential Campaigns*, 120.

40. Boller, *Presidential Campaigns*, 121–22.

41. Boller, *Presidential Campaigns*, 121–22.

42. John C. Waugh, *Reelecting Lincoln: The Battle of the 1864 Presidency* (New York, NY: Perseus Books, 2001).

43. Swint, *Mudslingers*, 32.

44. Paul Freedman and Ken Goldstein, "Measuring Media Exposure and the Effects of Negative Campaign Ads," *American Journal of Political Science* 43 (1999): 1189–208; Paul Fredman, Michael Franz, and Kenneth Goldstein, "Campaign Advertising and Democratic Citizenship," *American Journal of Political Science* 48 (2004): 723–41.

45. In *Mudslingers*, Kerwin Swint placed the 1964 and 1988 presidential elections as among the most negative campaigns in history.

46. Emmett H. Buell Jr. and Lee Sigelman, *Attack Politics: Negativity in Presidential Campaigns since 1960* (Lawrence, KS: University Press of Kansas, 2008), 29.

47. Goldwater quoted in Adam Cohen, *Nothing to Fear: FDR's Inner Circle and the Hundred Days that Created Modern America* (New York, NY: Penguin Books, 2009), 317.

48. Goldwater quoted in Gerald Garner, *Campaign Comedy: Political Humor from Clinton to Kennedy* (Detroit, MI: Wayne State University Press, 1994), 260.

49. Goldwater quoted in Robert Andrews, *The Columbia Dictionary of Quotations* (New York, NY: Columbia University Press, 1993), 303.

50. The Living Room Candidate, www.livingroomcandidate.org/commercials/1964.

51. Swint, *Mudslingers*, 31.

52. The Living Room Candidate, www.livingroomcandidate.org/commercials/1964.

53. The Living Room Candidate, www.livingroomcandidate.org/commercials/1964.

54. Kathleen Hall Jamison, *Packaging the Presidency: A History and Criticism of Presidential Campaign Advertising* (New York, NY: Oxford University Press, 1996), 220.

55. The Living Room Candidate, www.livingroomcandidate.org/commercials/1964.

56. The Living Room Candidate, www.livingroomcandidate.org/commercials/1964.

57. The Living Room Candidate, www.livingroomcandidate.org/commercials/1964.

58. Swint, *Mudslingers,* 272.

59. E. J. Dionne Jr., "Poll Shows Dukakis Leads Bush; Many Reagan Backers Shift Sides," *The New York Times*, May 17, 1988, A1.

60. CNN ad archive, www.cnn.com/ALLPOLITICS/1996/candidates/ad.archive/horton.mov.

61. Jamieson, *Dirty Politics*, 17.

62. The Living Room Candidate, www.livingroomcandidate.org/commercials/1999.

CHAPTER 7

1. Michael Barthel and Jeffrey Gottfried, "Majority of U.S. Adults Think News Media Should Not Add Interpretation to the Facts," *Pew Research Center*, November 18, 2016, http://www.pewresearch.org/fact-tank/2016/11/18/news-media-interpretation-vs-facts/.

2. Amy Mitchell, Katie Simmons, Katerina Eva Matsa, and Laura Silver, "Publics Globally Want Unbiased News Coverage, But Are Divided on Whether Their News Media Deliver," *Pew Research Center*, January 11, 2018, http://www.pewglobal.org/2018/01/11/publics-globally-want-unbiased-news-coverage-but-are-divided-on-whether-their-news-media-deliver/.

3. Mitchell et al., "Publics Globally Want Unbiased News Coverage."

4. Pew Research Center, July 2013, from http://pollingreport.com/media.htm.

5. Quinnipiac University, January 2017, and Bloomberg Politics Poll, December 2016, from http://pollingreport.com/media.htm.

6. Doris Graber, *Mass Media and American Politics*, 7th ed. (Washington, DC: CQ Press, 2006).

7. Michael Schudson, "The Objectivity Norm in American Journalism," *Journalism* 2 (2001): 149–70. See also Michael Emery, Edwin Emery, and Nancy L. Roberts, *The Press and America: An Interpretive History of the Mass Media*, 9th ed. (Boston, MA: Allyn & Bacon, 1999).

8. Schudson, "Objectivity Norm," 156, 158, 163.

9. Stephen J. Wayne, *Road to the White House 2004: The Politics of Presidential Elections*, 7th ed. (Belmont, CA: Wadsworth, 2004), 226.

10. Robert G. Kaiser, "The Bad News About the News," *Brooking Institution*, October 16, 2014, http://csweb.brookings.edu/content/research/essays/2014/bad-news-print.html.

11. Kaiser, "The Bad News About the News."

12. Dan Brown, "A History of Communication Technology," in *Communication Technology Update and Fundamentals*, ed. August E. Grant and Jennifer H. Meadows, 14th ed. (New York, NY: Focal Press, 2014), 9–20.

13. Aaron Smith, "Record Shares of Americans Now Own Smartphones, Have Home Broadband," *Pew Research Center* "FactTank," January 12, 2017, http://www.pewresearch.org/fact-tank/2017/01/12/evolution-of-technology/.

14. Brian Stelter, "Seeking More Viewers, MSNBC Turns Left," *New York Times*, August 21, 2008, www.nytimes.com/2008/08/22/business/media/22adco.html; Project for Excellence in Journalism, "The Color of News: How Different

Media Have Covered the General Election," October 29, 2008, www.journalism
.org/node/13436.

15. Jeffrey M. Jones and Zacc Ritter, "Americans See More News Bias; Most
Can't Name Neutral Source," *Gallup*, January 17, 2018, https://news.gallup.com/p
oll/225755/americans-news-bias-name-neutral-source.aspx.

16. Lymari Morales, "Majority in U.S. Continues to Distrust the Media, Perceive
Bias," *Gallup*, September 22, 2011, http://www.gallup.com/poll/149624/majori
ty-continue-distrust-media-perceive-bias.aspx.

17. John Sides, "Is the Media Biased Toward Clinton or Trump? Here Is Some
Actual Hard Data," *Washington Post*, September 20, 2016, https://www.washingt
onpost.com/news/monkey-cage/wp/2016/09/20/is-the-media-biased-toward-clinto
n-or-trump-heres-some-actual-hard-data/?utm_term=.a5cd0384e4c7.

18. Shanto Iyengar and Kyu S. Hahn, "Red Media, Blue Media: Evidence of
Ideological Selectivity in Media Use," *Journal of Communication* 59 (2009): 19–39.

19. Jay G. Blumler and Elihu Katz, eds., *The Uses of Mass Communications:
Current Perspectives on Gratifications Research* (Beverly Hills, CA: Sage, 1974);
Tomas Ruggiero, "Uses and Gratifications Theory in the 21st Century," *Mass Com-
munication & Society* 3, no. 1 (2000): 3–37.

20. Adam J. Schiffer, *Evaluating Media Bias* (Lanham, MD: Rowman & Littlefield, 2018), 17.

21. Tim Groseclose, *Left Turn: How Liberal Media Bias Distorts the American
Mind* (New York, NY: St. Martin's Press, 2011).

22. Center for Media and Public Affairs, "Election Watch '08: The Primaries,"
Media Monitor 22 (March/April 2008), https://cmpa.gmu.edu/wp-content/uploads/
2014/02/2008-4.pdf; Center for Media and Public Affairs, "Election Watch: Campaign 2008 Final," *Media Monitor* 23 (Winter 2009), https://cmpa.gmu.edu/wp-c
ontent/uploads/2014/02/2008-1.pdf.

23. Alexios Mantzarlis, "Not Fake News, Just Plain Wrong: Top Media Corrections of 2017," *The Poynter Institute*, December 18, 2017, https://www.poy
nter.org/fact-checking/2017/not-fake-news-just-plain-wrong-top-media-corrections
-of-2017/.

24. Jeffrey Gottfried and Elisa Shearer, "News Use Across Social Media Platforms 2016," *Pew Research Center*, May 26, 2016, http://www.journalism.org
/2016/05/26/news-use-across-social-media-platforms-2016/.

25. Laura Sydell, "We Tracked Down a Fake-News Creator in the Suburbs.
Here's What We Learned," *NPR*, November 23, 2016, https://www.npr.org/
sections/alltechconsidered/2016/11/23/503146770/npr-finds-the-head-of-a-covert-f
ake-news-operation-in-the-suburbs.

26. David Uberti, "Journalism Has a Plagiarism Problem," *Columbia Journalism
Review*, November 18, 2014, https://www.cjr.org/watchdog/journalism_has_a_plag
iarism_pr.php.

27. Thomas E. Patterson, *The Mass Media Election: How Americans Choose
Their President* (New York, NY: Praeger, 1980).

28. Thomas E. Patterson, *Out of Order: An Incisive and Boldly Original Cri-
tique of the News Media's Domination of America's Political Process* (New York,
NY: Vintage, 1994).

29. Thomas E. Patterson, "News Coverage of the 2016 General Election: How the Press Failed the Voters," *Shorenstein Center on Media, Politics and Public Policy*, December 7, 2016, https://shorensteincenter.org/news-coverage-2016-g eneral-election/. See note 14.

30. Center for Media and Public Affairs, "Campaign 2004—The Primaries," *Media Monitor* 18 (March/April 2004), www.cmpa.com/mediaMonitor/documents /marapr04.pdf.

31. Thomas E. Patterson, "News Coverage of the 2016 Presidential Primaries: Horse Race Reporting Has Consequences," *Shorenstein Center on Media, Politics and Public Policy*, July 11, 2016, https://shorensteincenter.org/news-coverage-2 016-presidential-primaries/.

32. Graber, *Mass Media and American Politics*, 221–22.

33. Patterson, "News Coverage of the 2016 Presidential Primaries."

34. Patterson, "News Coverage of the 2016 Presidential Primaries."

35. Tom Rosenstiel, Mark Jurkowitz, and Tricia Sartor, "How the Media Covered the 2012 Primary Campaign," *Pew Research Center*, April 23, 2012, http:// www.journalism.org/2012/04/23/romney-report/.

36. John Sides, "Media Coverage of the 2012 Election was Fair and Balanced After All," *Washington Post*, October 14, 2013, http://www.washingtonpost.com/ blogs/monkey-cage/wp/2013/10/14/media-coverage-of-the-2012-election-was-fai r-and-balanced-after-all/.

37. Center for Media and Public Affairs, "Election Watch '08: The Primaries."

38. Jacqueline Bacon, "Weeding the Field: The Lowest Circle," *Extra!* (September/October 2003), www.fair.org/index.php?page=1153.

39. Howard Kurtz, "Ted Koppel, Anchor Provocateur," *Washington Post*, December 10, 2003, C1.

40. Graber, *Mass Media and American Politics*, 222.

41. Patterson, "News Coverage of the 2016 Presidential Primaries."

42. Kiku Adatto, "The Incredible Shrinking Soundbite," *New Republic*, May 28, 1990.

43. Graber, *Mass Media and American Politics*, 222.

44. Larry J. Sabato, *Feeding Frenzy* (New York, NY: Free Press, 1993).

45. David Wright and Sunlen Miller, "Obama Dropped Flag Pin in War Statement," *ABC News*, October 4, 2007, abcnews.go.com/Politics/story?id=3690000 &page=1; Jennifer Parker, "Michelle Obama Defends Patriotism, Jokes of 'Girl Fight' on 'View,'" *ABC News*, June 18, 2008, abcnews.go.com/Politics/Vote2008/ story?id=5193627&page=1.

46. Patterson, "News Coverage of the 2016 General Election."

47. Patterson, "News Coverage of the 2016 General Election."

48. Patterson, "News Coverage of the 2016 General Election."

49. David R. Runkel, ed., *Campaign for President: The Managers Look at '88* (Dover, MA: Auburn House, 1989), 136.

50. Timothy Crouse, *The Boys on the Bus* (New York, NY: Random House, 1973).

51. W. Lance Bennett, *News: The Politics of Illusion*, 7th ed. (New York, NY: Longman, 2007), 171–3.

52. Center for Media and Public Affairs, "Campaign 2004—The Primaries."

53. Pew Research Center, "Winning the Media Campaign: How the Press Reported the 2008 General Election," October 22, 2008, https://www.pewresearch.org/wp-content/uploads/sites/8/legacy/WINNING-THE-MEDIA-CAMPAIGN-FINAL.pdf.

54. Thomas E. Patterson, "Pre-Primary News Coverage of the 2016 Presidential Race: Trump's Rise, Sanders' Emergence, Clinton's Struggle," *Shorenstein Center on Media, Politics and Public Policy*, June 13, 2016, https://shorensteincenter.org/pre-primary-news-coverage-2016-trump-clinton-sanders/; Patterson, "News Coverage of the 2016 Presidential Primaries."

55. Patterson, "Pre-Primary News Coverage of the 2016 Presidential Race"; Patterson, "News Coverage of the 2016 Presidential Primaries."

56. Wayne, *Road to the White House*, 230; "Campaign 2000 Final," *Media Monitor* 14 (November/December 2000).

57. Robert W. McChesney, *Rich Media, Poor Democracy: Communication Politics in Dubious Times* (New York, NY: The New Press, 2000).

CHAPTER 8

1. See "Presidential Debates and Their Effects," *Journalist's Resource*, October 16, 2012, http://journalistsresource.org/studies/politics/elections/presidential-debates-effects-research-roundup.

2. Quoted in Alexander Bolton, "Ten Game Changers That Could Decide the Race Between Obama and Romney," *The Hill*, June 3, 2012, http://thehill.com/homenews/campaign/230583-ten-game-changers-that-could-decide-the-presidency.

3. David Smith, "Trump Needs 'Game-Changing' Win in Next Debate to Salvage Election Chances," TheGuardian.com, October 7, 2016, https://www.theguardian.com/us-news/2016/oct/07/trump-clinton-second-presidential-debate.

4. Robert Schlesinger, "Sorry, Romney, Presidential Debates Are Rarely Game-Changers," *U.S. News & World Report*, October 3, 2012, https://www.usnews.com/opinion/articles/2012/10/03/sorry-romney-presidential-debates-are-rarely-game-changers.

5. Lydia Saad, "Presidential Debates Rarely Game-Changers," *Gallup*, September 25, 2008, http://www.gallup.com/poll/110674/presidential-debates-rarely-gamechangers.aspx.

6. Kayla Webley, "How the Nixon-Kennedy Debate Changed the World," *Time*, September 23, 2010, http://content.time.com/time/nation/article/0,8599,2021078,00.html.

7. History.com Staff, "The Kennedy-Nixon Debates," History.com, September 21, 2010, www.history.com/topics/us-presidents/kennedy-nixon-debates.

8. See the various accounts in Sidney Kraus, ed., *The Great Debates: Kennedy vs. Nixon, 1960* (Bloomington, IN: Indiana University Press, 1977); and History.com Staff, "The Kennedy-Nixon Debates."

9. There is some debate about accounts that suggest Kennedy bested Nixon because he looked better on television. For a good summary of this, see David Greenberg, "Rewinding the Kennedy-Nixon Debates: Did JFK Really Win Because He Looked Better on Television?" *Slate*, September 24, 2010, http://www.slate.com

/articles/news_and_politics/history_lesson/2010/09/rewinding_the_kennedynixon_debates.2.html. However, some credible evidence supports the notion that Kennedy's superior appearance had an impact. See James N. Druckman, "The Power of Television Images: The First Kennedy-Nixon Debate Revisited," *Journal of Politics* 65 (2003): 559–71.

10. Saad, "Presidential Debates Rarely Game-Changers."

11. See the "Debate Transcripts," Commission on Presidential Debates, accessed from http://www.debates.org/index.php?page=debate-transcripts.

12. "Debate Transcripts," Commission on Presidential Debates.

13. "Debating Our Destiny: The Ford/Carter Debates," *PBS*, September 24, 2000, http://www.pbs.org/newshour/spc/debatingourdestiny/doc1976.html.

14. Michael Reagan and Jim Denney, *The New Reagan Revolution: How Ronald Regan's Principles Can Restore America's Greatness Today* (New York, NY: St. Martin's Press, 2010), 46.

15. Saad, "Presidential Debates Rarely Game-Changers."

16. "Debate Transcripts," Commission on Presidential Debates.

17. Quote from "1980 Presidential Debates," *CNN*, 1996, http://www.cnn.com/ALLPOLITICS/1996/debates/history/1980/index.shtml. For further information about the impact of the "Amy speech," see Paul F. Boller Jr., *Presidential Campaigns: From George Washington to George W. Bush* (New York, NY: Oxford University Press, 2004), 367.

18. "Debate Transcripts," Commission on Presidential Debates.

19. "American President: A Reference Resource," Miller Center, University of Virginia, http://millercenter.org/president/carter/essays/biography/3.

20. Quoted in Marc A. Thiessen, "Like Reagan, Romney Can Still Win," *The Washington Post*, October 1, 2012, http://www.washingtonpost.com/opinions/like-reagan-romney-can-still-win/2012/10/01/01776f94-0bcb-11e2-bb5e-492c0d30bff6_story.html.

21. "Debate Transcripts," Commission on Presidential Debates.

22. M. J. Stephey, "Top Ten Memorable Debate Moments," *Time*, September 26, 2008, http://content.time.com/time/specials/packages/article/0,28804,1844704_1844706_1844712,00.html.

23. Rick Shenkman, "History Proves that Presidential Debates Matter," *History News Network*, September 22, 2004, http://historynewsnetwork.org/article/7478.

24. Saad, "Presidential Debates Rarely Game-Changers."

25. Bill Plante, "Game-Changing Presidential Debates Remembered," *CBS News*, October 2, 2012, http://www.cbsnews.com/news/game-changing-presidential-debates-remembered; and "Game-Changing Debate Moments," *NPR*, February 29, 2012, http://www.npr.org/2012/02/29/147654737/game-changing-debate-moments.

26. See, for example, Sean Sullivan, "The 10 Most Memorable Moments in Presidential Debates," *The Washington Post*, October 2, 2012, http://www.washingtonpost.com/blogs/the-fx/wp/2012/10/02/the-10-most-memorable-moments-in-presidential-debates.

27. Quoted in Nelson W. Polsby, Aaron Wildavsky, Steven E. Schier, and David A. Hopkins, *Presidential Elections: Strategies and Structures of American Politics*, 13th ed. (Lanham, MD: Rowman & Littlefield, 2012), 193.

28. Quoted in CNN Political Unit, "10 Debate Moments That Mattered," *CNN*, October 3, 2012, http://www.cnn.com/2012/10/02/politics/debate-moments-that-m attered.

29. Saad, "Presidential Debates Rarely Game-Changers."

30. "Debate Transcripts," Commission on Presidential Debates.

31. Jack Germond and Jules Witcover, *Wake Us When It's Over: Presidential Politics in 1984* (New York, NY: Macmillan, 1985), 9.

32. CNN Political Unit, "10 Debate Moments That Mattered."

33. CNN Political Unit, "10 Debate Moments That Mattered."

34. Saad, "Presidential Debates Rarely Game-Changers."

35. Frank Newport, "What History Tells Us About Second and Third Debates," *Gallup*, October 7, 2004, http://www.gallup.com/poll/13525/what-history-tells-abo ut-second-third-debates.aspx.

36. Saad, "Presidential Debates Rarely Game-Changers."

37. John Sides, "What Really Happened in the 1980 Presidential Campaign," *The Monkey Cage*, August 9, 2012, http://themonkeycage.org/2012/08/09/what -really-happened-in-the-1980-presidential-campaign. For further information, see Robert S. Erikson and Christopher Wlezien, *The Timeline of Presidential Elections: How Campaigns Do (and Do Not) Matter* (Chicago, IL: University of Chicago Press, 2012).

38. Sides, "What Really Happened"; and Erikson and Wlezien, *The Timeline of Presidential Elections*.

39. Sides, "What Really Happened"; and Erikson and Wlezien, *The Timeline of Presidential Elections*.

40. Germond and Witcover, *Wake Us When It's Over*. Also discussed in "Romney's Debate Performance Was Presidential Game Changer, Analysts Say," *Star-Ledger*, October 5, 2012, http://www.nj.com/politics/index.ssf/2012/10/romne ys_debate_performance_was.html.

41. Samuel L. Popkin, *The Reasoning Voter: Communication and Persuasion in Presidential Campaigns*, 2nd ed. (Chicago, IL: University of Chicago Press, 1994), 233.

42. Quote from James Stimson in John Sides, "Do Presidential Debates Really Matter?" *Washington Monthly*, September/October 2012, http://www.washingto n-monthly.com/magazine/septemberoctober_2012/ten_miles_square/do_presidenti al_debates_really039413.php.

43. Erikson and Wlezien, *The Timeline of Presidential Elections*. For a helpful summary, see also Sides, "Do Presidential Debates Really Matter?"

44. Erikson and Wlezien, *The Timeline of Presidential Elections*; Sides, "Do Presidential Debates Really Matter?"

45. Jeffrey M. Jones, "Romney Narrows Vote Gap After Historic Debate Win," *Gallup*, October 8, 2012, http://www.gallup.com/poll/157907/romney-narrows-v ote-gap-historic-debate-win.aspx.

46. John G. Geer, "The Effects of Presidential Debates on the Electorate's Pref- erences for Candidates," *American Politics Quarterly* 16 (1988): 486–501; and Erikson and Wlezien, *The Timeline of Presidential Elections*.

47. Quoted in Karen E. Crummy, "Obama, Romney Engage in University of Denver Presidential Debate," *The Denver Post*, October 3, 2012, http://www.denver-post.com/ci_21691794/obama-romney-prepare-take-stage-frst-debate.

48. Sides, "Do Presidential Debates Really Matter?"

49. David O. Sears and Steven H. Chafee, "Uses and Effects of the 1976 Debates: An Overview of Empirical Studies," in *The Great Debates*, ed. Sidney Kraus (Bloomington, IN: Indiana University Press, 1979). For more recent research, see Geer, "The Effects of Presidential Debates on the Electorate's Preferences for Candidates"; and Erikson and Wlezien, *The Timeline of Presidential Elections*.

50. Quoted in Miranda Green, "Presidential Debates Rarely Have Much Effect on Election Outcomes," *The Daily Beast*, September 29, 2012, http://www.thedailybeast.com/articles/2012/09/29/presidential-debates-rarely-have-much-effect-on-election-outcomes.html.

51. Stanley Kelley Jr., "Campaign Debates: Some Facts and Issues," *Public Opinion Quarterly* 26 (1962): 351–66.

52. Sides, "Do Presidential Debates Really Matter?"

53. Kathleen Hall Jamieson and David S. Birdsell, *Presidential Debates: The Challenge of Creating an Informed Electorate* (New York, NY: Oxford University Press, 1988): 131–32.

54. Jamieson and Birdsell, *Presidential Debates*.

55. Nielson, "Second Presidential Debate of 2016 Draws 66.5 Million Viewers," *Nielson.com*, October 10, 2016, https://www.nielsen.com/us/en/insights/news/2016/second-presidential-debate-of-2016-draws-66-5-million-viewers.html.

56. Frank Newport, "Viewers Deem Obama Winner of Third Debate, 56% to 33%," *Gallup*, October 25, 2012, http://www.gallup.com/poll/158393/viewers-deem-obama-winner-third-debate.aspx.

57. Newport, "Viewers Deem Obama Winner."

58. Frank Newport, "Debate Watchers Give Obama Edge Over McCain," *Gallup*, September 28, 2008, http://www.gallup.com/poll/110779/debate-watchers-give-obama-edge-over-mccain.aspx; and Newport, "What History Tells Us."

59. John Zaller, *The Nature and Origins of Mass Opinion* (Cambridge, UK: Cambridge University Press, 1992).

60. "Low Marks for Major Players in 2016 Election – Including the Winner," *Pew Research Center*, November 21, 2016, https://www.people-press.org/2016/11/21/voters-evaluations-of-the-campaign.

61. "Low Marks for the 2012 Election," *Pew Research Center*, November 15, 2012, https://www.people-press.org/2012/11/15/low-marks-for-the-2012-election/.

62. Thomas M. Holbrook, "Political Learning from Presidential Debates," *Political Behavior* 21 (1999): 67–89.

63. Holbrook, "Political Learning from Presidential Debates." See also Alan I. Abramowitz, "The Impact of a Presidential Debate on Voter Rationality," *American Journal of Political Science* 22 (1978): 680–90; and Lee Becker, Idowu Sobowale, Robin Cobbey, and Chaim Eyal, "Debates' Effects on Voters' Understanding of Candidates and Issues," in *The Presidential Debates*, ed. George Bishop, Robert Meadow, and Marilyn Jackson-Meadow (New York, NY: Praeger, 1978).

64. David J. Lanoue, "The 'Turning Point': Viewers' Reactions to the Second 1988 Presidential Debate," *American Politics Quarterly* 19 (1991): 80–95.

65. Steven H. Chaffee, "Presidential Debates—Are They Helpful to Voters?" *Communication Monographs* 45 (1978): 330–46; and Micahel Pfau, "Intraparty Political Debates and Social Learning," *Journal of Applied Communication Research* 16 (1988): 99–112.

66. Holbrook, "Political Learning from Presidential Debates"; and Sears and Chafee, "Uses and Effects of the 1976 Debates."

67. Abramowitz, "The Impact of a Presidential Debate."

68. Robert E. Denton and Gary C. Woodward, *Political Communication in America* (New York, NY: Praeger, 1990).

69. Donald P. Green and Ron Shachar, "Habit Formation and Political Behaviour: Evidence of Consuetude," *British Journal of Political Science* 30, no. 4 (2000): 561–73.

70. See, for example, Sears and Chafee, "Uses and Effects of the 1976 Debates"; and Geer, "The Effects of Presidential Debates."

71. See comments from Allan Lounden in Green, "Presidential Debates Rarely Have Much Effect."

72. See comments from Allan Lounden in Green, "Presidential Debates Rarely Have Much Effect."

73. Linda L. Swanson and David L. Swanson, "The Agenda-Setting Function of the First Ford-Carter Debate," *Communication Monographs* 45 (1978): 347–53.

74. Mike Yawn, Kevin Ellsworth, Bob Beatty, and Kim Fridkin Kahn, "How a Presidential Primary Debate Changed Attitudes of Audience Members," *Political Behavior* 20 (1998): 155–81.

75. William L. Benoit, Glenn J. Hansen, and Rebecca M. Verser, "A Meta-Analysis of the Effects of Viewing U.S. Presidential Debates," *Communication Monographs* 70 (2003): 335–50.

CHAPTER 9

1. Humphrey Taylor, "Myth and Reality in Reporting Sampling Error: How the Media Confuse and Mislead Readers and Viewers," *Polling Report,* May 4, 1998, www.pollingreport.com/sampling.htm.

2. Natalie Jackson, "HuffPost Forecasts Hillary Clinton Will Win With 323 Electoral Votes," *The Huffington Post,* November 7, 2016, https://www.huffpost.com/entry/polls-hillary-clinton-win_n_5821074ce4b0e80b02cc2a94.

3. Figures were obtained from a LexisNexis Academic Reference Search of Polls & Surveys, Roper Center, "Public Opinion Online," June 2, 2000, Question Number 185.

4. In this sense our objective is similar to Herbert Asher's, whose text *Polling and the Public: What Every Citizen Should Know,* 6th ed. (Washington, DC: CQ Press, 2004) not only is one of the leading textbooks in the field but also was an invaluable source of material for this chapter.

5. Tom W. Smith, "The First Straw? A Study of the Origins of Election Polls," *Public Opinion Quarterly* 54 (1990): 21–36.

6. See Susan Herbst, "Election Polling in Historical Perspective," in *Presidential Polls and the News Media*, ed. Paul J. Lavrakas, Michael W. Traugott, and Peter V. Miller (Boulder, CO: Westview, 1995).

7. From Herbst, "Election Polling in Historical Perspective," 26.

8. Robert S. Erikson and Kent L. Tedin, *American Public Opinion: Its Origins, Content, and Impact*, 7th ed. (New York, NY: Longman, 2005).

9. Peverill Squire, "Why the 1936 *Literary Digest* Poll Failed," *Public Opinion Quarterly* 52 (1988): 125–33.

10. Olav Kallenberg, *Foundations of Modern Probability*, 2nd ed. (New York, NY: Springer, 2002).

11. Herbert F. Weisberg, Jon A. Krosnik, and Bruce D. Bowen, *An Introduction to Survey Research, Polling, and Data Analysis*, 3rd ed. (Thousand Oaks, CA: Sage, 1996), 33.

12. Squire, "Why the 1936 *Literary Digest* Poll Failed."

13. Squire, "Why the 1936 *Literary Digest* Poll Failed," 10–14.

14. Squire, "Why the 1936 *Literary Digest* Poll Failed."

15. Courtney Kennedy and Hannah Hartig, "Response Rates in Telephone Surveys Have Resumed Their Decline," *Pew Research Center*, February 27, 2019, https://www.pewresearch.org/fact-tank/2019/02/27/response-rates-in-telephone-sur veys-have-resumed-their-decline.

16. For a full discussion on the subject of nonresponse bias in surveys, see Robert M. Groves, "Nonresponse Rates and Nonresponse Bias in Household Surveys," *Public Opinion Quarterly* 70 (2006): 646–75.

17. Mick P. Couper, "The Future of Modes of Data Collection," *Public Opinion Quarterly* 75 (2011): 889–908.

18. "Number of Internet Users in the United States from 2000 to 2016 (in Millions), Statista," *Statista*, last edited July 1, 2016, https://www.statista.com/statistics /276445/number-of-internet-users-in-the-united-states.

19. Stephen Ansolabehere and Brian F. Schaffner, "Does Survey Mode Still Matter? Findings from a 2010 Multi-Mode Comparison," *Political Analysis* 22 (2014): 285–303.

20. Don Dillman, Jolene D. Smyth, and Leah Melani Christian, *Internet, Mail, and Mixed-Mode Surveys: The Tailored Design Method* (Hoboken, NJ: John Wiley & Sons, 2009).

21. U.S. Census Bureau, Current Population Survey, November 2012.

22. Erikson and Tedin, *American Public Opinion*, 45.

23. Tom Rosentiel, "Determining Who is a Likely Voter," *Pew Research Center*, August 29, 2012, https://www.pewresearch.org/2012/08/29/ask-the-expert-determ ining-who-is-a-likely-voter.

24. David W. Nickerson and Todd Rogers, "Political Campaigns and Big Data," *Journal of Economic Perspectives* 28 (2014): 51–74.

25. "Bush Leads by Eight Points-or Two-Depending on Definition of Likely Voters," *PRNewswire*, October 20, 2004, www.prnewswire.com/cgi-bin/stories.pl?AC CT=105&STORY=/www/story/10-20-2004/0002289475. See also Robert S. Erikson, Costas Panagopoulos, and Christopher Wlezien, "Likely (and Unlikely) Voters and the Assessment of Campaign Dynamics," *Public Opinion Quarterly* 68 (2004):

588–601, for an in-depth exploration of the methods of measuring likely voters by the Gallup Organization.

26. Dana Blanton, "Fox News Poll: Clinton and Trump in a One Point Race Among Likely Voters," *Fox News*, September 15, 2016, https://www.foxnews.com/politics/fox-news-poll-clinton-and-trump-in-a-one-point-race-among-likely-voters.

27. Erikson and Tedin, *American Public Opinion*, 43.

28. Irving Crespi, *Pre-Election Polling: Sources of Accuracy and Error* (New York, NY: Russell Sage, 1988).

29. Erikson and Tedin, *American Public Opinion*, 43.

30. "An Evaluation of 2016 Election Polls in the U.S," *AAPOR*, https://www.aapor.org/Education-Resources/Reports/An-Evaluation-of-2016-Election-Polls-in-the-U-S.aspx.

31. "General Election: Trump vs. Clinton," *Real Clear Politics*, https://www.realclearpolitics.com/epolls/2016/president/us/general_election_trump_vs_clinton-5491.html.

32. "An Evaluation of 2016 Election Polls," *AAPOR*.

33. Gwern Branwen, "Was Nate Silver the Most Accurate 2012 Election Pundit?" *Center for Applied Rationality*, November 9, 2012, http://rationality.org/2012/11/09/was-nate-silver-the-most-accurate-2012-election-pundit/; Simon Jackman, "Pollster Predictive Performance, 51 out of 51," *Huffington Post*, November 7, 2012, http://www.huffngtonpost.com/simon-jackman/pollster-predictive-perfo_b_2087862.html.

34. Gary Smith, *Standard Deviations: Flawed Assumptions, Tortured Data, and Other Ways to Lie With Statistics* (New York, NY: Overlook, 2014), 27.

35. William G. Mayer, "Forecasting Presidential Nominations, or My Model Worked Just Fine, Thank You," *PS: Political Science & Politics* 36 (2003): 153–57.

36. See the various polls at "White House 2004: Democratic Nomination," *Polling Report*, 2004, www.pollingreport.com/wh04dem.htm.

37. Asher, *Polling and the Public*, 128.

38. "Clark Bows Out after Kerry Wins in South," *CNN*, February 13, 2004, www. cnn.com/2004/ALLPOLITICS/02/11/elec04.prez.main/index.html.

39. Mark Murray, "NBC/WSJ Poll: Carson Surges Into Lead of National GOP Race," *NBC News*, November 4, 2015, https://www.nbcnews.com/politics/2016-election/nbc-wsj-poll-carson-surges-lead-national-gop-race-n456006.

40. Mona Chalabi, "Trump or Clinton: Who Got the Biggest Post-Convention Bounce?" *The Guardian*, August 3, 2016, https://www.theguardian.com/us-news/2016/aug/03/trump-clinton-unpopularity-2016-election-prediction-winner.

41. Thomas Holbrook, "Campaign Dynamics and the 2004 Presidential Election," American Political Science Association, www.apsanet.org/content_5167.cfm.

42. Asher, *Polling and the Public*, 145.

43. Michal Addady, "Polls Paint Different Picture of Who Won Last Night's Debate," Fortune.com, September 27, 2016, http://fortune.com/2016/09/27/presidential-debate-polls-winner.

44. "Online Votes Declare Trump Debate Winner, Despite Media Consensus for Clinton," *Fox News*, September 27, 2016, https://www.foxnews.com/politics/online-votes-declare-trump-debate-winner-despite-media-consensus-for-clinton.

45. Steven Shepard, "Post-Debate Polls Show Trump Slump," Politico.com, September 30, 2016, https://www.politico.com/story/2016/09/donald-trump-hillary-clinton-post-debate-polls-228984.

46. Eric DuVall, "UPI/CVoter Poll: Clinton Retakes Lead With Post-Debate Bump," *UPI*, October 8, 2016, https://www.upi.com/Top_News/US/2016/10/08/UPICVoter-poll-Clinton-retakes-lead-with-post-debate-bump/2941475947664.

47. Stephen J. Wayne, *The Road to the White House, 2004: The Politics of Presidential Elections* (Belmont, CA: Wadsworth, 2004).

48. Smith, *Standard Deviations*, 125.

49. Asher, *Polling and the Public*, 78–80.

50. Sarah Dutton, Jennifer De Pinto, Fred Backus, Kabir Khanna, and Anthony Salvanto, "CBS News Poll: State of the Race the Day Before Election Day," *CBS News*, November 7, 2016, https://www.cbsnews.com/news/cbs-news-poll-state-of-the-race-the-day-before-election-day.

51. Some stories do not report the margin of error at all. See, for example, Carla Marinucci's story about Bush's six-point lead. Although not reported, the margin of error must have been at least three points, perhaps more. Carla Marinucci, "Poll Boosts Bush into a Slim Lead," *San Francisco Chronicle*, September 28, 2000, A3.

52. Humphrey Taylor, "Bush Leads Gore by Five Points," *Harris Poll #65*, October 28, 2000, www.harrisinteractive.com/harris_poll/index.asp?PID=127.

53. "Gore Edges Bush in CBS News Poll," *CBS News*, October 17, 2000, www.cbsnews.com/stories/2000/10/18/politics/main242058.shtml.

54. Asher, *Polling and the Public*, 79–80.

55. Nate Silver, "Why FiveThirtyEight Gave Trump a Better Chance Than Almost Anyone Else," *FiveThirtyEight*, November 11, 2016, https://fivethirtyeight.com/features/why-fivethirtyeight-gave-trump-a-better-chance-than-almost-anyone-else.

CHAPTER 10

1. David R. Mayhew, *Congress: The Electoral Connection* (New Haven, CT: Yale University Press, 1974), 81–82.

2. Joseph A. Schumpeter, *Capitalism, Socialism and Democracy* (New York, NY: Harper, 1942); Robert A. Dahl, *A Preface to Democratic Theory* (Chicago, IL: University of Chicago Press, 1956).

3. "Electoral Competition Survey," Pew Research Center for the People & the Press, October 2006. The survey results reported here were obtained from searches of the iPOLL Databank and other resources provided by the Roper Center for Public Opinion Research. The 71 percent figure excludes those who answered "don't know" or refused to answer.

4. James C. Miller III, "Incumbents Advantage," Citizens for a Sound Economy Foundation, economics.gmu.edu/working/WPE_98/98_05.pdf.

5. Samuel Kernell, "Toward Understanding 19th Century Congressional Careers: Ambition, Competition, and Rotation," *American Journal of Political Science* 21 (1977): 669–93.

6. David Brady, Kara Buckley, and Douglas Rivers, "The Roots of Careerism in the U.S. House of Representatives," *Legislative Studies Quarterly* 24 (1999): 489–510.

7. David R. Mayhew, "Congressional Elections: The Case of the Vanishing Marginals," *Polity* 6 (1974): 295–317.

8. See also Jacobson, *Politics of Congressional Elections*, 26–31.

9. Box-Steffensmeier, "A Dynamic Analysis of the Role of War Chests in Campaign Strategy," 352–71.

10. Roger H. Davidson, Walter J. Oleszek, Frances E. Lee, and Eric Schickler, *Congress and Its Members*, 15th ed. (Washington, DC: CQ Press, 2016),127.

11. Davidson, Oleszek, Lee, and Schickler, *Congress and Its Members*, 127.

12. Davidson, Oleszek, Lee, and Schickler, *Congress and Its Members*, 127.

13. Davidson Oleszek, Lee, and Schickler, *Congress and Its Members*, 128.

14. Stephen Hess, *Live from Capitol Hill: Studies of Congress and the Media* (Washington, DC: Brookings Institution, 1991); Timothy E. Cook, *Making Laws and Making News: Media Strategies in the U.S. House of Representatives* (Washington, DC: Brookings Institution, 1990).

15. "In addition to senators and representatives, the president, cabinet secretaries, and certain executive branch officials [are also] granted the frank." See "January 22, 1873: Senate Ends Franked Mail Privilege," *U.S. Senate, Historical Minutes*, 1851–1877, www.senate.gov/artandhistory/history/minute/Senate_Ends_Franked_Mail_Priviledge.htm.

16. Morris P. Fiorina, "The Case of the Vanishing Marginals: The Bureaucracy Did It," *American Political Science Review* 71 (1977): 177.

17. Norman J. Ornstein, Thomas E. Mann, and Michael J. Malbin, *Vital Statistics on Congress, 1989-90* (Washington, DC: CQ Press, 1990), 154.

18. Morris P. Fiorina, *Congress: Keystone of the Washington Establishment*, 2nd ed. (New Haven, CT: Yale University Press, 1989).

19. For Senate members, see http://www.senate.gov/senators/contact/; for members of the House, see http://www.house.gov/representatives/.

20. Michael J. Robinson, "Three Faces of Congressional Media," in *The New Congress*, ed. Thomas E. Mann and Norman J. Ornstein (Washington, DC: American Enterprise Institute, 1981).

21. See, for example. R. Douglas Arnold, *Congress, the Press, and Political Accountability* (Princeton, NJ: Princeton University Press, 2004).

22. Davidson, Oleszek, Lee, and Schickler, *Congress and Its Members*, 128-130.

23. For the classic treatment of this, and other legislative norms geared toward the goal of reelection, see Mayhew, *Congress*.

24. "Cost of Election," OpenSecrets.org, Center for Responsive Politics, https://www.opensecrets.org/overview/cost.php?infl=N&display=P.

25. See, for example, any of the quadrennial "Financing the [Year] Election" books, the first of which was by Herbert E. Alexander, *Financing the 1960 Election* (Princeton, NJ: Citizens Research Foundation, 1962), the latest of which is David B. Magleby, Anthony Corrado, and Kelly D. Patterson, eds., *Financing the 2004 Election* (Washington, DC: Brookings Institution, 2006). See also Peter L. Francia, John C. Green, Paul S. Herrnson, Lynda W. Powell, and Clyde Wilcox, *The Financiers*

of Congressional Elections: Investors, Ideologues, and Intimates (New York, NY: Columbia University Press, 2003).

26. Robert G. Boatright, *Interest Groups and Campaign Finance Reform in the United States and Canada* (Ann Arbor, MI: University of Michigan Press, 2011).

27. Megan Messerly, "Freshman Democrats Build Cash-on-Hand Advantages Before Races Heat Up," *The Nevada Independent*, July 16, 2019, https://theneva daindependent.com/article/freshman-democrats-build-cash-on-hand-advantages-before-races-heat-up.

28. Anthony King, *Running Scared: Why American's Politicians Campaign Too Much and Govern Too Little* (New York, NY: Martin Kessler, 1997).

29. Paul S. Herrnson, *Congressional Elections: Campaigning at Home and in Washington*, 7th ed. (Washington, DC: CQ Press, 2016), chapter 5.

30. Francia et al., *The Financiers of Congressional Elections*.

31. Herrnson, *Congressional Elections*, chapter 2.

32. Gary W. Cox and Jonathan N. Katz, "Why Did the Incumbency Advantage in U.S. House Elections Grow?" *American Journal of Political Science* 40 (1996): 478–97.

33. Herrnson, *Congressional Elections*, chapter 2.

34. This example was taken from Michael D. Robbins, "Gerrymander and the Need for Redistricting Reform," October 25, 2006, www.fraudfactor.com/ffgerry-mander.html.

35. David Lublin, *The Paradox of Representation: Racial Gerrymandering and Minority Interests in Congress* (Princeton, NJ: Princeton University Press, 1997).

36. Juliet F. Gainsborough, *Fenced Off: The Suburbanization of American Politics* (Washington, DC: Georgetown University, 2001); see also Peter L. Francia and Jody C Baumgartner, "Victim or Victor of the 'Culture War'? How Cultural Issues Affect Support for George W. Bush in Rural America," *American Review of Politics* 26 (Fall/Winter 2005–2006): 349–67; and Seth C. McKee, "Rural Voters and the Polarization of American Presidential Elections," *PS: Political Science & Politics* 41 (2008): 101–8.

37. Bill Bishop, *The Big Sort: Why the Clustering of Like-Minded America Is Tearing Us Apart* (New York, NY: First Mariner Books, 2008).

38. Gregor Aisch, Adam Pearce, and Karen Yourish, "The Divide Between Red and Blue America Grew Even Deeper in 2016," *The New York Times*, November 10, 2016, https://www.nytimes.com/interactive/2016/11/10/us/politics/red-blue-di vide-grew-stronger-in-2016.html.

39. Quoted in Bill Bishop, "No We Didn't: America Hasn't Changed as Tuesday's Results Would Indicate," *Slate*, November 4, 2008, https://slate.com/news-an d-politics/2008/11/no-we-didnt-america-hasn-t-changed-as-much-as-tuesdays-result s-would-indicate.html.

40. Ronald Brownstein, "How the Election Revealed the Divide Between City and Country," *The Atlantic*, November 17, 2016, https://www.theatlantic.com/po litics/archive/2016/11/clinton-trump-city-country-divide/507902/.

41. Jacobson, *Politics of Congressional Elections*, 122–27.

42. Davidson, Oleszek, Lee, and Schickler, *Congress and Its Members*, 92.

43. Richard F. Fenno Jr., *Home Style: House Members in Their Districts* (New York, NY: Longman, 2003).

44. Jay Goodliffe, "The Effect of War Chests on Challenger Entry in U.S. House Elections," *American Journal of Political Science* 45 (2001): 830–44.

45. More recently, see James E. Campbell and Steve J. Jurek, "The Decline of Competition and Change in Congressional Elections," in *The United States Congress: A Century of Change*, ed. Sunil Ahuja and Robert Dewhirst (Columbus, OH: Ohio State University, 2003).

CHAPTER 11

1. Louis Nelson, "Trump Definitely Has Mandate," *Politico*, November 13, 2016, https://www.politico.com/story/2016/11/rudy-giuliani-trump-mandate-231290.

2. Eugene Scott, "Conway: Trump 'Has Been Given a Mandate,'" CNN.com, November 9, 2016, https://www.cnn.com/2016/11/09/politics/donald-trump-kellyanne-conway-mandate/index.html.

3. Hayley Hoefer, "A Trump Mandate?" *U.S. News & World Report*, November 9, 2016, https://www.usnews.com/opinion/views-you-can-use/articles/2016-11-09/does-president-elect-donald-trump-have-a-mandate.

4. Joan Walsh, "The Obama Mandate," *Salon*, November 6, 2012, http://www.salon.com/2012/11/07/the_obama_mandate. Italics added.

5. David Weigel, "Yes, There Is a Mandate for Higher Taxes," *Slate*, November 7, 2012, http://www.slate.com/blogs/weigel/2012/11/07/yes_there_is_a_mandate_for_higher_taxes.html.

6. See Jon Meacham, *American Lion: Andrew Jackson in the White House* (New York, NY: Random House, 2008), 141.

7. See Sidney M. Milkis and Michael Nelson, *The American Presidency: Origins and Development, 1776–2014* (Washington, DC: CQ Press, 2015).

8. Quoted in Leonard D. White, *The Jacksonians: A Study in Administrative History* (New York, NY: Macmillan, 1954), 23. For further information, see Daniel Feller, "The Bank War," in *The American Congress: The Building of Democracy*, ed. Julian E. Zelizer (New York, NY: Houghton Mifflin, 2004).

9. Quoted in Robert Dahl, "Myth of the Presidential Mandate," *Political Science Quarterly* 105 (1990): 355–73.

10. Sidney M. Milkis and Emily J. Charnock, "History of the Presidency," in *Guide to the Presidency and the Executive Branch*, 5th ed., ed. Michael Nelson (Washington, DC: CQ Press, 2013), 128.

11. Quoted in Julia R. Azari, "Institutional Change and the Presidential Mandate," *Social Science History* 37 (2013): 483–514.

12. Quoted in Julia R. Azari, *Delivering the People's Message: The Changing Politics of the Presidential Mandate* (Ithaca, NY: Cornell University Press, 2014), 55.

13. Quoted in Dahl, "Myth of the Presidential Mandate," 355.

14. Hedrick Smith, "Reformer Who Would Reverse the New Deal's Legacy," *The New York Times*, January 21, 1981, http://www.nytimes.com/1981/01/21/us/reformer-who-would-reverse-the-new-deal-s-legacy.html.

15. Azari, *Delivering the People's Message*, 23.

16. Quoted in Steven T. Dennis, "Barack Obama Claims Mandate on Taxing the Rich," *Roll Call*, November 9, 2012, http://www.rollcall.com/news/barack_obam a_claims_mandate_on_taxing_the_rich-218921-1.html.

17. Quoted in Dennis, "Barack Obama Claims Mandate."

18. Azari, "Institutional Change and the Presidential Mandate"; and Azari, *Delivering the People's Message*.

19. Catherine S. Manegold, "The 1994 Election: The G.O.P. Leader; Gingrich Now a Giant, Claims Victor's Spoils," *The New York Times*, November 12, 1994, http://www.nytimes.com/1994/11/12/us/the-1994-election-the-gop-leader-gingr ich-now-a-giant-claims-victor-s-spoils.html.

20. Robert J. Samuelson, "The Public Trust: Handle with Care," *The Washington Post*, January 4, 1995, A15.

21. Quoted in William Branigin, "Democrats Take Majority in House; Pelosi Poised to Become Speaker," *The Washington Post*, November 8, 2006, http://www.washingtonpost.com/wp-dyn/content/article/2006/11/07/AR2006110700473.html.

22. "Republicans Capture House in Historic Wave, Claim 'Mandate' to Shrink Government," *Fox News*, November 3, 2010, http://www.foxnews.com/politic s/2010/11/03/republicans-capture-house-historic-wave-make-gains-senate.

23. Andrew C. McCarthy, "The Republican Congress Has a Mandate," *National Review*, January 15, 2015, http://www.nationalreview.com/article/396403/repub lican-congress-has-mandate-andrew-c-mccarthy.

24. Rush Limbaugh, "The Republicans Have a Huge Mandate—Whether They Know It or Not," *The Rush Limbaugh Show*, November 3, 2014, http://www.rush-limbaugh.com/daily/2014/11/03/the_republicans_have_a_huge_mandate_whe ther_they_know_it_or_not.

25. Jake Johnson, "'A People's Wave' Rebukes Trump: Democrats Retake US House with Mandate to Chart Bold Progressive Course," *Common Dreams*, November 7, 2018, https://www.commondreams.org/news/2018/11/07/peoples-wa ve-rebukes-trump-democrats-retake-us-house-mandate-chart-bold-progressive.

26. Maxine Waters, "Waters Statement on the 2018 Midterm Election Results," *U.S. House Committee on Financial Services*, November 7, 2018, https://financi alservices.house.gov/news/documentsingle.aspx?DocumentID=401642.

27. Quoted in Dahl, "Myth of the Presidential Mandate," 364.

28. See, for example, Lawrence J. Grossback, David A. M. Peterson, and James A. Stimson, *Mandate Politics* (New York, NY: Cambridge University Press, 2006); and Patricia Heidotting Conley, *Presidential Mandates: How Elections Set the National Agenda* (Chicago, IL: University of Chicago Press, 2001).

29. Quoted in Jake Sherman, "John Boehner: No Tax Hike on Top Earners," *Politico*, November 5, 2012, http://www.politico.com/news/stories/1112/83363.html.

30. Grossback, Peterson, and Stimson, *Mandate Politics*.

31. See for example, Azari, *Delivering the People's Message*; and Grossback, Peterson, and Stimson, *Mandate Politics*.

32. Amy E. Gangl, Lawrence J. Grossback, David A. M. Peterson, and James A. Stimson, "Mandate Elections and Policy Change in Congress" (paper presented at the annual meeting of the Midwest Political Science Association, April 1998, Chicago, IL), http://www.polmeth.wustl.edu/media/Paper/gangl98.pdf.

33. George C. Edwards III, Kenneth R. Mayer, and Stephen J. Wayne, *Presidential Leadership: Politics and Policy Making*, 10th ed. (Lanham, MD: Rowman & Littlefield, 2018), 110.

34. Stanley Kelley, Jr., *Interpreting Elections* (Princeton, NJ: Princeton University Press, 1983).

35. Samuel L. Popkin, *The Reasoning Voter: Communication and Persuasion in Presidential Campaigns* (Chicago, IL: University of Chicago Press, 1991), 155.

36. Edwards, Mayer, and Wayne, *Presidential Leadership*.

37. Kelley, *Interpreting Elections*, 126–28.

38. For an informative summary on this point, see John Sides, "The 2012 Election Was Not a Mandate," *The Monkey Cage*, November 7, 2012, http://themonkeycage.org/2012/11/07/the-2012-election-was-not-a-mandate.

39. Larry M. Bartels, "Partisanship and Voting Behavior, 1952–1996," *American Journal of Political Science* 44 (2000): 35–50; and Michael S. Lewis-Beck, William G. Jacoby, Helmut Norpoth, and Herbert F. Weisberg, *The American Voter Revisited* (Ann Arbor, MI: University of Michigan Press, 2008).

40. Morris P. Fiorina, *Retrospective Voting in American National Elections* (New Haven, CT: Yale University Press, 1981); Karen M. Kaufmann, "Disaggregating and Reexamining Issue Ownership and Vote Choice," *Polity* 36 (2004): 283–99; and Danny Hayes, "Candidate Qualities through a Partisan Lens: A Theory of Trait Ownership," *American Journal of Political Science* 49 (2005): 908–23.

41. Gabriel S. Lenz, "Learning and Opinion Change, Not Priming: Reconsidering the Priming Hypothesis," *American Journal of Political Science* 53 (2009): 821–37.

42. George C. Edwards III, *At the Margins: Presidential Leadership of Congress* (New Haven, CT: Yale University Press, 1989), 149.

43. Paul S. Herrnson, *Congressional Elections: Campaigning at Home and in Washington*, 6th ed. (Washington, DC: CQ Press, 2013).

44. George F. Bishop, *The Illusion of Public Opinion: Fact and Artifact in American Public Opinion Polls* (Lanham, MD: Rowman & Littlefield, 2005), 145–46.

45. See the section "Do Elections Matter?" in Steven K. Medvic, *Campaigns and Elections: Players and Processes* (New York, NY: Routledge, 2014).

46. Exit poll results for the 2012 election were obtained from "Presidential Election Results," *NBC News*, November 6, 2012, http://elections.nbcnews.com/ns/politics/2012/all/president/#.XVlY_OhKhPY.

47. Exit poll results for the 2016 election were obtained from "Exit Polls," *CNN*, November 23, 2016, https://www.cnn.com/election/2016/results/exit-polls.

48. Grossback, Peterson, and Stimson, *Mandate Politics*.

49. Thomas Ferguson and Joel Rogers, "The Myth of America's Turn to the Right," *The Atlantic*, May 1986, http://www.theatlantic.com/past/docs/issues/95dec/conbook/fergrt.htm.

50. Gil Troy, *Morning in America: How Ronald Reagan Invented the 1980s* (Princeton, NJ: Princeton University Press, 2005).

51. William E. Leuchtenburg, *The FDR Years: On Roosevelt and His Legacy* (New York, NY: Columbia University Press, 1995).

52. Jeffrey W. Coker, *Franklin D. Roosevelt: A Biography* (Westport, CT: Greenwood Press, 2005), chap. 8.

53. Dahl, "Myth of the Presidential Mandate."

54. Dahl, "Myth of the Presidential Mandate."

55. Jon R. Bond and Richard Fleisher, eds., *Polarized Politics: Congress and the President in a Partisan Era* (Washington, DC: CQ Press, 2000).

56. Edwards, Mayer, and Wayne, *Presidential Leadership*, 356–58.

57. George C. Edwards III, *Overreach: Leadership in the Obama Presidency* (Princeton, NJ: Princeton University Press, 2012).

58. "USA Today/Pew Poll: Health Care Law Faces Difficult Future," *USA Today*, September 23, 2013, http://www.usatoday.com/story/news/politics/2013/09/16/usa-today-pew-poll-health-care-law-opposition/2817169.

59. Chris Cillizza, "What Effect Did Health-Care Reform Have on the Election?" *The Washington Post*, November 7, 2010, http://www.washingtonpost.com/wp-dyn/content/article/2010/11/07/AR2010110705311.html.

60. Jeff Nesbit, "What Donald Trump Will Do With His Mandate," *Time.com*, November 9, 2016, http://time.com/4564256/donald-trump-mandate/.

61. Bradford Richardson, "Donald Trump Campaign Says It Has a 'Mandate'," *The Washington Times*, November 13, 2016, https://www.washingtontimes.com/news/2016/nov/13/donald-trump-campaign-says-it-has-a-mandate/.

62. Jim Norman, "Solid Majority Still Oppose New Construction on Border Wall," *Gallup*, February 4, 2019, https://news.gallup.com/poll/246455/solid-majority-opposes-new-construction-border-wall.aspx.

63. Dahl, "Myth of the Presidential Mandate," 365.

64. Dahl, "Myth of the Presidential Mandate," 366.

Index

Page locators in italics refer to boxes, figures, and tables

pack journalism, 102
Palin, Sarah L., 62, 66, 67, 68, 71, 72, 73–74, 103
Parker, Alton, 46
parliamentary systems, 34
participation by citizens, 13, 116–17
partisan core, 10–12
partisan dealignment, 2
partisan identification, 3–4
partisan voters, 1–2
    independent "leaners" as, 6, 8–9, 12
    voting in elections, 1952–2016, 7
party-building activities, 49
party platform, 41–42
"party switchers," 8
party system, 34
Patterson, Thomas, 98
Paul. Ron, 99
Pelosi, Nancy, 55, 154
Pence, Michael R. (Mike), 65, 66, 67, 71, 72–73
Perot, Ross, 38, 110
Perry, Rick, 129
personalized campaign messages and appeals, 21
person-to-person contact, 21
persuadable voters, 9, 10, 55, 114
petition signature requirements, 39
Pew Research Center, 124, 125
photo identification, 26
"Phryne Before the Chicago Tribunal" (Gillam), 46, 47
Pinckney, Charles, 77
plurality (most votes), 34, 36
plurality-winner rules, 19, 34
policy mandate, 156–57
policy proposals, 152
political action committees (PACs), 51, 51, 145
political efficacy, sense of, 15
political parties
    ambivalence about, 29
    as broad-based coalitions, 61

decline attributed to, 2
issues, stances on, 41–42
rules for candidates, 39
See also Democratic Party; Republican Party
political system, 34
Polk, James, 153
polls, 3–4, 119–34, 127
    applying national results to state-by-state contest, 132–33
    basics of public polling, 120–23
    biased samples, 123
    checklist, 133
    definition of, 121
    follow-up questions, 126
    forecasting models, 119
    fundraising and, 54
    how to determine likely voters, 125–26
    margin of error, 131–32
    mixed-mode survey designs, 124–25
    multistage cluster sampling, 122, 123
    nonprobability samples, 124
    nonresponse bias, 124
    online, 124–25, 130
    postconvention numbers, 129–30
    preprimary, 128–29
    presidential preference, 125–26
    pseudo, 123–25
    random sampling, 122, 123
    random variation, 131
    registered vs. likely voters, 126
    representative sample, 121–22
    samples, data, and reporting, 130–31
    secret ballot/face-to-face, 126
    self-selected samples, 124
    stratified sampling, 122, 123
    straw polls, 120
    systematic sampling, 122, 123
    telephone surveys, 124